UNDERSTANDING BASIC ECONOMICS

This book is part of the
WORLD CONTINUING EDUCATION SERIES

L. C. Michelon, Consulting Editor

UNDERSTANDING
BASIC
ECONOMICS

L. C. Michelon

Reuben E. Slesinger

THE WORLD PUBLISHING COMPANY
Cleveland and New York

Published by THE WORLD PUBLISHING COMPANY
2231 West 110th Street, Cleveland, Ohio 44102

Published simultaneously in Canada by
Nelson, Foster & Scott Ltd.

Revised Edition (Parts 1, 2 & 3). First Printing (Part 1), 1967

Library of Congress Catalog Card Number: 68–16448

Printed in the United States of America

CONTENTS

Part Three · COMPARATIVE ECONOMIC SYSTEMS

FOREWORD

This book is intended to provide an interesting, practical, and comprehensive review of basic economics.

It differs from traditional textbooks because it is less concerned with abstract models designed for professional economists. Rather, it is intended for the businessman who wants an introductory overview of practical economics, for the citizen who wants to learn more about how our economy operates, for the conference leader who needs help in conducting economic discussions, for the teacher who seeks a better understanding of economic fundamentals, and for the student who is interested in the world of business and what makes it tick.

The study of economics can be approached in three basic ways:

1. The *positive* approach, which seeks to uncover fundamental principles that apply under all circumstances and at all times. Actually, there are few such positive statements since economics is concerned largely with human behavior under the stress of conflicting economic demands.

2. The *normative* approach, which is more typical of economics discussions because it describes human behavior and adds judgmental qualifications. For this reason, the economists who deal in a normative manner—and most of them do—state their assumptions, objectives, and the pros and cons of various solutions. There are many normative statements in this book.

3. The *applied* approach, which analyzes a specific problem by the use of relevant economic tools. It deals with questions like how to price an article, what changes may be expected in market demand, or how unemployment compensation can best be administered.

In this book the authors relate the *applied* and *normative* approaches. They ask *how* and *why* a particular phenomenon affects the basic characteristics of our economy. This approach will help the reader to examine public statements about our economic system, and it should sharpen his ability to distinguish economic reasoning from propaganda.

The material for this book has been drawn, in part, from booklets prepared by the following authors, in conjunction with Mr. Michelon:

The Anatomy of Free Enterprise	Dr. Robert L. Darcy Associate Professor of Economics Ohio University
Who Sets Prices?	Dr. Jules Backman Research Professor of Economics New York University
The Role of Management	Dr. Billy J. Hinton Professor of Economics and Business Administration and Dean, School of Applied Arts Southwest Texas State College
Impact of Automation and Technological Change	Dr. Walter Buckingham Head of Department of Economics Drexel Institute of Technology
The Problem of Inflation	Dr. Samuel J. Mantel, Jr. Associate Professor of Economics Case–Western Reserve University
Foreign Trade: The Challenge of a Changing World	Dr. Gerhard Rosegger Associate Professor of Economics Case–Western Reserve University

The authors are grateful to these men for their valuable contributions to this book.

L.C.M.
R.E.S.

UNDERSTANDING BASIC ECONOMICS

PART ONE

ECONOMIC PRINCIPLES

1

THE ANATOMY OF
FREE ENTERPRISE

OUR DYNAMIC AMERICAN ECONOMY

During its history, the United States has undergone substantial changes in its economic structure, accompanied by a growing complexity in its economic problems. Just consider the dramatic changes we have experienced since 1800.

In those days the typical farmer worked his own land, wore homespun clothes, and lived in a house that he built with the part-time help of neighbors. Traders and craftsmen worked primarily for themselves. Annual money income was small, and prices were low. Emphasis was placed on real earnings—on the goods and services that an individual could buy with his labor. Very little income resulted from property rights or absentee ownership.

Each town or village exchanged its goods within a small marketing area because of the difficulties of transportation and communication.

Although the price of food was low, the costs of some manufactured goods were quite high. For example, west of the Alleghenies, a suit of clothes might cost as much as a good-sized farm.[1]

All in all, the typical American of the early nineteenth century was self-sufficient, but his standard of living was much lower than ours is today.

Since that time employment in agriculture, forestry, and fishing has dropped from about 75 per cent of the labor force to less than 10

---

[1] Based on a lecture by Asher Isaacs, *How the U.S. Grew Strong,* University of Pittsburgh Workshop in Economic Education, 1954.

per cent.[2] Today, therefore, the typical American could exist on his own for only a short while, because our economic system is completely interdependent. We produce little for our own use, and we are forced to rely on the market for goods, services, jobs, and income.

Perhaps the turning point in American history came with a series of advances in the textile and related industries, soon after the War of 1812.[3] Rapid mechanization, geographical growth, and improved transportation made possible mass production and mass marketing methods. New problems began to manifest themselves—instability of employment, fluctuations in industrial production, and monetary and banking crises. Continuing changes have added to the complexities of the economic environment, and it is often difficult for the citizen to discern the principles by which the economy operates.

The system of free enterprise capitalism is based on principles that cannot be changed without affecting the fundamental nature of the system. These principles are at the heart of a free enterprise economy, and public policy must heed them, or the principles themselves may be sacrificed for expediency.

But what, you may ask, are the basic principles behind our American economic system? Well, to discuss those principles intelligently, let us first get an idea of how our economic system works.

HOW OUR ECONOMIC SYSTEM WORKS

Economics starts with the well-known fact that people are very hard to satisfy. It is an unusual person who is content and has everything he wants. Most of us want all kinds of things we don't have. The man who doesn't own an auto usually wants one. The person who has an auto wants a new one, or perhaps a second car. The same is true with thousands of goods and services—houses, appliances, clothes, vacations, and all the rest.

To have everything we wanted would be extremely difficult because the economic system must first produce the many things we would like to have. We must intelligently combine *material, manpower, money, management, methods,* and *machines* to get a wide variety of goods and services produced efficiently. And unfortunately, at any given time, our supply of resources for producing goods and services is never great

---

[2] Arnold B. Barach, *U.S.A. and Its Economic Future* (New York: The Macmillan Company, 1964), p. 14; and *Economic Report of the President,* U.S. Department of Commerce, 1966, p. 232.

[3] *See* Douglass C. North, *The Economic Growth of the United States* (New York: W. W. Norton and Company, 1966), pp. 66 ff., pp. 179 ff.

enough to satisfy every conceivable want. This is true for several reasons. For one thing, there are only 24 hours in a day and 365 days a year. For another, there is just so much manpower, capital, raw material, and technology. Thus there is a limit to what we can produce at any given time, whereas the things we would like to have are limited only by our expectations and imaginations.

Every economy, therefore, finds itself on an economic merry-go-round: first, human wants are virtually unlimited; second, productive resources are definitely limited; and third, no one can have anything unless someone works to produce it.

EVERY ECONOMIC SYSTEM MUST MAKE FOUR DECISIONS

Our economy tries to solve the fundamental economic problem of relative scarcity by producing as many goods and services as it can and by distributing them as fully and fairly as possible. But to do this our economic system must decide:

- *How much* to produce in total, with the existing production resources and technology available
- *What* and *how much* to produce of the millions of different goods and services that could be produced

- *How* to produce these goods and services efficiently
- *Who* will get *what share* of the goods and services produced

These decisions, in turn, can be made in two basic ways:

- By government planning
- By the decentralized decisions of individuals, as reflected in a competitive market place

We shall next examine how these decisions are made in our free enterprise system.

Freedom of Choice

In our American economic system, every individual helps make these important economic decisions by exercising his freedom of choice in the market place. Whenever you buy anything, in effect you cast a "dollar vote" for that particular product or service and the business which produced it.

When a company turns out something that is popular, the company is encouraged to expand and to make more of that product or service available. On the other hand, if a company turns out an unsatisfactory product, the product usually goes off the market and the company may go out of business, unless it adapts to the changing situation.

In this simple way you and your fellow shoppers make the key economic decisions in our society. You really determine *what* and *how much* is going to be produced—and *by whom*.

You and other customers also force efficiency in production by how you cast your dollar votes or hold them back. To win your favor, producers turn out more attractive products or services and offer them at competitive prices.

The last decision—who gets what share of the goods and services produced—also depends to a large extent on the market place. Just as you will pay a higher price for products you value highly, so too, an employer will pay more to those with rarer or greater skills. Their jobs are better paid, and, as a result, this enables the people with skills to buy more of the goods and services available.

As you can see, then, *free choice* in the market place is an important characteristic of free enterprise. By exercising free choice, consumers make the important economic decisions rather than having them made by government directives or planners.

The Competitive Market Place

Free choice leads to another characteristic that is not found to the same extent in communist or socialist systems. Free enterprise relies on market competition as the best way of making our key economic decisions. Under communism or socialism, government planners decide which products will be produced and who will produce them. The customer's choice is generally to buy or not to buy. There are few competing products through which the consumer can register his satisfaction or disapproval. The shopper who wants something different in style, design, or color is often out of luck. Since most products are standardized and simplified, there is very little consumer choice or individuality.

Under free enterprise everybody takes part in the planning process. Individuals and families plan their own economic lives, budgeting to buy the things they would like to have as well as those they must have. Their total buying plans make up the national market. Business firms strive to meet their demands in terms of quality, designs, and prices. Each company tries to do a better job than its competitors because in that way it can win a larger number of consumer dollar votes.

Competition, working within a free market, gives the consumer the best value for his money—and the widest selection of goods and services from which to choose.

Unfortunately, some people have the idea that our free enterprise system is unplanned and inefficient. They confuse "economic planning" with centralized decision-making by government officials. However, if we judge an economic system by its results, then the people of the United States, under free enterprise, have realized the highest standard of living and the greatest degree of freedom in the history of the world. If these are the results we want, then our free enterprise system must certainly be "well-planned" and efficient.

Besides *free choice* and *competition,* there is a third important characteristic of free enterprise. This characteristic is found in the answer to the question of how our economy gets people to work, to produce, and to take the risks of going into business for themselves. Three possibilities suggest themselves:

- By training people for assignment to specific jobs
- By forcing them to do what we want done
- By offering incentives

The United States was founded on the principle of personal freedom and individual dignity. Our freedoms would mean very little if someone had the power to force us to work at certain jobs or if business firms were required to turn out certain products. So incentives are the real motivating force behind our economic system.

Our Incentive System

Our competitive, free enterprise system rewards those whose contributions are more valuable. In this way free enterprise uses the carrot, rather than the stick.

Business firms and service companies that offer reliable products and services, good performance, and low prices stimulate the consumer's willingness to buy.

Since workers are producers as well as consumers, our economy offers them the incentive of a higher standard of living through better job opportunities over the years.

From the businessman's point of view, the possibility of earning a profit is the basic incentive that stimulates him to start new businesses, to expand existing ones, and to produce the goods and services which are in demand.

In a purely personal way, we all want to profit. We want to improve and get ahead. We want our children to be better off than we have been. We want to lay aside money in savings, insurance policies, pension plans, and home ownership. Moreover, if an employee is to achieve security, it is important that his company make a profit. For only a profitable company can provide him with good working conditions, adequate income, continued employment and advancement, and medical insurance, pensions, and other fringe benefits.

Incentives, then, take their rightful place along with free choice and competition as cornerstones of our free enterprise system.

Now, let us pick out another of our economy's basic characteristics from these alternatives:

1. Government subsidies
2. Wage and price controls
3. Private ownership of resources

The Right to Call It Mine

There is no doubt that free enterprise is characterized by the right of private ownership. In our country a person can own a house, a car, or a boat. He can own a small business—and if it is successful, he can add to his stock of material resources and watch it grow.

His savings and investments are his to use as he wishes. His savings may insure a college education for his children, provide for retirement, or represent a nest egg for his family in an emergency. His savings involve risk, however. If inflation takes place, his savings may decline in value. He will not be able to buy as much as he could have bought on the day on which he earned the money.

We could not have a free enterprise economy without a sound system of private property, protected by our laws and legal systems. Without private property we would lose a powerful incentive that has helped make our country as successful as it is.

Personal freedom, individual incentives, market allocation by competitive factors, private property—these are prime ingredients of free enterprise. They are, as well, the sound bases to universal economic progress. No better substitutes have been found for providing freedom and plenty in our times. These four pillars of our free enterprise system have made possible the greatest degree of freedom and the highest standard of living in the history of the world. With only about 6 to 7 per cent of the world's population and land area we produce about 30 per cent of the oil and 45 per cent of the motor vehicles. And we consume more than a third of the world's goods and services.[4]

U. S. POSITION IN THE WORLD, EARLY 1960s

Each symbol represents 10 per cent of world total.

SOURCE: Arnold B. Barach, *USA and Its Economic Future,* a Twentieth Century Fund Survey (New York, The Macmillan Company, 1964), p. 4.

Our nation's economic progress is the result both of our economic system and of an additional factor that has played a very important role in our long-term rise in living standards. It is one of the following:

1. Rising prices

2. Machinery and technology

3. Government regulation and control

[4] Barach, *op. cit.,* p. 4.

WE MUST PRODUCE MORE
TO HAVE MORE

Economists agree that <u>machinery and technology</u> are most important because they lead to increased efficiency—what economists call increased productivity. Productivity increases are important because, in the long run, we can have more as a nation only if we can produce more. Most economists agree that improved technology and more and better tools per worker have been primarily responsible for our rising productivity and our higher living standards over the years.

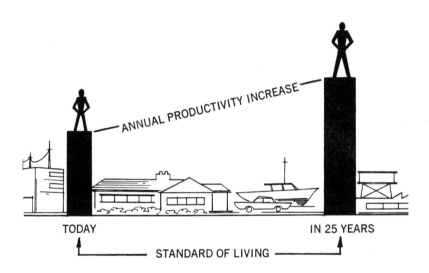

IT'S NO SECRET AFTER ALL

The secret of our economy's phenomenal success is really no secret after all. As a matter of fact the important ingredients are so obvious that some people make the mistake of considering them unimportant. We have become the world's most prosperous nation because our people are free to work out their own futures. We encourage them to improve their skills and talents, and then back them up with modern tools which many of us help to provide by voluntarily investing our savings in private industry with the hope of earning a profit.

Discussion Questions

1. Highlight the significant changes that have taken place in the American economy since 1800.

2. What basic problems are faced by every economy?

3. What is meant by freedom of choice? Give examples from your experience.

4. How is the public protected from inferior goods in a free enterprise system?

5. Discuss this statement: "Under free enterprise, everybody takes part in the planning process."

6. Discuss this statement: "Competition gives everyone the best value for his money."

7. What incentives are provided by our free enterprise system?

8. Discuss this statement: "There is no place for government under a free enterprise system."

9. List and describe the basic pillars of a free enterprise system.

10. What roles do profits perform in our economy?

11. Present the main facts that depict the economic position of the United States in the world.

12. Discuss this statement: "Competition is the best regulator of business and industry."

13. What role does risk play in our economy?

14. Describe how management coordinates natural resources, human labor, and raw materials during the production of goods and services.

15. Discuss this statement: "The economic welfare of a nation depends upon the number of people and the resources at their command."

16. Describe how the institution of private property functions within our American economy.

17. Describe some of the frictions that hamper the full operation of the basic principles of our economic system.

18. Is the study of economics concerned with philosophy, human behavior, and social institutions?

19. In today's complex society, do individual wants exert a guiding influence on our society? If so, by what methods does the individual translate his wants and desires into effective action?

20. Discuss this statement: "The free-market mechanism should be used unconditionally for the purpose of achieving economic goals for the future."

Circle the T or F (True or False) before each statement:

T F 1. The competitive nature of our economic system promotes economic progress.

T F 2. A competitive price tends to balance the quantity demanded with the quantity supplied.

T F 3. A communistic system doesn't need capital because the government controls production.

T F 4. Government controls are as effective as competitive prices in organizing production.

T F 5. It's better to work for equality of opportunities than to reduce inequalities of income.

T F 6. There's little interrelationship between a society's economic and political systems.

T F 7. The living standards of communist and socialist countries have improved because of more capital equipment per worker.

T F 8. Socialist countries tend to achieve overall economic growth by diverting production resources from consumer goods to capital equipment.

T F 9. Government intervention in our economic system has increased considerably in the last fifteen years.

T F 10. Decentralized decision making in an economic sense is important to our basic freedom.

ANSWERS

10. T	8. T	6. F	4. F	2. T
9. T	7. T	5. T	3. F	1. T

2

PRODUCTIVITY: THE MAGIC LAMP OF PROGRESS

A basic criterion of our economy's success is how well it produces the goods and services which all of us need or want. And, as stated in the last chapter, our ability to produce is determined by our productive efficiency—what we customarily call our productivity as a nation.

The output of our American economic system is the result of three interrelated mechanisms and institutions:

1. The factors of production—*land, labor, capital,* and *entrepreneurship*
2. Competitive pricing and free markets
3. The money and banking system

We shall now examine the subject of increased productivity to see how it comes about and what it means to our future as a nation.

The story of Aladdin's lamp dramatizes a basic hope in all of us: we would not be human if we did not dream of a magic lamp which would give us everything just for the asking. Many of the early Greek stories tell of the wondrous powers conferred upon those who searched for and found certain objects. A good example is Jason and the Golden Fleece. During the Middle Ages, alchemists and sorcerers tried for years, without success, to change ordinary metals into gold. Later, Ponce de Leon crossed the Atlantic in search of a fountain of youth which would keep people perpetually young. The prospectors of the early West sought the big strike and the easy life. A whole generation of them risked everything in search of El Dorado, the legendary country of gold. Throughout history people have searched, in one way or another, for the magic

14

lamp that would provide them with the goods and services of a new and plentiful life.

This chapter tells the story of the MAGIC LAMP of our economy, which has made possible a whole stream of near miracles we take for granted—autos, airplanes, air conditioners, wonder drugs, electronics, nuclear energy, and space vehicles.[1] Any one of these would have made Aladdin, the alchemists, or Ponce de Leon stare in wonder and amazement.

PRODUCTIVITY: THE ROAD TO HIGHER LIVING STANDARDS

Our standard of living consists of the amount, quality, and variety of goods and services we can buy in the market place. Intangibles, like the leisure time at our disposal, are also included in our standard of living. But most of us prefer to think of our living standard in terms of real goods and services.

Now it is easy for us to take these goods and services for granted. But how are they produced? What problems would we face if we found ourselves in other circumstances? Let us pretend for a minute. Suppose your home, your car, and all of your modern conveniences were suddenly taken away and you were left in a wilderness without appliances, supplies, or tools of any kind. What would you do?

Well, you would soon realize how tough it is to produce even the basic necessities of life—the food for your next meal, some clothes, and particularly a few tools to help you get things done.

Would you like to catch a fish? If so, where will you get the hook or the net? Would you like to hunt some game? Where is the gun, the bow and arrow, or any weapon to help you do the job effectively? Immediately, you would appreciate how unproductive a person is without tools. To build a crude shelter, you would need an axe to cut down trees and to prepare the lumber. Then you would need something to fasten the pieces together. It also would be necessary to develop material for a roof and something for the doors and windows.

While all this was going on, you would have to spend time making clothes and hunting for food. Then you would have to plan ahead and add to your supply of tools, so that you could produce more and better

---

[1] For a detailed account of the record of U.S. economic growth, see Richard T. Gill, *Economic Development: Past and Present* (Englewood Cliffs, N.J.: Prentice-Hall, 1963), ch. 4.

things with less effort as time went on. Without tools your standard of living would depend on what you personally could do—and unfortunately, you would not be able to do much until more and better tools were available. Very soon, two things become quite clear: to achieve a higher standard of living, you must produce more and better goods and services; and to produce goods and services efficiently, you need more and better tools with which to work. As your supply of tools increases, your ability to make clothes, to build a house, and to hunt food improves along with your standard of living. The things we take for granted—the tools we have built up over the years—are what really help make our country productive. Take them away, and we find it very hard to produce.

The main point is simple. Our country's standard of living depends upon the goods and services that we, as a nation, can produce. This, in turn, depends upon the productiveness of our economic system. That is why economists say, "We can have more if we produce more." We must raise the production of our country's goods and services before we can increase our national consumption and enjoy a rising standard of living.

That is how rising productivity leads to economic growth and higher living standards. It is truly our "Magic Lamp of Progress."

WHAT PRODUCTIVITY REALLY MEANS

The word "productivity" is confusing, so let us examine it. Briefly, productivity is a way of comparing "output" with "input." The *output* consists of the quantity and quality of goods or services that are produced. The *input* consists of money, manpower, materials, machines, and methods—that is, all the resources needed to produce. There is an improvement in efficiency—which is the same as an increase in productivity—whenever we are able to get more output without a proportionate increase in input.

During World War II, we increased production by putting more people and mechanical equipment to work and by working them longer hours. This was not really an increase in productivity, since more production resources and effort were needed. To increase efficiency we must do a better production job with the resources at hand. Thus productivity is increased whenever we are able to combine production resources in such a way that we get more or better output without a similar increase in input.

Although "output per man-hour" is often used to measure changes in

productivity, this measure does not take into account the increased use of mechanical equipment nor the other important ways in which productive changes may come about. For example, if an employee works on a product and turns out 96 pieces a day, his output per man-hour for an eight-hour day is 96 ÷ 8, or 12 pieces an hour. Assuming that we install more or better machinery and improve the methods of production, this same employee is able to produce, say, 15 pieces an hour. Can we say that the entire increase in output per man-hour represents greater productivity? The answer is "no," because we had to add more or better machines and do more engineering to achieve this result. Therefore the net increase in efficiency is less "when everything is considered." So a measure like "output per man-hour" is not as accurate as it should be, nor does it tell us how the increased efficiency came about.

We must always consider the capital cost required to make our employees more productive. And we must pay dividends or interest to the investors who furnish the tools that make the jobs easier, safer, more productive, and more rewarding.

There is another important point to keep in mind. Production includes services as well as goods, so we also have productivity improvements where services are concerned. But how do you measure a person's productivity when he furnishes a service? How do you count or measure the impact of a new method or a good idea? Many people— like scientists, engineers, accountants, industrial relations specialists, administrators, doctors, lawyers, dentists, and teachers—work at jobs where no product is involved. They do not produce something physical that can be counted or measured. But they do furnish services which people want. Improvements in their ability to furnish services are as important as other people's efficiency in producing goods.

To raise our standard of living, we must increase the productivity of each person in our economy, whether he produces goods or furnishes services. Everyone has an important part to play in improving productivity and raising living standards.

HOW INCREASED PRODUCTIVITY COMES ABOUT

Some people believe that increased productivity requires only that we work harder. Actually the best ways to increase productivity involve a combination of more and better tools, more education and higher skills, more efficient production methods, and a wiser use of time and money. Let's discuss how greater productivity can be achieved.

Consider what a farmer can do to increase the crop yield on his farm. He may try to increase his farm yield by rotating his crops. He puts his *idea* to work—and over a period of time he produces more from the same amount of land. His good idea introduced a better *method,* which raised his productivity. Thus he is better off because he can produce more with less effort.

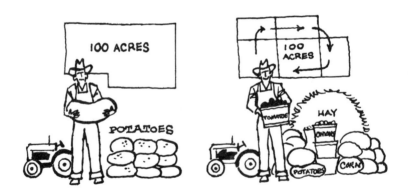

The farmer may increase his farm yield through the better use of *raw material,* like fertilizer. If he is successful, he produces more from the same amount of land. He can improve his "value productivity" by doing a better job of *managing* his time and money. He may, for example, plant five acres of land in a crop that will give him a better return than some other crop. In this case a better management of the same time and money makes him more productive. Or he may decide to improve his efficiency by using more and better *mechanical equipment* —like a new tractor, combine, or automatic milker. As he adds more and better tools, he can accomplish more because mechanical equipment puts more horsepower at his finger tips. But remember—and this is important—this equipment is expensive and it requires the farmer to make a larger investment and take greater risks to stay in business. On top of that, the tools will have to be maintained, repaired, replaced, housed, and used safely. He will not need as much muscle power, but he will have to work intelligently. In our modern economy increased productivity is seldom the result of more muscle power on the part of employees. It generally comes about by doing away with muscle power and substituting mechanical power in its place. This, in turn, demands a higher degree of skill on the part of the worker.

All in all the farmer raised his productivity in several ways. In the first case he applied a new idea and better method. In the second he made a better use of raw material. In the third he managed his time and money to better advantage. In the fourth he invested in more and better tools and took extra risks. In each case, the work required more "brain power" and less "brawn power."

Firms can increase their productivity in much the same way. They must start with their resources of production—money, materials, machines, methods, and manpower—all of which should be efficiently co-ordinated by management. These resources are the input factors— what is put into the business to produce. When this input is used more efficiently, the output of goods and services is greater than before. Thus, a company can increase its productivity only when it makes better use of its production resources.

Following are some examples of tools which have enabled industry to increase productivity. The steel industry has continuous rolling mills, basic oxygen furnaces, and improved blast furnaces and coke ovens. The oil industry has catalytic crackers and automatic controls keyed to electronic devices. The auto industry has ultra modern production processes, improved quality-control equipment, and better assembly techniques. The banking field has electronic bookkeeping and check screening devices that are revolutionizing this part of our economy.

We know, too, how carefully prepared materials increase our efficiency of production. In the steel industry, the pre-preparation of raw materials has increased the productivity of blast furnaces. In medicine, new drugs and antibiotics have shortened many illnesses and have permitted doctors to care for more patients in a given period of time.

There are endless ways in which we can improve our productivity by doing things in a more efficient way. Generally, this requires the development of better methods through good ideas. For example, better packaging and combined rail-truck movements have increased the efficiency of moving goods long distances over land.

We also know that productivity can be improved by making a better use of capital in a business. This can be done by reducing unnecessary inventories or by making better investments in products, plant sites, or equipment.

From all this we can see that increased productivity—increased efficiency—comes about whenever we make a better use of the factors of production. Therefore, we increase a company's productivity when we make continuous improvements in the use of money, materials, methods, and machines as well as of manpower. Moreover, we must share the increased productivity with investors, customers, and employees. We must look to investors for the better tools needed in the future; to our customers, for the growing markets for our products or services; and to our employees, for the skill and sense of job responsibility that lead to future growth and progress.

JOB RESPONSIBILITY AND FUTURE PROGRESS

Let's pause for a moment to see what happens when we're not productive enough. For one thing, when we're not productive enough, our production costs go up, and with higher costs go higher prices and an inability to compete.

Furthermore, when a company or industry cannot keep its production costs in line, substitute materials or products will take away some or all of its markets. On top of that, foreign producers will be quite willing to move in with more of their products and services. After all, there is nothing sacred about a particular industry or company. It may be important today, but so were kerosene lamps at one time.

We must realize that business firms are not immortal. They can remain in business as long as they meet the basic conditions of survival: *low cost, high quality, competitive prices, adequate profits,* and *appealing products.* When firms meet these conditions, they are productive and they can survive. As a result, all of us prosper because future opportunities and personal security depend upon enterprises that are efficient and competitive over the years.

Unfortunately, some people have the idea that their personal efforts have little impact on the overall efficiency of the firm for which they work, especially if they are one of hundreds or thousands of employees. Nothing is further from the truth, for a company is no better than its employees. Improving productivity is a company-wide challenge at all levels of the organization. For most people this means working more effectively—doing their regular jobs a little better. There are countless ways in which we can participate, ways which seem small but which have a tremendous effect on the profitability of the employer.

Some of us can save time, which often slips through our fingers. Others can come up with good ideas for doing our jobs better—or more easily, or faster, or more safely. Some of us can help reduce waste and scrap; others can improve quality and avoid needless claims. Sales, ad-

TO A PRODUCTIVE FUTURE

vertising, and engineering can help develop even better customer relations and product knowledge. Simple savings in the office can help—like caring for equipment and keeping reusable envelopes. This may sound silly, but a large mail-order company saved millions of dollars over the years by training its employees to wrap packages in such a way that paper and string were effectively but economically used.

The important point is that we are not talking about big changes that only top management can make; we are talking about day-to-day jobs which, if done well, can spell the difference between a successful company and a mediocre one.

' What, in general, makes an employee productive over a period of time? First, an employee is generally productive when he is able to do his job well. This depends largely on whether his supervisor has adequately trained him to do his work correctly and efficiently. Good supervision is important because a well-trained employee is usually a productive one. Second, a productive employee has a sense of job responsibility, which compels him to do what is right. Employees who want to progress have this sense of responsibility. They want to achieve a standard of excellence far above the minimum needed to hold onto their jobs. Such employees do their best every day. They work safely at all times, take care of equipment, and use materials efficiently. They come up with good ideas for improving their job performance and for making the company a more aggressive factor in its industry. A sense of job responsibility will help the employee as well as the employer. It will help the local community, for its well-being, too, depends upon the success of the business firms located in its area. A responsible person is also an asset to his family, company, community, and country. He incorporates the individualism and independence we all respect and admire. He stands on his own feet, and he makes his own way.

CONCLUSION

Increased productivity is essential to economic progress because it determines our nation's future standard of living.

Productivity is hard to measure accurately because it refers to services as well as goods, and it implies improvements in all production resources—money, materials, methods, machinery, and manpower.

Rough measurements of our country's overall productivity have been made by economists and by private research organizations. Most of them agree that our productivity, in terms of output per man-hour, has increased more than 2 per cent a year, compounded, throughout the century.[2]

This rate of annual improvement may seem small, but it has led to striking changes in our way of life. Compare the differences in today's living standards with those of the past. We take for granted the autos, airplanes, refrigerators, radios, telephones, powered lawn mowers, television, air conditioning, and the other conveniences made possible by increased productivity. Yet we had almost none of these fifty years ago.

If we can raise our national productivity by 3 per cent a year, we can double our standard of living in less than twenty-five years. Naturally that would mean an even better life in goods and services, as well as more leisure time with our families and friends. Over and above personal benefits, increased productivity will help us solve many of our national problems. It will help us in our fight against inflation. It will help us provide the resources we need for national defense. It will make possible more and better schools and municipal improvements. It will help us care for the aged, for the disabled, and for the young people in our schools.

Greater national production through increased productivity has been the key to progress in the past. It will be a sure road to better living in the future. That is really our magic lamp in America. How does it operate? By simply taking our good ideas, putting them to work on the production resources at hand, and doing our job well in an atmosphere of freedom and productivity.

Discussion Questions

1. Identify and discuss the factors of production.
2. Why is productivity termed the "road to higher living standards"?
3. Describe and illustrate what is meant by "output-per-man-hour."
4. How can there be an improvement in productivity in the service sector of our economy? Can you measure it?
5. How can the better use of raw materials influence productivity?
6. Discuss how "brain" and "brawn" are related to productivity.

---

[2] Edward F. Denison, *Sources of Economic Growth in the United States,* Committee for Economic Development, U.S. Department of Commerce, 1962; and *Economic Report of the President,* U.S. Department of Commerce, 1966, p. 245.

7. What meanings are connoted by the word, "capital"?

8. How can increased productivity help American industry compete against foreign firms? Give several examples.

9. How is increased productivity related to economic progress?

10. List the important factors that have contributed to increased productivity in the United States.

11. Describe some of the technological forces that are affecting the size of the business unit.

12. Discuss this statement: "The end of all production is consumption."

13. How does specialization make our economy more complex?

14. Discuss this statement: "Land, labor, and capital must be combined, organized, and directed if production is to succeed."

15. What are the disadvantages of division of labor as we know it today?

16. What facts would you look for if you were to go to another country to observe agricultural or industrial production methods?

17. Discuss this statement: "Labor productivity is largely a reflection of the work force's educational attainments."

18. How does specialization increase output per worker?

19. Discuss this statement: "The division of labor has really reduced the skill of the typical worker."

20. Would economic scarcity diminish by a corresponding amount if production should increase by 25 per cent between 1970 and 1980?

Circle the T or F (True or False) before each statement:

T   F   1. Increased national productivity will raise living standards.

T   F   2. Education and training are essential to higher productivity.

T   F   3. Labor is the sole productive factor in our economy.

T   F   4. More capital equipment per worker is required to obtain higher real wages over the years.

T   F   5. Increases in productivity result in unemployment.

T   F   6. Research is a capital investment that increases productivity.

T   F   7. Our living standards have increased as more capital equipment has been employed.

T   F   8. Our overall production of goods and services is determined by the quantity and quality of our country's production resources.

T   F   9. It's better to apply all increases in productivity to higher wages so that we can increase purchasing power.

T   F   10. Our national production cannot go up unless productivity increases.

ANSWERS

10. F   8. T   6. T   4. T   2. T

9. F   7. T   5. F   3. F   1. T

3

WHO SETS PRICES?

In recent years it has become customary to analyze the field of economics by what are called *micro* and *macro* approaches. Micro-economics is concerned with the decision-making processes of those who buy and sell—basically, consumers and producers. Therefore, micro-economics concerns itself with questions of demand, supply, costs, and prices. Macro-economics deals with the total economy. It examines the national income and the level of economic activity. It tries to find out why this level is high or low, growing or declining, and how it can be stimulated by outside forces. Macro-topics include monetary and fiscal policy, unemployment and business cycles, and economic stabilization.

The next few chapters will deal with micro-topics. This chapter will examine the pricing process by asking the question, "Who sets prices?"

PRICES AND THE MARKET PLACE

Competitive prices cannot exist unless there is a free market place where buyers and sellers can meet. And, when the free market is the balancing force, the resulting prices reflect a general equilibrium between the forces of supply and demand.

Why does coffee sell for, say, 75 cents a pound and bread for 31 cents a loaf? Some people say it all depends on supply and demand in the market place. Others argue that such prices are simply set by those who produce or sell the item. There is no doubt that all prices paid by consumers are set by businessmen, ranging from executives in large corporations to the local grocer and barber. In this sense, every price charged in a drug, bakery, stationery, or shoe store is set by administrative action. However, this does not mean that the price is going to stay there or that the businessman can set prices at any level he desires.

He must consider many factors—special product characteristics, competition, the level of demand, costs, prices of substitute products, anti-trust laws, public opinion, and political and legal considerations. Furthermore, if he sets a price at a level which consumers are unwilling to pay, he will lose business and may end in failure.

SPECIAL PRODUCT CHARACTERISTICS

The nature of the product has a definite influence on the price charged by a company. Fresh peas, for example, are subject to greater and more frequent price changes than canned or frozen peas. The need to dispose of perishable supplies before they spoil is quickly reflected in the price. Bananas are another case in point.

Machinery is something else again. In this case the buyer is less concerned about the price he pays for the machine than with the machine's ability to turn out products that he can sell at a profit. On the other hand the sale of colored television sets can be stimulated by price reductions, while price cuts may be less effective with black-and-white sets unless new features are added.

Some products, like automobiles, furniture, and appliances, are durable. When incomes decline, consumers tend to use these products longer than usual, even though their prices may have been reduced substantially. Nondurable goods like foods and gasoline are used up in one operation and must be replaced frequently. In these instances price reductions will have an immediate effect on consumer demand.

When raw materials or labor make up a large proportion of total costs, as in the case of meat or shoes, changes in these costs are customarily reflected in the price of the finished product. But for products like drugs, raw material costs are not as important as outlays for research and development.

THE ROLE OF COMPETITION

A company's price policies are also affected by domestic and foreign sellers of similar products and by the prices of close substitutes. The number of competing companies may range from a few, in industries like aluminum, to hundreds, in the case of textiles. Other industries, like steel, may consist of ten or more large companies and numerous smaller ones. For all these the competition is severe.

Typical competitive pressures may be illustrated by gasoline. Since the gasolines of different companies are readily substitutable, all brands tend to have identical prices in a given area.

Besides these pressures, no company can ignore the competition from substitute products. Cotton producers are forever fighting the competition from Dacron ®, Orlon ®, and other synthetic fibers. The price of aluminum affects the price of copper and steel. Producers of butter must take into account the price of margarine. Moreover, foreign competition is particularly heavy in products like cotton goods, carpets, transistor radios, cameras, steel, turbine generators, and chemicals. The illustration shows that our imports of steel mill products now drastically exceed our exports—a dramatic change from the situation before 1960.

All of these factors emphasize the truth that the rugged competition of the free market system plays a key role in a company's pricing decisions. The ultimate effect is to upgrade quality and reliability as well as to lower prices.

Follow the Leader

Companies may follow the leadership of other companies when making price changes. Price leadership and followership usually take place in industries whose products are relatively standardized or have substitutes —like gasoline, milk, and steel.

The initiative for changing prices generally falls on one or a few of the companies in an industry. When one firm raises its price, it is usually in response to powerful market forces which are also affecting its rivals. However, price leaders are not always followed when they raise prices. And where they are not followed, their price increases usually are

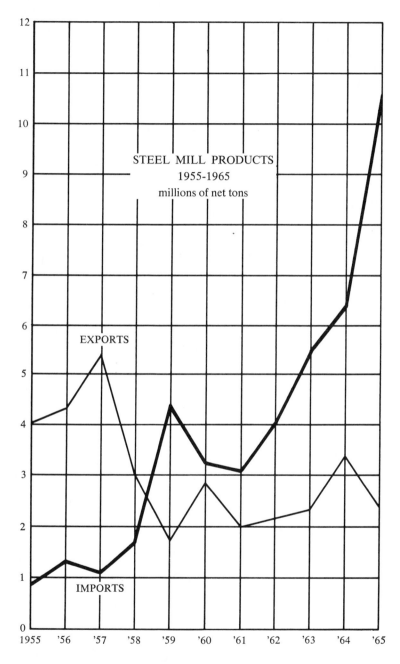

STEEL MILL PRODUCTS
1955-1965
millions of net tons

EXPORTS

IMPORTS

SOURCE: "Foreign Trade Trends," *Iron and Steel,* 1966 Edition (New York: American Iron and Steel Institute, 1966), p. 6.

rescinded. This has happened in a variety of products, including chemicals, gasoline, aluminum, paper, and steel.

The consistent matching of prices by all sellers need not indicate an agreement among companies. Indeed, such agreements are illegal. Competitive pressures provide the motivation for "price followership," because similar products tend to sell at about the same price.

Demand Characteristics and Price Policies

A key factor in price policy is the demand characteristic of the product or service sold. Demand, in turn, is influenced by the level of consumer income, habits, tastes, and availability of substitute products.

Businessmen are keenly aware that consumers will shift to substitute products if "the price is right." For this reason, they build customer loyalty by better quality, service, delivery, advertising, and so on.

The company that takes advantage of a temporary demand situation by charging a price higher than its competitors may profit for a short period of time. However, it may lose out in the end because of public ill will.

Companies producing new products or services may consider broadening the market by lowering prices. But other companies must decide whether a lower price will raise their volume of sales high enough to compensate for the loss in revenue per unit.

Costs and Prices

Costs are important, but they are just one factor in setting prices. There is no doubt that a company cannot indefinitely sell its products at a loss and stay in business. It can sell some of its products at a loss to offer a full line, or it can even operate in the red for a time. But to survive, it must obtain enough income from all of its sales to cover total costs and earn a profit.

Unfortunately, many people believe that a company adds up its costs for a given product and then simply sets a price high enough to provide a liberal margin of profit. To be sure, all sellers would like to do this, but there is no assured way of doing so. The level of demand, competition, and other factors often make it impossible to get a price high enough to recover all costs on every product. Profits may be reduced or even converted into losses.

In reality, price more often determines the costs that can be incurred. This is particularly evident in women's apparel, which is usually sold on a price-line basis. The price determines the cost which can be absorbed. If costs go down, it is possible to offer a better quality dress at the same price. When costs go up, they may be accompanied by a deterioration in quality. There may be times, too, when higher costs are absorbed by reducing the size of a product which is sold at the same price. A good example is a bar of chocolate candy.

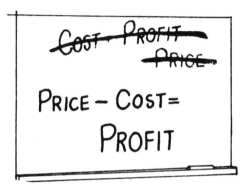

Costs play an even less important role where new products are concerned. Production costs cannot be accurately determined until the market is tested and some idea is obtained as to the volume of sales. But the volume of sales, in turn, depends upon the price.

Cost-price relationships are important. The price you can get under prevailing conditions of demand and competition usually determines the costs you can incur.

Excess Capacity and Prices

Excess capacity is another consideration in pricing. A good example of excess capacity is the effort of air lines to fill seats by offering special rates when wives travel with husbands, when children accompany parents, or when students travel at special times. It may come about because of a temporary decline in demand, improvements in response to competitive pressures, a permanent decline in demand, or an overestimation of the market.

Excess capacity affects the degree of competition and a company's pricing decisions. Heavy overhead costs continue even when a plant operates below its capacity. At lower levels, however, overhead costs must be recovered from fewer units of output. This, in turn, raises unit costs. To help cover overhead charges, new orders may be accepted even though lower prices must be quoted.

At times price cutting becomes so severe that too much business is accepted at prices which involve substantial losses. This often happens in milk or gasoline price wars. There is a limit, however, to the amount that can be sold at special prices if a company is to avoid bankruptcy.

Political Pressures

In recent years, political pressures have had an important impact on pricing policies. Appeals and threats by government officials, known as "jawbone controls," as well as investigation by congressional committees, have definitely influenced the pricing actions of companies in some industries. Obviously, these pressures tend to upset the workings of a free market system.

Public Relations and Price Policies

There are times when companies feel compelled to give reasons why they have raised or lowered their prices. Actually, companies are free to charge their prices as long as they operate within the law. But, if their prices are too high, no company explanation will make up for the unwillingness of consumers to buy the product. In many instances companies do not charge all they can get at a particular time because they are more interested in their long-term position than in temporary profits.

After World War II, industries like steel, automobiles, and farm implements did not raise their prices as much as they could. Long-run considerations influenced management not to "charge what the traffic would bear." Some people, therefore, were able to buy these products at relatively low list prices and resell them at much higher prices.

Our country's antitrust laws cast a long shadow over pricing decisions because any agreement with competitors to fix prices is automatically illegal. Moreover, companies must charge the same price to different business buyers of the same or similar quantities of a product. Otherwise they are guilty of price discrimination under the Robinson-Patman Act.

The trouble is that court decisions can make today's legal pricing illegal tomorrow. After a recent court decision, for example, the discount structure was substantially altered because canners were permitted to buy cans as well as to rent closing machines. Producers of shoe machinery, business machines, bowling-alley equipment, and the like must now price for sale as well as for lease.

The so-called "fair-trade laws" permit retail prices to be fixed for many trademarked and branded products, including drugs and appliances. But the courts have set aside some state laws, thus eliminating the effectiveness of fair-trade pricing in these areas. Thus, knowing what is legal and what is not is no simple matter in today's complex economy.

The Role of Personal Judgment

There is no way to feed the many factors affecting prices into a computing machine and to come out with the "right" price. Competition, demand, public relations, political pressures, and legal factors cannot be assigned numbers which add up to a price. Moreover, these factors assume varying importance at different times and for different products. The "feel" of the market by the price maker is more significant than his adeptness with a calculating machine. That is why simple formulas for pricing are not infallible. The price maker must adapt himself to the market place and furnish goods and services which are in demand at a price that consumers are willing to pay. If he services his customers' needs better than do his competitors, he can generally sell at more competitive prices and realize an improved return on his effort and resources.

In the last analysis, the competitive market system sets the boundaries within which companies must conduct their business—and will ultimately determine their success or failure.

Discussion Questions

1. Distinguish between micro- and macro-economics.
2. Describe several micro problems with which you are familiar.
3. What factors determine prices in the market place?
4. How does the relative durability of goods affect their market behavior?
5. Discuss this statement: "The American economy is highly competitive."
6. Describe how foreign trade affects competition? Give some current examples.
7. Does the practice of "follow the leader" mean that competition has failed?

8. What demand characteristics must be considered in the determination of market prices?

9. Discuss this statement: "Total costs determine prices."

10. Give your opinion on whether fair-trade laws are really fair.

11. How does excess capacity affect prices?

12. Describe how political pressures affect prices.

13. When might a company sell below its costs of production? Can you mention specific cases?

14. How are price policies in basic industries linked with public relations?

15. Explain the influence of personal judgment in the setting of prices.

16. What is meant by "a feel of the market"?

17. How do antitrust laws influence prices?

18. Discuss this statement: "The competitive market merely sets the outside boundaries for pricing, but that's all it does."

19. What restrictions or forces may keep a company from raising its prices at will?

20. Discuss this statement: "Price really determines the costs that can be incurred."

Circle the T or F (True or False) before each statement:

T   F   1. Consumers play a vital role in setting prices.

T   F   2. The price of a product is really determined by the cost of producing it.

T   F   3. Competitive markets tend to balance the quantity demanded with the quantity supplied.

T   F   4. The price of a product should not be allowed to rise above a customary or traditional level.

T   F   5. A good way to protect consumers from high prices is to have the government keep prices down.

T   F   6. The government has clear rules regarding monopolistic practices in industry.

T   F   7. Monopolies are easier to maintain than—say—fifty years ago.

T   F   8. Competition tends to keep prices at the lowest level consistent with a reasonable profit.

T   F   9. There's no good reason why a rock and roll singer should make more money than a tool and die maker.

T   F 10. Wages are really prices.

ANSWERS

10. T	8. T	6. F	4. F	2. F
9. F	7. F	5. F	3. T	1. T

4

THE ROLE OF
DEMAND AND SUPPLY

We have described the general factors that determine how prices are set, as well as the competitive conditions that prevail in the market place. Now we take a look at demand and supply analysis—the tools that economists use to explain how competitive prices are arrived at in the market place.

The words "demand" and "supply" are used in everyday conversation and in newspapers and magazines. As used in economics, however, these terms mean something quite different from what the typical person has in mind. For example, demand does not mean simply "how much of something we would like to have." Nor does supply denote "how much of something there is." When the word "demand" is used in economic reasoning, it means *how much of a product or service people are willing to buy at various prices which might prevail in the market place.* And when economists use the word "supply," they refer to *how much of the item sellers are willing to put on the market at various selling prices.*

Naturally, the competitive interplay of demand and supply—of buyers and sellers—determines what market prices will prevail. These market prices, in turn, will move up and down with changes in demand and supply. With this in mind we shall look more closely at the demand side, which illustrates the basic psychology of buyers.

DEMAND

The basic rule of demand is summed up in this statement: *All other things being equal, people will generally buy more of an item when its price is low. They will usually buy less when its price is high.* You will notice the phrase, "all other things being equal." This is included because, at any other time or with any given item, the rule may not apply. Thus, lower prices may give people the impression that prices will go still lower—and so, they may temporarily refuse to buy, despite lower prices. Or lower prices could be a disadvantage—as, for example, with certain perfume, dress, or cosmetic lines.

As a general rule, though, people shop for bargains, and so they are more apt to buy when prices are lower rather than when they are higher than normally prevailing prices. This, of course, is the basis of most sales held periodically by department stores.

You can see this principle at work if you consider the situation that faces most housewives when they buy a week's supply of groceries. To lure the housewife, most supermarkets run special sales and frequently use "loss leaders." In other words, they may sell some items below cost to get housewives to buy other items at more profitable prices. Sales on meat, fruits, and vegetables are often used for this purpose. Meanwhile, most housewives are quite clever at picking up bargains. They compare items for quality, size, and other factors before they buy. They may even buy different items at adjoining stores to save on their overall shopping bill. And all other things being equal, the critical factor in their decision to buy is usually the price.

Now, let us imagine a housewife going into a store to buy a week's supply of meat. She studies the various cuts and prices of meat, and she notices that beef is selling at a much higher price than, say, chicken. She may decide to buy chicken in place of beef, particularly if the price of beef is significantly out of line. In any event, she and other housewives will usually buy more of any one item—in this case, chicken— if its price is sufficiently lower than substitute items. Consumers are able to substitute, and as long as they can, they will vary their demand for products with an eye to pricing. We can show a hypothetical demand for chicken, depending upon its price. For example the housewives in a given area might be willing to buy the following amounts of chicken at the various prices shown:

> 5,000 lbs. of chicken at 60 cents a lb.
> 10,000 lbs. of chicken at 50 cents a lb.
> 15,000 lbs. of chicken at 40 cents a lb.
> 20,000 lbs. of chicken at 30 cents a lb.

Their overall demand for chicken at these prices can be illustrated by a demand curve, as follows:

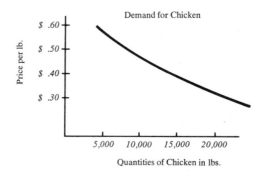

Demand for Chicken

Quantities of Chicken in lbs.

This curve shows that the quantity of chicken that would be demanded is less at higher prices than at lower prices. The same would hold true for other meats commonly used by the family. And as we said earlier, this illustrates the psychology of a buyer, who usually seeks greater value for his money. The hypothetical demand curve shown is oversimplified, and does not represent the actual demand curves that might exist, but the principle is essentially the same.

SUPPLY

Obviously, a person who *sells* meat is not going to follow the psychology of a buyer. He is going to try to get the best price he can for the meat he puts on the market. So, from a supply point of view, the following basic rule prevails:

All other factors being equal, sellers will furnish more of an item at higher prices, and they will furnish less of an item at lower prices. However as conditions change, lower costs of production may make it profitable to offer increased amounts at lower prices.

This general principle can be seen in the following figure, which shows a supply curve going upward to the right.

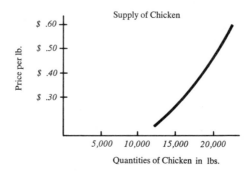

Supply of Chicken

Quantities of Chicken in lbs.

It is easy to see why sellers would be willing to increase the quantities supplied at higher prices.

First, if prices move up and costs lag somewhat behind, sellers will make more profits on everything they sell. They are then encouraged to increase production and to expand their operations. On the other hand, lower prices will not encourage them to expand, unless their production costs are falling fast enough to justify their taking advantage of a broader market. The marketing of color television sets is a good example of how falling costs and lower prices expand the overall market and ultimately increase the total profit a seller might make. The seller also may be forced to lower his asking price because of competitive factors arising from increased productive capacity in an industry.

Second, higher prices usually permit relatively inefficient producers to operate, and their inefficiency results in higher costs. Typical is crude oil. You have perhaps seen some oil wells operating while others are shut down. As a rule, the price of crude oil determines which wells can operate profitably and which must be capped until such time as the price of crude oil moves up high enough to permit marginal wells to operate. Or take the case of copper. When copper is low in price, high cost mines cannot operate at all. Only efficient mines can operate under the extremely competitive conditions that often prevail. Here again, higher prices permit marginal facilities to operate and thus encourage an increase in the quantity of copper supplied.

Let us get back to meat. When meat goes up in price, farmers are encouraged to ship cattle, lamb, and hogs to market. The meat packer, too, is encouraged to carry a bigger inventory and to increase his production costs, because he can recoup his higher costs by higher prices. Thus he may truck in beef from longer distances, or pay overtime to see that meat is made available at the prices offered.

To summarize, then, a supplier will usually furnish more of an item if his profit margins go up, if increased production costs can be covered by higher prices, or if inefficient properties or facilities come into operation because of higher prices.

THE EQUILIBRIUM POINT
AND THE MARKET PRICE

Our hypothetical demand and supply curves for chicken are combined in the illustration on the next page.

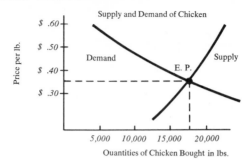

Supply and Demand of Chicken

In highly competitive markets, demand and supply will be working against each other constantly. Momentary equilibriums will be established from time to time, depending upon where the two curves intersect. The intersection point is called the equilibrium point (EP) because, at that point, the quantity demanded equals the quantity supplied. In the illustration the equilibrium point is at about 17,500 lbs. of chicken.

Competitive prices tend to move toward the equilibrium point because of the rational market behavior of buyers and sellers. If, for example, the price of chicken were considerably above the intersection point, the quantity of chicken supplied would exceed the quantity demanded at that price. Inventories would increase, and meat packers would have to mark down their prices or cut back their production to bring it in line with the prevailing levels of sales. On the other hand, if the price of chicken were considerably below the equilibrium point, the quantity of chicken demanded would be greater than the quantity supplied, so prices would be bid up by consumers wanting more chickens.

Our simplified demand and supply analysis may give us the fallacious idea that competitive prices remain stationary at the equilibrium point. Yet we know from our experience that the prices of products and services are constantly changing. So, let us see why there is a constant fluctuation in competitive market prices.

WHY COMPETITIVE PRICES CHANGE

If demand and supply determine competitive prices, it follows that prices will change with changes in demand and supply.

Changes in Demand

In economics we distinguish two kinds of demand changes: *nominal* and *real*. For example, in the following dual illustration, we show the two kinds of demand changes.

As we lower price, the quantity demanded is increased—and we know ahead of time that this will happen provided we lower the price. This change in quantity demanded exists *right in the curve,* so we call it *nominal,* meaning a change in name only. On the other hand, we can have a *real* change in demand—and this can be shown by *moving the demand curve to the left or right,* as you can see from the illustration. This is quite different from the nominal change in demand brought about by lower prices.

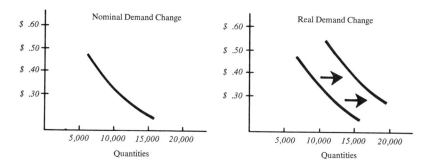

For example, a real increase in demand—that is, when the curve moves to the right—may come about because:

1. The taste of consumers has changed
2. The income of consumers has gone up
3. The prices of close substitutes have increased

Consider the changing tastes of consumers. Recently people have become quite conscious of their weight, and there has been a great deal of discussion about high-cholesterol diets. As a result the entire pattern of consumer spending has changed for sherbet, skimmed milk, eggs, cream, candy, fatty meats, and other products. These changes in consumer tastes have affected the demand characteristics of such products. Some have shown real increases, while others have experienced real decreases.

It is not hard to see why changing consumer income would affect overall demand. If a new company moved into a small community and caused a local boom, there would no doubt be a real increase in the demand for houses, churches, home lots, automobiles, furniture, transportation, education, doctors, and other goods or services associated with growth areas. Today, there are such areas of growth in the Southeast, the Far West, in the Rocky Mountain states, and in the Northwest. Also, when a new suburban community springs up, there is an immediate need for public facilities—water, sewers, education, and the like.

Finally, the *prices of close substitutes* affect the equilibrium price at any given time. If butter rises sharply in price, more oleomargarine probably will be sold. If beef skyrockets in price, people will switch to other meats or to cheaper cuts of beef, like hamburger or short ribs. If conventional bacon goes out of sight, people may discontinue eating bacon altogether, or they may switch to Canadian bacon or picnic hams. Or if regular bacon jumps in price, Canadian bacon may also go up in price.

In any event the real demand for an item may go up when people's incomes rise, tastes change, or the prices of close substitutes increase. Naturally, the reverse of these would lead to a real decrease in demand for any given product.

Real Changes in Supply

As we said before, suppliers are willing to offer for sale more of a product when its price is higher. In the long run, however, they may offer more of a given product at lower prices if lower costs permit them to do so and the demand for the product is relatively elastic. Thus, in the long term, the quantity of most items offered for sale tends to increase with lower prices, *provided technology lowers production costs sufficiently to permit this to happen.*

Students of demand and supply analysis are often confused by this, and they believe they have found apparent contradictions to the original argument. But over long periods of time, increased quantities supplied are possible at lower prices because costs of production play an important role in the willingness of a supplier to furnish items at any price level.

Most mass-production industries are the result of the broadening of the market for consumer goods and services. The market is broadened by lowering the price and by increasing demand. A good example is the automotive industry, which started out as a high-price and high-cost industry with a limited demand. When the first cars were produced, they cost $3,000 to $4,000 or more. This was too much for the times, and so only limited production was possible. The mass market for automobiles developed when Henry Ford was able to lower the costs of production and sell his Model "T" for about $400. Meanwhile, rising incomes, better quality levels, and a growing population have made the new mass automotive market possible at present price levels.

Another example is the market for color television sets, which has expanded as prices have come down. The lower prices, in turn, are being made possible by changes in the technology of tube making and by solid-state modifications.

It is possible for the real supply of an item to increase if:

- Cheaper ways are found for producing the product
- Product prices can be increased, thus raising profit margins
- No better profits can be made in alternate product areas

On the other hand, the real supply of a product or service may go down when:

- Costs go up
- Prices fall, thus cutting into profit margins
- Better profits are available in other product areas

Changes in Demand and Supply Considered Together

We may now have given the impression that we can consider changes in demand separately from changes in supply. In fact this is possible for purposes of economic analysis. But the equilibrium price established in a competitive market is the result of demand and supply factors working on each other.

For example, there has been a tremendous increase in the demand for television sets since they first came on the market. If we ignored the supply side, the price of television sets should have gone completely out of sight. Yet television sets are priced quite low in comparison to their original prices, and they are of much higher quality. Prices did not go out of sight because the supply increased substantially as the technology of production was improved. Also, the greater consumption of sets that we have experienced has been the result of lower prices made possible from the supply point of view. We can illustrate this dynamic trend on a supply and demand chart as follows:

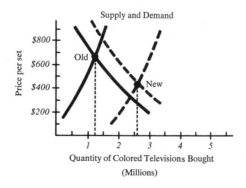

Supply and Demand

Quantity of Colored Televisions Bought
(Millions)

The same tendency for demand and supply to influence each other over the years can be seen in such diversified items as kitchen appliances, oil and gas products, automotive production, and in virtually all consumer goods areas.

THE IMPORTANCE OF COMPETITIVE PRICES

The important role of competitive prices is seldom realized by the typical student. As illustrated by the above analysis, when demand and supply factors operate freely in a competitive situation, they act as a basic organizing device for the entire economic system.

Consumers' votes, freely cast in the market place, and producers' votes, freely determined by their investment decision, really determine how the nation's overall production resources are going to be allocated.

When consumers want more of an item, they reflect it in their market demand for the item. When producers see that they can make adequate profits by producing certain goods and services, they commit their production resources to the area of greatest consumer demand. So, in the long run, consumers decide freely where production resources will be used and what goods and services will be produced. Competitive prices also help direct production resources to the areas of highest priority. And these high priority areas are again determined by the votes of consumers.

Without competition our economic system could not be as flexible nor as efficient as it is, and it would lack the dynamic quality of a living organism.

LIMITATIONS ON COMPETITIVE MARKET PRICES

Naturally it is more difficult for businesses and individuals to succeed when rigorous competition prevails. It is only human nature, therefore, to try to avoid the effects of competition. Moreover, the government, through various programs and legal means, tends to overrule competition in many areas of our economic system. We are all familiar with government interferences with the competitive price mechanism. Over the years, for example, the government has supported the prices of key farm commodities. This has been tantamount to fixing prices, because the farmer has been guaranteed a price for certain farm products regardless of their true competitive position in the market place. Also, by inserting basic conditions and guidelines in its contracts, the government has specified the acceptable level of wages to be paid, and in many cases, this level has exceeded the prevailing wage rates in many communities.

In the case of public utilities and transportation, monopolies have been accepted as desirable because duplicate companies furnishing gas, electricity, water, or telephone service are considered uneconomic. In these cases, the "natural" monopoly is justified by detailed public regulation of the rate structures of the various companies.

In the private sector we have had many instances where companies have tried to fix prices or monopolize a given area to avoid the rigors of competition. That is why the antitrust laws were placed on the statute books, and have been carefully enforced ever since. Unfortunately these laws have not been clear in their original intent or in their application, and many companies have been found guilty of antitrust infractions despite their belief that they were acting in a truly competitive manner. We shall say more about antitrust legislation later on in this book.

Labor has long had the practice of trying to eliminate competition in wage rates. The fundamental purpose of union agreements is to freeze wage levels over periods of time, regardless of what market conditions may dictate. Also, trade unions like the building trades have prevented the construction of prefabricated buildings by building codes which favor on-the-site manual-type skills. Thus, carpenters, electricians, plumbers, and others who want to protect their position in a local construction market try to keep out prefabricated structures by building-code restrictions.

CONCLUSION

The fact that so many people try to avoid competition in the market place should teach us how important it is to the preservation of the public interest.

Competition organizes the economic system more efficiently and more fairly than any other alternative method. So from our point of view, it is impossible to talk about a free market economy unless there is vigorous competition among the producers and consumers of goods and services.

Economic systems which have tried to plan the economy, without using competition as the controlling element, have usually failed to provide the volume of goods and services that make up a high standard of living—and in the process, they have eliminated personal freedom as well. If we want a high standard of living with commensurate freedom, we must maintain vigorous competition in all areas of our economic system.

Discussion Questions

1. What does the word "demand" really mean?
2. Summarize the basic rules of demand.
3. Why might consumers not buy when prices are falling?
4. Why is the typical demand curve negatively sloped?
5. How are prices and quantities related in a typical demand schedule?
6. Why does a typical supply curve slope upward and to the right?
7. Comment on this statement: "Higher prices permit inefficient producers to operate."
8. Distinguish between *demand* and *quantity demanded*.
9. How do demand and supply interact to develop an equilibrium point?
10. Explain what happens when the market place is displaced from the point of equilibrium.
11. Why do competitive prices change?
12. What is meant by a real change in demand? An increase in demand? A decrease in demand?
13. Is there an increase in demand if a person is willing to buy three of an item at $5.00 each or four at $3.00? Explain.
14. What factors cause a real change in demand?
15. What is the significance of the phrase, "All other things remaining equal"?
16. What is meant by a change in supply?
17. What influence does technology have in changing supply?
18. What is the difference between *quantity supplied* and *supply?*
19. Discuss this statement: "It is far more difficult for a business to succeed when competition is vigorous."
20. Is there an increase in supply when a supplier is willing to offer six items at $10, but nine at $11? Explain.

Circle the T or F (True or False) before each statement:

T   F   1. Competitive markets tend to balance the quantity demanded with the quantity supplied.

T   F   2. When the demand for a product goes up, its price tends to go up, all other factors equal.

T   F   3. When prices go up, producers generally increase their production.

T   F   4. When the supply of an article is greater than the quantity demanded, the price usually goes up a little.

T   F   5. When the price of a product goes up, the price of a close substitute may go up.

T   F   6. If the demand for a product remains the same, an increase in its supply will probably lower its price.

T   F   7. The equilibrium point is where the demand and supply curves intersect.

T   F   8. Scarcity means that there are not enough production resources to satisfy all conceivable economic wants.

T   F   9. A real change in demand is demonstrated by moving the demand curve to the right or to the left.

T   F   10. An increase in demand is inevitably followed by an increase in price.

ANSWERS

1. F   3. T   5. T   7. T   9. T
2. T   4. F   6. T   8. T   10. F

5

THE COMPETITIVE CHALLENGE AT HOME AND ABROAD

In our competitive economy, millions of people work for business concerns and farms to produce the thousands of different goods and services people need and want. In 1965, for example, about 19 million persons were employed by manufacturing and mining, 13 million in trade, 12 million in finance and services, 4 million in transportation and public utilities, and 3.2 million in construction. Agriculture accounted for another 4.5 million, and more than 10 million were employed by the various units of government.[1]

These individuals and businesses are trying to profit from their economic activity. What, then, insures that these purely private activities will serve the public interest? In our economy, when consumers and producers are free to act in their own behalf, their activities are guided toward the public interest by competition. Competition works to our advantage when we go out to buy the goods and services we want. It is competition, too, that makes our business firms produce efficiently.

This chapter discusses three main points about competition:

- How important competition is to our economy
- The different types of business competition
- What we must do to remain competitive

[1] Board of Governors of the Federal Reserve System, *Historical Chart Book,* 1966, p. 81; and *Economic Report of the President,* U.S. Department of Commerce, 1966, p. 238.

HOW IMPORTANT COMPETITION
IS TO OUR ECONOMY

As we said before, there are two basic ways of directing economic activities toward the public interest: *by government control* or *by competition in the market place.*

Competition eliminates the need for a master plan to coordinate our national production. We need no central authority to decide what or how much to produce. No law says that we must make steel in Cleveland or cheese in Wisconsin. We leave those decisions to freedom of choice and competition in the market place. Control by government action is generally less flexible and tends to cripple personal initiative and freedom. But private enterprise, when backed by vigorous competition, encourages the best from all of us and helps protect our personal freedoms. We prepare ourselves for a better job because we naturally improve our ability when we compete with others. When we bowl or play golf, we tend to do better with stiff competition. Do you remember when you raced with other children to see who could run the fastest? Later on, you may have played on a team against other teams. You probably did your best when you faced keen competition.

Suppose we didn't face this kind of competition. Would we push ourselves to accomplish as much as we are capable of? Probably not. Competition is a spur to personal initiative, and without it, we are not apt to do our best.

Business firms are a lot like people. They do their best when they operate in competitive markets. They go all out when they know that other companies may step in and turn out a better, cheaper, or more attractive product. Competition enables us to know whether our business firms are performing to the best of their capabilities. And it is competition that keeps our economic system at the peak of efficiency at all times. With this in mind, let us describe the three basic types of competition we meet in the economic arena:

1. Competition between domestic companies in the same industry
2. Competition between different industries
3. Competition from foreign producers

Competition Between Companies in the Same Industry

When companies compete with one another, they try to meet the customer's requirements of price, quality, performance and service. You would not buy a suit of clothes if you knew you could get as good a suit for less money. The same thing applies to the products your company makes. If its prices are not competitive, your sales department faces a very difficult job.

However, there is a lot more to competition than price. Certainly, quality is a decisive factor. When your customers buy something, they want your products to be as good in quality as the best at that price.

Then, customers want performance. No one likes to buy an article that works at one time but not at another. You expect and demand reliable performance over the life of the product—and that is why some companies have a better reputation than others. The price and apparent quality of two competing products may appear the same in the beginning, but a company's reputation eventually depends upon the trouble-free performance of its products. Finally, there is the all-important factor of service. Difficulties may arise during the lifetime of an article, so adjustments or minor repairs may be needed. The important thing is to back up the product with quick and dependable service. Nothing is more irritating than to buy a product, have something go wrong with it, and then not be able to get prompt or dependable service.

Remember, too, that prompt and reliable service applies to more than products. The clerk in a store, the waitress in a restaurant, the attendant in a gas station, the person at a ticket counter, the salesman representing his company—everyone who meets the customer and deals with his needs and problems—has an opportunity to keep his company's customers satisfied. It is a lot easier to say "service" than it is to deliver it day-after-day on the job; yet this is what we must do if we want to stay competitive.

Thus, when a company competes for a growing share of the industry's market, it must meet the difficult standards of *competitive prices, high quality, good performance,* and *excellent service.* Crucial "word-of-mouth" advertising comes from customers who are satisfied with the products they buy. This means that a company's employees must do their share to keep it competitive in all of these areas. Anything less will weaken its competitive position, make their jobs less secure, and their future opportunities more difficult to realize.

Competition Between Different Products or Industries

There is increasing competition between different products or industries. To a large extent this represents competition between different materials or types of service. For example, the plastics industry is comparatively young and aggressive. One result is that many items are packaged in plastic containers rather than in containers made from glass, wood, aluminum, or steel.

Glass, meanwhile, is more widely used in automobiles and buildings. Compare an old office building with a new one. Notice how metal walls and glass have taken the place of brick or cut stone.

Another example is coal, which has been fighting a competitive battle with oil and gas. And, of course, these have been competing with one another as well as with electricity. In the transportation field, airplanes are competing with railroads, trucks, busses, and steamships.

So, as you can see, there is a never-ending competition between industries for new customers and new markets for their products. When an industry wins, the result means more customers and more jobs for the people working in that industry. But when it loses, it means fewer customers and fewer jobs.

Competition does indeed bring more success to some than to others, but that is the objective of the system and the price of progress. Competition forces us to be appreciative of our customers, to be realistic about day-to-day operations, to plan for the future, and to be prepared to meet competitors in the market place.

Progressive companies carry on continuous research programs to gain new markets or to recapture markets that are being lost to other companies and industries. But research alone cannot do the job. To win, a company must have the best combination of research and development, production performance, and aggressive selling methods.

Competition from Foreign Producers

There is increased competition between companies at home and those abroad. Count the foreign cars the next time you take a drive. Or walk through a department store and check the number of products made in other countries. You will surely agree that competition from foreign producers is getting more intense.

There are two main reasons for this increased competition. First, the industrial plants of most foreign countries have been completely rebuilt since World War II. They have modern plants and well-trained employees, and are aggressive competitors in the world's markets.

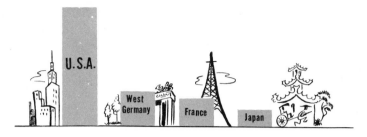

COMPARATIVE WAGE$

Second, foreign production costs are often low by our standards. As a result, they frequently can produce products more cheaply than we can.

In the past we made up this difference in production costs by using ultramodern equipment which made our operations more productive. But foreign concerns now have modern equipment capable of high quality, low cost production.

Thus, we face a renewed competitive challenge at home and abroad. It is imperative, then, that we take a close look at the things we must do to remain competitive.

WHAT WE MUST DO TO REMAIN COMPETITIVE

There are several ways in which a company can improve its ability to compete:

Research and development

Diversification

Design and styling

Aggressive marketing and selling

Effective cost reduction

Intensive research is leading us into a new era, paced by rapid advances in electronics, metallurgy, and physics. This means that a large part of our competitive effort is taking place right in our research laboratories, and for that reason, competent and aggressive research personnel are going to be very important to us.

Stiff competition is forcing industry to develop new materials, new products, and new processes. Today's product may have to be replaced tomorrow by something better. We see this every day in the pharmaceutical business, where one drug or antibiotic may replace another almost overnight. This trend requires that many companies develop a "product mix" that balances one product life against another to insure profitable operation over the long run. That is why companies are constantly striving for greater diversification.

Emphasis on research is being paced by dramatic changes in design and styling, which make consumers long for the new and the different.

Besides research and design, we need aggressive marketing and sales. As a consequence, companies are improving the competitive position of their products by catering to special markets, stressing product quality, and doing a better selling job. No industry can sit still and rest on its laurels. It must improve, and it must adapt to its customers.

Finally, a competitive company is always cost-conscious. This is so essential that we have devoted the next chapter to the need for competitive costs.

CONCLUSION

The most important conclusion of this chapter is that competition is essential if we are going to get the best possible performance from our business firms.

A second key point is that all of us have a job to do if we want our economy and our companies to remain competitive. It does not matter whether we are in the plant or in the office, a salesman or a research employee. Everyone has a part to play.

We need the good ideas of employees who are close to the job and know it in its finest details.

We need understanding salesmen who can mirror the needs of customers, for we cannot compete unless we relate production to customers' needs.

We need research, engineering, and marketing personnel, who can come up with new products, better designs, and market them attractively.

We need capable managers who can plan ahead, develop a good product mix, for strategic markets, and lead a successful competitive team.

We need money to buy the tools required to produce more and better products. Here investors play a vital role in our ability to compete.

By being competitive—and staying competitive—we can insure the future success of our companies and contribute to the security and future opportunities of our economic system.

Discussion Questions

1. How important is competition to the effective working of our American economy?

2. Comment on this statement: "Government control is inconsistent with competition."

3. When is government control more efficient than competition?

4. What different kinds of competition does American industry face today?

5. How does inter-industry competition differ from intra-industry competition.

6. How do research and development affect competition?

7. What is meant by brand competition?

8. Discuss this statement: "Foreign competition should be eliminated."

9. How do the production costs of foreign industries affect the competitive framework of our economic system?

10. What are the prerequisites to keep American industry competitive?

11. How does an effective "product mix" affect competition?

12. How can employees enhance the competitive position of their companies?

13. What is management's role in meeting the competitive pressures of the market place?

14. Why is competition relied upon more in the United States than in most other countries?

15. Why has government been providing more services in recent years?

16. Why is it necessary to regulate some businesses in a free enterprise system?

17. Name as many regulated industries as you can.

18. What factors might the government consider when regulating the rates of an electric power company?

19. Why does government find it necessary to operate some enterprises and provide some services to its citizens?

20. What is meant by "non-price" competition?

Circle the T or F (True or False) before each statement:

T F 1. We are relatively self-sufficient as a nation.

T F 2. There is little foreign competition in industries like textiles, steels, or electronics.

T F 3. A product mix tuned to consumer markets tends to improve a company's competitive condition.

T F 4. Higher costs can be absorbed by higher prices in most situations.

T F 5. Business firms operate best in highly competitive markets.

T F 6. Substitute competition increases as research and development continue to grow.

T F 7. Non-price factors are important in a company's ability to compete.

T F 8. A large number of mergers is an indication of the competitive nature of our economy.

T F 9. The government has a responsibility to keep our economy competitive.

T F 10. The basic industries of the United States are non-competitive.

ANSWERS

1. F	3. T	5. T	7. T	9. T
2. F	4. F	6. T	8. T	10. F

6

COMPETITIVE COSTS

To remain competitive at home and abroad, a company must keep its costs down and its efficiency of production up. This is more easily said than done, but there are sensible courses of action that can be taken.

First, we should agree that our standard of living would suffer if vigorous competition were not on the job encouraging efficiency and prog-

PRICES • FOREIGN GOODS | PRICES • U.S. GOODS

ress. And if this is true, our best long-term solution is to attack a main part of our competitive problem: *The high cost structure of American products.*

Our costs are high because virtually everything that goes into the production cycle has gone up in price: research and development, material costs, wages and salaries, transportation, taxes, and selling and administrative expenses.

The impact of rising costs can be emphasized by a familiar daily experience. Not long ago, one of the authors bought a new automobile from a dealer with a good reputation. The author's wife looked over the interior, while he checked into its horsepower, performance, and economy of operation. They discussed the car at some length with the salesman, and finally reached what must be the most painful of all questions: "How much does it cost?" This is the crucial point, where a sale is made or lost, setting in motion a series of consequences which may lead to more customers and more jobs, or to a downturn in business for the dealer and manufacturer.

They bought the car after the usual offers and counter-offers—and, looking back, it was a good deal. It was quality product at a competitive price, and they got the assurance that it would be backed up and serviced by a reputable manufacturer and dealer. We relate this simple story because there are not many words as commonly used or as decisive as the simple phrase, "How much does it cost?"

- We use it every day when we go shopping.
- We use it when we buy appliances and furniture—or have painting, repairs, or odd jobs done.
- Companies, large and small, ask this question when they buy materials, tools, or other goods and services used in their operations.
- Government agencies ask it when they advertise for bids on supplies, defense contracts, and construction projects.

The fact is . . . we are all cost-conscious when we buy something. Everybody tries to stretch a dollar, and for that reason, our wallet or purse is a very sensitive area. Under these circumstances, there are three essential ingredients to success in business:

- *Make* a quality product or furnish a service that people really want.
- *Produce* it at a competitive cost.
- *Sell* it at an attractive price.

These ingredients can be stated in the simple formula:

$$\text{Sales Income} - \text{Total Costs} = \text{Profit or Loss}$$

We can make a profit when our sales income is greater than our total costs, including taxes. Otherwise, we have four main choices:

- Increase sales income.
- Reduce costs.
- Raise prices to cover higher costs.
- Switch to other products, or limp along and perhaps go out of business.

There are many good reasons why these alternatives cause their share of problems for management.

THE SALES-COST SQUEEZE

Many factors affect sales income, such as the basic demand for the product and its general attractiveness, quality, reliability, and performance. Then there is the reputation of the company, its marketing and sales aggressiveness, competition from domestic and foreign producers, and general business conditions.

Therefore, the level of sales often depends on factors beyond management's control. Even the most successful companies may experience severe competition and a drop in sales. When demand drops or competition gets keen, product prices become weak and profit margins thin.

When sales cannot be increased, the best thing to do is to reduce costs, because something can be done about that part of the "success formula." Companies tend to get flabby during good times, so there's room for improvement when things get tough. Today, it is imperative that we improve our cost position as a nation. Production costs have been rising steadily since the end of World War II. For a while, these higher costs could be covered by higher prices because the demand for goods and services was growing and competition was not as vigorous as it is today.

But in recent years production costs have continued to climb during periods of declining business, with increased foreign and domestic competition, and even when weaker prices prevailed. As a result, profit

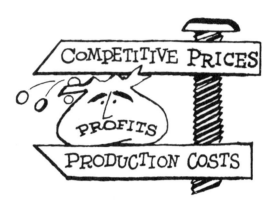

margins have been cut to the point where the typical company earns less than 6 cents on each dollar of sales. In other words, 94 cents or more of each sales dollar is used to pay bills of one kind or another.

For 1965, for example, the all-industry median was 5.5 per cent or 5.5 cents of profit on each dollar of sales. The 5.5 industry median means that half the industries showed percentages above 5.5 cents and half below that figure. The comparable percentage for 1964 was 5.0. The range in 1965 was from 11.1 cents per dollar of sales in mining to a low of 2.8 cents in food and beverages.[1]

COMPETITION CHANGES THE PICTURE

This trend to high costs and its effects are easy to see in the motel business. There was a time when travelers were content with clean, modern rooms at reasonable rates. But before long they upgraded their standard of living on the road. They demanded—and they got—private phones, free television, swimming pools, entertainment, dining facilities, ice-making machines, free newspapers, free breakfasts, and next-stop reservation service. Meanwhile, construction costs rose sharply, as lobbies were added as well as air conditioning, paved roads and parking areas, picture windows, landscaping, and fancy entrances.

[1] "The Fortune Directory of the 500 Largest United States Industrial Corporations," *Fortune,* Vol. LXXIV, No. 2 (July 1966), pp. 250–251.

Even so, the owner could sometimes manage, provided other newer or larger motels did not open in the same area. But as a rule, he was not that lucky. When competition moved in, he probably found himself with more rooms but more vacancies per night throughout the year. All in all, he might end up with more money invested, greater capacity, increased costs, higher taxes, bigger risks, a lot more money going through the till, and less profit per dollar of sales at the end of the year. Obviously, you have to be on your toes to survive and succeed under these conditions.

There is not much difference between this example and what has happened to the typical American business firm. Most companies expanded after World War II, increasing their output of old products and adding capacity for new goods or services. Specifications and quality levels were continually pushed up. This meant intensive research and development, which in turn required more and better equipment and facilities. Higher nonproduction costs entered the picture as scientists, engineers, research, and other staff personnel were added to the pay roll. During this period, too, the cost of everything was going up—raw materials, employment costs, state and local taxes, machinery and tools, construction costs, plant sites, transportation, and maintenance.

This is what has happened to one large company in a key industry since 1946:

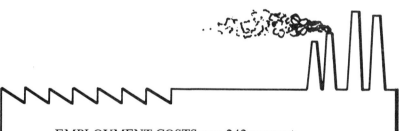

EMPLOYMENT COSTS rose 242 per cent.
CONSTRUCTION COSTS increased more than 140 per cent.
HEAVY EQUIPMENT costs went up 150 per cent.

All other costs, including raw materials, rose sharply, and these costs were reflected in smaller profit margins as time went on.

Taxes—particularly local and state—took a bigger bite. In 1965, income taxes alone took an average of 41 cents out of each dollar of corporate profits.[2] Out of the remaining money the company must pay dividends and have funds left to reinvest in the business to help it stay competitive.

This is not an unusual situation, nor is it limited to one company or industry. Across the country higher costs and closer profit margins on sales have been the rule rather than the exception.

RISING COSTS POSE A LONG-TERM PROBLEM

For some time after World War II higher production costs and higher taxes were covered by strong customer demand and by capacity operations which permitted companies to make maximum use of capital investment. But as downturns in business occurred—and as domestic and foreign competition became intense—cost control became essential to economic survival even during periods of good business activity.

When a business is comparatively small, like a motel, the owner knows from day to day how things are going and what he must do to survive or to prosper. He has the urge to do something because his life savings are most likely at stake. But in a large company, the employee may not immediately see the long-term effects of high production costs. Moreover, where such a company is concerned, there may be an unavoidable time lag between knowing that costs are rising and being able to do something about them. This is caused, in part, by the nature of a company's activities.

For example, basic research and construction projects cannot be discontinued every time there is a drop in business. What do you do with a plant that is half finished, which you don't need now, but may require in a year or two? What do you do with employees in training who don't contribute to your present productive effort but who will do so in the future? What do you do with an expensive research program that you can dispense with today but that may insure the company's life in the long run? In other words, how do you balance the short-term need to cut costs with the future soundness of the company?

These are the tough decisions a company's management must make, and there is no sure way of making them correctly. If you put yourself in management's shoes, your responsibility is to organize and to administer a company so that it can:

---

[2] *Federal Reserve Bulletin* (November 1966), pp. 1706–7.

- *Produce* efficiently
- *Sell* its output
- *Plan* ahead intelligently
- *Succeed* in the future

Your planning generally is based on what is going well and what is doing poorly. If a product line is doing well, you will most likely expand and commit more of the company's production resources to that effort. This will mean more and better jobs within the company and greater employment opportunities within companies that supply the machinery and materials needed for the expansion. But when the product is doing poorly, you may be forced to cut back production, reduce job opportunities, switch to another product, or go out of that particular business.

In any event, success will come to your company only if you produce efficiently at competitive costs and sell profitably in a competitive market.

COSTS ARE EVERY EMPLOYEE'S BUSINESS

It is important to remember that cost control is not simply top management's responsibility. There is a great deal that every employee can and should do, since each employee has a lot to lose if his company cannot keep its costs in line with competitors. In such circumstances, it may have to raise its prices and thus encourage its customers to drift to other companies. Along with its customers may go the very jobs upon which the employee and the total economy depend for their future growth.

The inevitable effects of high costs can be described in a series of simple statements:

- Higher costs may mean higher supply prices and fewer customers.
- Fewer customers mean fewer jobs.
- Therefore, higher costs and higher prices may mean fewer jobs in the long run.

But the opposite is also true:

- Competitive costs make possible competitive prices.
- Competitive prices generally mean more customers and more and better jobs.
- Therefore, competitive costs mean more and better jobs.

You may say, "That's fine, but what can the typical employee do to help out?" Let's see what he can do.

Accountants classify costs as *fixed* and *variable*. They also talk about *controllable* and *non-controllable* costs. There are some costs about which an employee can do very little—for example, property taxes and insurance. These are pretty well fixed, and are not controllable by the employee. On the other hand, many expenses go up and down with the level of production—like raw materials, man-hours of work, simple tools, general supplies, heat, and light. These are known as variable costs.

The key point, however, is that there are no set variable costs for a given level of production, because every step in the production process can be improved if all employees do their individual jobs better. Thus higher costs are every employee's business because costs accumulate at every job position within a company.

THE FACT IS . . . EVERY PENNY COUNTS

All kinds of items make up a company's costs—raw materials, blueprints, automobiles, trucks, telephone, light, heat, outside services, office machines, wrapping paper, string, postage stamps, paper towels, paper clips, and rubber bands. Employees have many opportunities to economize in the use of these items.

In recent years the typical company has earned a net profit of less than 6 cents on each dollar of sales. The rest of the money went for manpower, materials, plant expenses, taxes, and other costs. Thus, cost savings of only 1 or 2 per cent could improve profits dramatically.

The typical manufacturing company has to sell more than $15 worth of goods to earn $1 in net profit. But this $1 profit could be earned by reducing costs by $2. Taxes would probably take away about $1 of the saving, leaving $1 in profit after taxes. Put another way, it takes $15 in sales to earn about the same profit as $2 in cost reduction. The ratio is almost 8 to 1 in favor of cost dollars.

Cost dollars are "high-powered dollars," because every dollar saved is a dollar earned before taxes.

Here is another example from everyday life. If a child goes into a supermarket and playfully tears open the top of a box of cookies that sells for 35 cents, the store would probably have to sell $25 worth of groceries to cover the loss! Its margin of net profit, if it is a typical chain, is probably about 1½ cents on the dollar, and so it would require additional sales of $25 to make up for the 35-cent loss.

This shows how important it is for industry to be cost-conscious, for a saving in cost of 35 cents in the above example might be much easier than an increase in sales of $25. Here we are not talking merely about big items over which the employee has little control; we are really talking about saving a few pennies here and there throughout a company or organization.

Costs, of course, can be prevented in many ways, for instance by:

- Reducing the cost of maintaining and of repairing equipment
- Extending the life of tools, or keeping them in better shape to reduce scrap
- Reducing start-up and shut-down time, or cutting down on absenteeism
- Doing the job more efficiently

- Saving on the use, storage, and transportation of supplies and raw materials
- Working more safely and eliminating accidents—and all they mean in heartache, loss of income, and insurance claims

A company's ability to compete depends on the efforts of all of its employees and representatives. It starts with employees in the research laboratory, and continues through every step of design, production, sales, and service. Everyone who handles an order, helps make the product, guards its quality, maintains equipment, does the paper work—everyone in fact who works for a company plays an important part in its ability to compete.

Just offhand, what if someone bet us a thousand dollars that we couldn't improve our individual jobs by, say, 5 per cent? Most of us could find a way to make that kind of improvement. For many companies, this is actually the difference between remaining competitive or falling by the wayside.

Perhaps our big handicap, after spending years on a job, is the tendency to develop a set routine. To make changes for the better, we must look at our job from a new point of view. In a sense we have to look at it as though we had never seen it before. Increased job efficiency means doing something a little bit better, and probably a little bit differently.

We can use our job knowledge to discover new and better ways of doing things—ways that will save materials, raise quality, eliminate scrap, reduce start-up time, improve product flow, cut inventories, or improve customer service. It is really impossible to mention all of the different ways, because every job represents a new challenge.

AMERICA'S HIGH AND RISING EMPLOYMENT COSTS

We use the term "employment cost" because some people are only conscious of their hourly wage and take-home pay. They overlook the deductions on their pay check, and often forget that a company pays for many benefits and taxes that never appear on their pay check stub.

The supplemental wage payments that an employee may never see on his check stub include insurance and pension plans, hospitalization, workmen's compensation, unemployment compensation, paid vacations, paid holidays, and social security taxes. Recently, the French National Institute of Statistics compared employment costs in the United States with the leading countries of Europe. At that time, it found our employment costs to be as much as three to four times as high as West Germany, Switzerland, Britain, Belgium, France, and Italy.

To compete with the lower employment costs abroad requires the very best in every one of us. Anything less will have the effect of "exporting

American jobs" to other countries. On the other hand, we can definitely hold our own if we improve the efficiency of our operations.

Discussion Questions

1. Explain how American industry can be competitive despite its high-cost structures.

2. Comment on this statement: "High wage costs have made American industries non-competitive in nature."

3. Explain how foreign competition has affected the following industries:
   a. Steel
   b. Automobiles
   c. Electronics
   d. Housing

4. Discuss the significance of the question, "How much does it cost?"

5. Describe the key factors that determine a company's profit or loss.

6. Which is more manageable?
   a. Costs?
   b. Prices?

   Justify your answer.

7. Describe the nature of a sales-cost squeeze. Give specific examples.

8. Discuss this statement: "Companies get flabby during good times."

9. About what percentage of the sales dollar goes for profits in the typical manufacturing firm?

10. Show how competition has caused some costs to increase.

11. Distinguish between controllable and non-controllable costs.

12. Discuss this statement: "Taxes are an important cost factor."

13. What can a businessman do to combat the long-run increase in his production costs?

14. What is the difference between fixed and variable costs? Give several examples.

15. Why does the rate of profit rise more rapidly above the break-even point?

16. How do standards and routine procedures increase production costs?

17. What can be done about the rising employment costs in the United States?

18. How do rising costs affect the flow of investment funds?

19. Give several examples of how variable costs can be reduced.

20. How does volume of operations affect the fixed cost per unit of product?

Circle the T or F (True or False) before each statement:

T F 1. The alternative cost of buying a given product is the other goods or services that cannot be bought.

T F 2. Dollars of sales will result in more net income than the same number of dollars saved by cost reduction.

T F 3. There is no profit below the break-even point.

T F 4. The best way to lower the break-even point in a competitive market is to raise prices.

T F 5. Cost dollars are "high-powered dollars" because any savings go directly into income before taxes.

T F 6. The fixed costs of doing business include depreciation and interest on borrowed money.

T F 7. Waste and scrap are substantially the same.

T F 8. Cost consciousness is a psychological problem that's easy to overcome.

T F 9. An employee who saves 50 cents a day can make a real impact on his company's overall operation.

T F 10. Marginal costs are usually higher than average costs.

ANSWERS

10. T	8. F	6. T	4. F	2. F
9. T	7. F	5. T	3. T	1. T

7

PROFITS, ECONOMIC GROWTH, AND SECURITY

Different economic systems use different approaches to reach their growth goals. Our economy uses profits as the key incentive to economic growth. When industry is prosperous, employment and economic progress follow. But when industry is depressed, unemployment and lower living standards usually prevail. Indeed, a little adversity can ruin the profit picture of a company. Moreover, businessmen are motivated by expectations of future profits, so it is important that their outlook be optimistic if industry is to increase its output and provide more jobs.

This chapter describes the role of profits in our economy by discussing how profits:

- Help preserve economic freedom
- Promote economic growth
- Build personal security and job opportunities

PROFITS HELP PRESERVE ECONOMIC FREEDOM

An economic system is the way people organize themselves to produce the goods and services they want over the years. This requires the efficient use of materials, machines, methods, manpower—and, of course, the money to pay for them. We also need capable management, or we could not produce effiiciently the volume of goods and services that make up our high and rising standard of living.

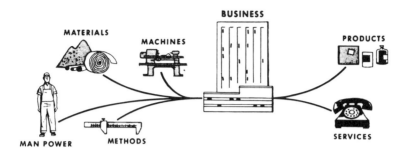

As we said earlier, no economic system can produce all of the conceivable things its people would like to have, so it must balance unlimited wants with its limited resources of machines, manpower, materials, and money. And to do this every economic system must decide:

- *What to produce* of the many things that people would like to have
- *How much* of each good or service to produce
- *How to produce* these efficiently

In our economy these decisions are made by consumers who are free to buy whatever they please with the money they have. In a very real sense, every dollar they spend is a vote of confidence for the goods or services they want produced.

On the other hand, a lack of consumer dollars automatically tells a producer that people do not want his products. This forces him to produce the type of goods and services that people will buy, and to do so at attractive prices.

So our changing dollar votes literally force the shift of production resources from one company or industry to another, as changes take place in our consumer demands. We do not rely on state planners to order what should be produced or how resources should be allocated. We attract the resources by using incentives, and by this method we preserve our economic freedoms.

FREE ENTERPRISE ECONOMY

STATE PLANNED ECONOMY

To attract manpower, we pay adequate wages. To get raw materials, we pay the going market price. To entice investment capital, we hold out to investors the possibility of a profit. And here's where profit plays a key role. Without profit there would be few good reasons for stockholders or creditors to let us use their money. And if we cannot use their money, we cannot buy the resources of production. When we can't buy the resources of production, there will be fewer tools, less production, and insufficient jobs.

PROFITS INSURE ECONOMIC GROWTH

For these reasons, profit is a key incentive to economic growth and to the efficient use of production resources.

To A Growing Economy

Someone must provide the tools we need to produce and to remain competitive. Someone must supply the capital to develop our natural resources and to pay for raw materials. Someone must furnish the money to hire the skilled employees and the capable management we need to run our companies. And, in our economy, a large part of the money required is made available by people who save their money and invest it with the idea of earning a profit.

People often think of a company's profit as so many dollars in the bank—but, by and large, this is not so. A part of its profits is paid out in dividends to stockholders, but the remainder is plowed back into the company to provide more and better machinery, plant, and equipment.

When people receive regular dividends, they are more inclined to let businessmen use more of their money. But when a company does not earn a profit, there is no money to pay out or to plow back. You would not lend someone your hard-earned money if you knew he would not be able to pay you back. It is no different with a company. Unless a company pays its bills and makes a profit, few people are going to lend it money or buy its stock. That is only common sense.

What, then, encourages the growth of our economy? Well, we can highlight three basic steps:

- Economic growth takes place when we make full and efficient use of our natural resources, machines, and manpower.
- We make the fullest use of these resources when people have the incentive to save and to invest their money in private industry.
- The proven incentive is the possibilty of earning a profit on invested savings.

PROFITS BUILD JOB SECURITY AND NEW JOB OPPORTUNITIES

In the years ahead we are going to see a sharp rise in our population and a big increase in the need for schools, hospitals, utilities, and roads. On top of that, there will be new products and new materials coming out of our research laboratories—all of which should make our lives easier, safer, and more prosperous. However, these developments require large amounts of capital to make them realities.

Some people have the idea that a rising population automatically guarantees a booming economy. Yet places like India and China prove unmistakably that a large population without a sound economic system is no guarantee of progress.

During the coming years we must provide millions of productive jobs for the flood of young people pouring out of our high schools and colleges.

To make these jobs possible, we must have the tools and equipment that our new workers need to produce future goods and services. All told, we shall probably need about $800 billion in new investment money during the 1970s—far more than at any time in our history. Healthy profits will help us raise this investment money and provide the new tools needed for our future work force.

For all of these reasons, a profitable company is a most beneficial institution. It creates more and better job opportunities for its employees. It serves the public's interest by producing more and better goods and services over the years. It generally assures job security. It gives employees a chance to retrain for better jobs when their skills are made obsolete by technical changes. It guarantees the community a pay roll and a future. Without a profitable company, the typical worker

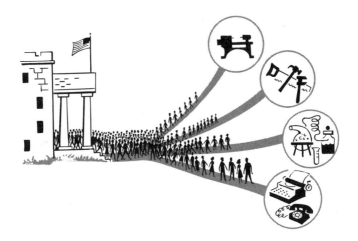

would live in constant fear of what was going to happen to him and his family.

Unfortunately, some people have the idea that companies are immortal. They seem to think that every large company will be around permanently, regardless of business conditions or the market for its products. The facts, however, are quite different. All of us can remember well-known companies that are no longer around. They just could not meet the basic conditions of survival: modern products, low costs, high quality, competitive prices, and adequate profits.

If competition does its job properly, inefficient and unprofitable companies are not likely to survive indefinitely. And if they do survive, they will be marginal firms that furnish no degree of security to their employees. On the other hand, a profitable company means a better future for everyone—consumers, employees, investors, suppliers, and the government.

- *Consumers* gain, because a profitable company usually produces quality goods and services at attractive prices.
- *Employees* are better off, because profits build economic growth, with better job opportunities, greater security, and a higher standard of living.
- *Investors* benefit, since they are reasonably sure of a satisfactory return on their savings.

- *Suppliers* are better off, because a profitable company buys a large part of its materials and services from other firms in the economy.
- The *government* benefits, since profits are an important source of government revenue.

Today corporate profits provide a full 30 per cent of the federal government's income and a big share of local and state taxes. In this way profitable companies help provide schools, hospitals, roads, and many other public services that will be required in greater volume in the future.

WE CAN HELP KEEP OUR
BUSINESS FIRMS PROFITABLE

American industry will continue to have trouble staying profitable because of high operating costs and keen competition at home and abroad. Generally, a profitable company has to be efficient, or it wouldn't succeed in our competitive economy. And keeping a company fit is the responsibility of every employee who works for it. There are many things we can do to help keep our company competitive and profitable— about as many different ways as there are people in a company.

One final word about profits and the prices of capital equipment. People sometimes forget that high prices affect a company just as they do the average consumer. As a matter of fact, rising prices make it very hard for industry to replace old tools and to buy new ones. Modern and efficient tools are essential to the over-all productiveness of our country. When tools are up-to-date, we can turn out more and better products, and do so at lower costs and cheaper prices. Our ability to compete and to remain profitable depends largely on the "youthfulness" of our capital equipment. When our machines and tools are old or obsolete, we just can't compete because we just can't be efficient. A study by Fordham University emphasized that one-third of our country's tools and equipment were obsolete, and that $70 billion worth (or more) would become obsolete by 1970. During the next decade obsolescence will be a bigger factor than ever because of research discoveries and rapid technological advances. Our big problem is to replace tools and equipment as soon as they are no longer efficient. When this cannot be done by depreciation allowances, profits play an important role. For when a company plows back a part of its profits, it helps provide some of the money for the new and better tools we need.

COST ORIGINALLY $10,000

REPLACEMENT COST $15,000

WHAT PROFITS DO

Let's review briefly how profits help consumers, workers, investors, and the government:

- Profits encourage people to invest their savings in private industry. Their money buys the production resources we need to turn out the goods and services which make up our high and rising standard of living.

- When profits are healthy and growing, they attract more and more investment money, and by so doing, they guarantee the long-range economic growth of the nation.

- Healthy profits are essential if we are going to provide job security and growing job opportunities for the millions of young workers who will be entering our labor force.

- Profits encourage companies to buy more goods and services from supplier firms, fostering economic growth and development.

- Profits help pay for the new and better tools we need to keep industry strong and competitive. And in the future, this need will be greater than ever before.

- Profits provide a large share of government revenue at the local, state, and federal levels.

These are the reasons why profits are a key incentive to economic growth. Like the spark plugs in a car, profits are small in size but they keep the economy moving ahead.

Discussion Questions

1. How do national economic goals differ among different economic systems?
2. What key incentives does the American economy use to promote economic growth?
3. What problems are common to all economies?
4. How do state-planned economies differ from free enterprise economies in seeking answers to these problems?
5. How are profits related to the preservation of economic freedom?
6. Comment on this statement: "Profits contribute to economic growth."
7. How does increasing an economy's stock of capital assets affect its economic growth?
8. Show how the various sectors of the economy gain as economic growth takes place.

9. How can an individual employee help increase the profitability of his firm?

10. In what ways are profits related to job security?

11. Give examples of a favorable and an unfavorable environment for economic growth in the American economy.

12. Discuss this statement: "We are doing a good job of preserving the leading incentives responsible for economic growth in the private sector."

13. Why does the United States need economic growth?

14. How does economic growth in your state and community compare with that of the United States as a whole?

15. To what extent is growth related to natural resources? To human resources?

16. Present supporting data to show the rate of growth in the United States in this century.

17. What influence does education have on economic growth?

18. What forces are basically responsible for our extraordinary economic growth during the last century? In your opinion, what forces will contribute to such growth in the future?

19. List some of the economic possibilities available to today's high school and college students.

20. How is the Gross National Product related to over-all economic growth?

Circle the T or F (True or False) before each statement:

T   F   1. There are few business risks when times are good.

T   F   2. Profits after taxes for all corporations average more than 15 per cent of the national income.

T   F   3. A company's profit level determines what its prices are going to be.

T   F   4. Profits are a reward for taking business risks.

T   F   5. Profits measure the efficiency of management.

T   F   6. Rates of profit should be higher in some industries than in others.

T   F   7. Bondholders don't have to be paid when a company skips its dividend to the stockholders.

T   F   8. Profit on sales is a good measure for comparing companies in different industries.

T   F   9. Profit on investment is a good way to size up companies in different industries.

T   F   10. High profits are ethically untenable.

ANSWERS

10. F	8. F	6. T	4. T	2. F
9. T	7. F	5. T	3. F	1. F

8

THE ROLE OF MANAGEMENT

The term "economics" is derived from the Greek *oikonomike, oikos* meaning "the sum of one's possessions" and *nomos* meaning "management." As used by the Greeks the term came to describe the art of prudent and systematic household management.

The early Greeks had a healthy respect for a person who could manage his family affairs economically and use resources prudently and to good advantage. Similarly, in today's complex and competitive world, few things are as important to our country as the efficient management of commerce and industry. Our economic system depends for its success upon having efficient management to convert the nation's production resources into the largest possible amount of quality goods and services for consumers. How well we succeed depends on how efficient we are—and to a large extent, that depends on the kind of management we have.

Indeed, the survival of a free enterprise system depends on efficient management, because management must maintain the flow of sales between a company and its customers. It must come up with new and better products, more attractive designs, adequate service and performance, lower costs, and constant capital improvements. It must guide the company's operations in the best interests of employees, customers, stockholders, and the community.

As *employees,* we depend on effective management for continued employment and future security. As *customers,* we look to management to provide the thousands of quality products and services available at competitive prices. As *investors,* we depend on sound management to use our savings wisely and to provide a fair return from profitable operations. As *communities,* we need profitable companies because their pay rolls, contributions, and taxes help support vital activities like education, charitable drives, hospitals, and other community programs.

Sound management is essential in a broader sense, too. The real question today is whether we will survive as a free nation or will join the civilizations that no longer exist. And, if the past twenty years are prologue to the future, we face difficult problems, revolutionary changes, dynamic challenges, and unsurpassed opportunities.

Politically, we live in a divided world dominated by the fear of nuclear weapons. Culturally, we are seeing the masses of the world stirring with a rampant nationalism that is sweeping across entire continents. Economically, we are experiencing an aggressive invasion of our domestic and foreign markets by friend and foe alike. As a result, American industry is having to find changing markets and is undergoing a revolution in production methods, tremendous increases in capital requirements, new and different personnel needs, complicated government regulations and controls. All this adds up to an industrial way of life quite different from that of the past.

We must now concern ourselves with the crucial problem of national and industrial survival, and this survival depends more on the quality of our human resources and the effectiveness of management than on any other factor. With these things in mind, let us take a minute to consider what management really does. Actually, management must:

- Direct other people and see that the work gets done
- Bring about healthy changes that will insure business survival and growth
- Run the company so that it can compete in today's markets

MANAGEMENT'S GOAL—A BETTER
AND MORE SECURE FUTURE

All three obligations are important management responsibilities. But perhaps management's most important job is to bring about healthy changes to insure business survival and growth.

Management assures business survival and growth through constructive and positive change. Today's performance is the result of management decisions made months ago. Tomorrow's future depends on difficult decisions that are now being made, decisions that will bring about changes in product, in design, in financing, in marketing, and in manufacturing methods—all aimed at giving the company a better chance to survive in the never-ending competitive battle.

Even so, planning and directing business growth and survival are far more complicated than knowing what changes are necessary and then carrying them out. If you had to plan a company's future, which of the following factors do you think would have the greatest effect on your plans?

- Product improvements desired by customers
- Manufacturing methods used by your competitors
- Your company's financial resources

BUYING SUCCESS ON THE INSTALLMENT PLAN

Again, all three answers have a crucial bearing on business decisions. In the long run, however, a company is distinctly limited by the financial resources at its disposal. Therefore, management must constantly weigh what should be done against what the company can afford to do.

No company can do everything it would like to do for its employees, stockholders, customers, and the community. Expansions which create new job opportunities, new and improved products which increase a company's strength in the market place, community contributions, and scores of other benefits depend on profits and financial strength. A company without adequate finances cannot do these things, no matter how good its intentions.

Management has to budget the company's future success in step-by-step increments, year after year. This requires decisions as to which projects can be started immediately, and which should be put off because the company cannot afford them.

MANAGEMENT'S RESPONSIBILITY
TO THE EMPLOYEE

Now, let us consider management's responsibility to those who have a vital interest in the company. We'll start with the company's employees. What should an employee expect from his company?

- Steady, full-time employment
- An opportunity to practice his particular skill or profession
- A constantly rising standard of living

Unfortunately, management cannot really create steady work nor a rising standard of living for a company's "employees," and that word includes management personnel. Management helps make those benefits possible by planning for business survival and growth. But it takes all employees to make the benefits real. High productivity, careful craftsmanship, and efficient production and sales are some of the ways that employees can help management achieve the goals of steady work and better job opportunities.

Management's basic responsibility is to provide each employee with an opportunity to earn a competitive income by practicing his particular skill or profession. Every other employee benefit depends upon how well employees take advantage of the opportunities offered by their jobs.

The employee depends on management to supply him with work and

with up-to-date tools and facilities to do that work. Management must supply specialists to keep these tools and facilities in good shape, a sales force to bring in the orders, and engineers to design the company's products and to figure out the best ways to produce them. Management supplies raw materials and arranges for delivery of the finished products.

Most important of all, management must analyze changes in the market place and make plans for the company's future stability, so that employees can have reasonable expectancy of continued employment.

Management, however, must depend on all of its employees to produce efficiently and with craftsmanship. It is only when management and all other employees work together toward a common goal that benefits like improved wages, working conditions, and better living standards can become a reality.

MANAGEMENT'S RESPONSIBILITY TO THE STOCKHOLDER

What about the stockholder? What does he expect from the management of a company in which he has invested his hard-earned savings?

- A chance to sell his stock at a profit
- A return on his investment in the form of dividends
- Sound, well-planned business growth over the years

Stockholders naturally are interested in realizing a return on their investment in the form of dividends. And, of course, they want the market price for their stock to go up. But a stockholder's main concern is the sound and continuing growth of the business in which he has invested his

money. In the long run this alone will assure his dividends and enhance the value of his investment.

America's 20 million stockholders come from all walks of life and the overwhelming majority of them are not speculators. The stockholder who is investment-conscious wants to see his company survive and prosper. That is why management must run the company profitably and plow back some of the profit to provide new products, better facilities, and the aggressive research and development that help a company move ahead of its competitors.

MANAGEMENT'S RESPONSIBILITY TO THE CUSTOMER

Now, what about the customer? Do his demands conflict with those of the employee and the stockholder? What is it that the customer wants from management?

- The lowest possible price
- A well-made product he can rely on
- A reliable and prosperous company that is likely to stay in business

The first two choices are obviously important. But in a fundamental way, they depend on the third.

Some people may consider it strange that a customer should be interested in the survival of the company from which he buys. After all, isn't the customer really after the lowest possible price, whether the company makes out or not?

Let us suppose that you are planning to make a substantial purchase— maybe an automobile, a camera, a home appliance, or some other item from which you expect long and reliable service. You look at two or more competing brands, and they seem to meet your general requirements. One is the product of a well-known company that has a fine reputation. The other product is cheaper, maybe even looks good. You wonder how it can be made at that price. You have heard that the company is having financial trouble and may not stay in business.

The chances are that you will buy the product turned out by the successful and well-established company, for you would have few doubts about its quality, reliability, and service guarantees.

It is management's job to see that the company's products are the best in the market so that buyers will be satisfied and will become repeat customers in the future.

MANAGEMENT'S RESPONSIBILITY
TO THE COMMUNITY

But what about the community in which the company is located? What is the most important thing that the community should expect of management?

- Leadership in community affairs
- Tax money to support local government
- Business survival and growth

A company's contribution to the community cannot really be measured by its tax dollars or by its participation in civic and welfare activities, because its most important contribution fundamentally is business survival and growth.

A growing company is essential to the community because it provides a source of jobs that bring new residents to the community and keep them there. At regular intervals the company pours substantial pay rolls into the community through its employees. These pay rolls generate the trade that keeps the community's stores, banks, restaurants, theaters, service stations, dry cleaning and laundry establishments, bowling alleys, and scores of other private enterprises in business. Thus a community's entire economy is tied in great measure to the growth of its companies and industries. Sometimes this is not realized until it is too late. Responsible management can help make a community aware of this fact, but

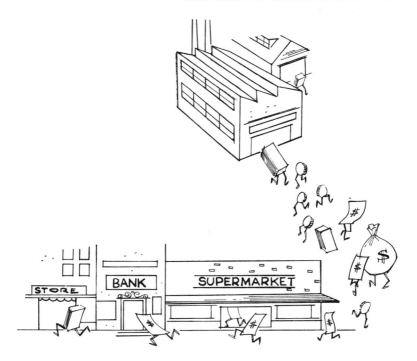

management alone cannot create a favorable business climate for industry. Everyone in the community must help.

Today, many communities are in trouble because they have not encouraged industry to move into their areas, or because they may have made it difficult for their industry to compete.

REVIEW—THE RESPONSIBILITIES OF MANAGEMENT

We will continue to progress as a nation if we encourage everyone through personal and corporate incentives to upgrade his skills and talents, to assume business risks, and to work co-operatively to overcome the challenge we face.

It means meeting competition at home and abroad by turning out more and better products at lower cost—in short, by improved efficiency of production.

It requires that we keep sufficient capital flowing into private industry by making sure that investors earn an adequate return on their savings.

It implies a mobile work force with employable skills, which can earn high and rising wages through productive performance.

All of these, in turn, assume sound management that can take our country's resources and use them wisely to meet changing market opportunities as they develop in the years ahead.

Moreover, our communities should do all they can to generate a business climate that will encourage established companies to stay, enable new industries to move in, and keep pay roll dollars and other benefits flowing for everyone's best interest.

Discussion Questions

1. How does the study of economics relate to management?
2. How does the survival of free enterprise relate to management?
3. How does effective management affect employees, customers, and investors?
4. What is the responsibility of management to the community? To the state? To the nation?
5. How is business management related to government and politics?
6. Describe some of the fundamental challenges faced by business management today.
7. How is change related to progress?
8. How does adequate financing affect a company's future potential?
9. What are the main things that employees can rightfully expect from their companies?
10. What responsibilities does management have to the stockholders?
11. How do adverse changes in the market place affect management responsibilities?
12. Discuss this statement: "Customers always want the lowest possible price."
13. Give illustrations of business leadership in your community.
14. What are some of the community's costs of business failure?
15. Why is management "everybody's business"?
16. Discuss this statement: "The growth of large corporations has meant the end of individual proprietorships."

17. Who assumes the responsibility for risk-taking in our modern business system?

18. Discuss 'this statement: "Management must pursue economic objectives."

19. Why should management care for and feed new ideas?

20. Discuss the statement: "Business management today is a highly specialized science."

Circle the T or F (True or False) before each statement:

T   F   1. A set of management rules can be developed which will be applicable in most circumstances.

T   F   2. Managerial jobs differ so widely in scope and content that no practical generalizations about management are possible.

T   F   3. A basic management function is planning, which includes setting objectives and specifying the steps needed to reach them.

T   F   4. Decision making under conditions of uncertainty is typical of our economy.

T   F   5. Mergers and acquisitions are greater in number than ten years ago.

T   F   6. Wages can be scientifically determined, so there need be no argument if management and union will just act rationally.

T   F   7. Complexity and specialization combined with rapid changes are making improved communication essential in industry.

T   F   8. Communication problems are inherent whenever management makes decisions, solves problems, induces innovation, or capitalizes on technological change.

T   F   9. In deciding whether a new course of action will be helpful in attaining his objectives, a manager must consider whether the returns are worth the time, effort, and risk.

T   F   10. With all the new products coming out, managers would be wise to wait and see what's going to happen before they embark on new product development.

ANSWERS

1. F	3. T	5. T	7. T	9. T
2. F	4. T	6. F	8. T	10. F

9

THE ABC'S OF
FINANCIAL
STATEMENTS

This chapter will describe in detail the financial statements which companies use to measure their economic performance. These statements are essential to effective management, and a knowledge of them will prove valuable in personal financial planning.

All of a company's detailed accounting records ultimately lead up to:

- The Income Statement
- The Balance Sheet

The Balance Sheet and Income Statement complement each other, and they provide a wealth of information about a company.

The Income Statement is more popularly known as a profit and loss statement, or more simply as a "P-and-L" statement. It reviews the company's performance over a period of time—a month, a quarter, or a year.

The Income Statement *reports sales, costs and taxes,* and *whether the company made a profit or loss* for the period. Naturally, how the company fared during the period affects its Balance Sheet.

The Balance Sheet tells us the financial health of a company as of a given date, say December 31, 1966. It tells us *what the company owns* and *what it owes,* and it measures the company's net worth in dollars and cents.

The Income Statement fits in between two successive balance sheets like this:

Dec. 31, 1966 Balance Sheet

±1967 Income Statement (Profit, Loss and Disbursements)

Dec. 31, 1967 Balance Sheet

Thus, the Income Statement for 1967 builds on the 1966 Balance Sheet, and generates the 1967 Balance Sheet

WHAT THE BALANCE SHEET ITEMS MEAN

A balance sheet consists of assets and liabilities. *Assets* are generally shown on the left, and they represent items that the company *owns*. *Liabilities* and *Stockholders' Equity* are usually shown on the right. These are items which are *owed* to others or to the company's stockholders. The two sides always balance because:

Assets = Liabilities + Stockholders' Equity
Stockholders' Equity = Assets − Liabilities

With this in mind, let's describe the *Asset* side of a balance sheet for a mythical XYZ Company, as of December 31, 1966. All assets are classified according to how soon they can be converted into cash. Cash comes first, then marketable securities, and so on. Plant and equipment are at the bottom.

Current Assets include cash or assets that can be converted into cash within a year. *Cash,* of course, consists of currency or money on deposit in the bank. *Marketable Securities* represent investments of idle cash which may not be needed immediately in the business. The invested money should be available on reasonably short notice, so the securities must be readily marketable and have a minimum price fluctuation. The approved practice is to show marketable securities at cost.

Accounts Receivable represent moneys which have not been collected from customers to whom goods have been sold. Such customers are usually given 30, 60, or 90 days in which to pay. Some customers fail to pay their bills, so provision is made for bad debts.

Inventories consist of raw materials, partially finished goods, and goods ready for shipment. Inventories are usually valued at *cost or market,* whichever is lower.

These *Current Assets* are "working assets" because they're constantly being converted into cash. Inventories, when sold, become accounts receivable. Receivables become cash, and cash is used for paying expenses.

Moving down the asset side, the *Investment in Unconsolidated Subsidiaries* represents the cost of buying the capital stock of another company. The word *subsidiary* implies that more than 50 per cent of that company's stock is owned by the parent company. When most of the stock is owned, a *Consolidated Balance Sheet* may be issued.

ASSETS

Current Assets		
Cash		$ 950,000
Marketable Securities, at Cost		1,550,000
(Market Value $1,570,000)		
Accounts Receivable	$2,100,000	
Less: Provision for Bad Debts	100,000	2,000,000
Inventories		1,500,000
Total Current Assets		$6,000,000
Investment in Unconsolidated		
Subsidiaries		300,000
Property, Plant, and Equipment		
Land	$ 150,000	
Buildings	3,800,000	
Machinery	950,000	
Office Equipment	100,000	
	$5,000,000	
Less: Accumulated Depreciation	1,800,000	
Net Property, Plant, and Equipment		3,200,000
Prepayments		100,000
Total Assets		$9,600,000

The next item—*Property, Plant,* and *Equipment*—is commonly called the company's *Fixed Assets.* Accordingly, this category includes land, buildings, machinery, equipment, furniture, automobiles, trucks, and so on.

Depreciation represents the decline in value of a fixed asset because of wear and tear or the passage of time.

The resulting figure doesn't reflect present market value nor future replacement cost. The general accounting rule is to use original cost, less accumulated depreciation to the date of the balance sheet.

Our sample balance sheet shows a total figure for the company's accumulated depreciation. This is the total accumulated depreciation for all buildings, machinery, and office furniture. Land is not subject to depreciation, so its cost remains the same from year to year.

Net Property, Plant, and *Equipment* is the valuation of the company's investment in fixed assets, after accounting for accumulated depreciation.

Prepayments may arise from situations like this. Let's say the company paid its insurance premium for a three-year period, or perhaps leased computing machines and paid rental on them for two years in advance. As of the date of the balance sheet, there would exist an asset that had not as yet been used up.

Well, so much for the *Assets*. Now, let's take a look at the *Liability* side. The term *Current Liabilities* stands for items that will come due within a year. *Current Assets* and *Current Liabilities* are considered companion items because current assets are the prime source from which current debts are paid.

Accounts Payable are what the company owes in the course of its regular business, and it usually pays these bills within 30, 60, or 90 days. Money owed to a bank or other lender is listed under *Notes Payable,* since a promissory note has been given by the borrower.

As of any given day the company owes salaries and wages to employees, pension funds, fees to attorneys, insurance premiums, and similar items. These items of expense are grouped under *Accrued Expenses Payable.*

Taxes are stated separately under *Federal Income Tax Payable.*

Total Current Liabilities represent the sum of all of the items listed —and in this case, they add up to $2,500,000.

Long-Term Liabilities include debts which come due after one year. In this sample balance sheet, the only long-term liability is the 5% First Mortgage Bonds, due in 1970. In this case the bondholders were given a promissory note in which the company agreed to repay the debt in 1970 and to pay interest at 5% a year. The words "First Mortgage" mean that, if the company doesn't pay off the bonds, the bondholders have a claim on the company's assets, which can be sold to satisfy the debt.

Stockholders' Equity, or *Net Worth,* represents the stockholders' interest in the company and it is made up of three categories:

- Capital Stock
- Capital Surplus
- Retained Earnings

Capital Stock represents ownership shares in the company. Part of this ownership interest is made up of *Preferred Stock,* which has preference over common shares as regards dividends or distribution of assets in case of liquidation. The preferred stock is *5% cumulative, $100 par value,* which means that each share is entitled to $5 in dividends each year before any dividends are paid to the common stockholders. The word "cumulative" means that, if a dividend is not paid, the amount of the dividend accumulates in favor of the preferred shareholders and the dividends in arrears must be paid before dividends are paid on the common stock.

LIABILITIES

Current Liabilities
Accounts Payable	$1,000,000	
Notes Payable	850,000	
Accrued Expenses	300,000	
Federal Income Taxes Payable	350,000	
Total Current Liabilities		$2,500,000

Long-Term Liabilities
First Mortgage Bonds, 5% Interest,
due 1970   2,700,000

Total Liabilities $5,200,000

STOCKHOLDERS' EQUITY

Capital Stock:
Preferred Stock, 5% Cumulative, $100 Par Value Each; Authorized, Issued, and Outstanding 6,000 Shares	$ 600,000	
Common Stock, $5 Par Value Each; Authorized, Issued, and Outstanding 300,000 Shares	1,500,000	
Accumulated Retained Earnings	2,300,000	
Total Stockholders' Equity		4,400,000
Total Liabilities and Stockholders' Equity		$9,600,000

Common Stock is the ordinary ownership interest on which dividends are paid at the discretion of the Board of Directors. Such dividends may be high in prosperous times or non-existent when times are bad.

Accumulated Retained Earnings, or *Earned Surplus,* refers to the profit the company has plowed back into its operations over the years. When a company is successful, it will have some money left over each year, after paying dividends on its stock. This retained income is put to work for the benefit of the stockholders.

WHAT THE BALANCE SHEET FIGURES TELL US

The balance sheet tells us a great deal about the financial health of a company, particularly when you combine the various figures. For example, the company's "Working Capital" can be determined by subtracting "Current Liabilities" from "Current Assets":

WORKING CAPITAL

Current Assets	$6,000,000
Minus Current Liabilities	2,500,000
Working Capital	$3,500,000

A healthy working capital position means that the company can meet its obligations, expand its sales volume, or take advantage of opportunities as they come along. But what is a comfortable amount of working capital? To help answer this question, we use what is called the *Current Ratio*. This is obtained by dividing the *Current Assets* by the *Current Liabilities:*

CURRENT RATIO

$$\frac{\text{Current Assets}}{\text{Current Liabilities}} = \frac{\$6,000,000}{\$2,500,000} = \frac{2.4}{1} \text{ or } 2.4 \text{ to } 1$$

Most management specialists like to see at least $2 in current assets for every $1 of current liabilities.

Companies with a small inventory and good accounts receivable can operate with a lower ratio than companies with a larger inventory selling their products on credit. For this reason we also use what is called the *Quick Assets Ratio,* to provide additional information. This ratio is found by dividing the company's quick assets by its current liabilities, as follows:

QUICK ASSETS

Current Assets	$6,000,000
Minus Inventories	1,500,000
Quick Assets	$4,500,000

NET QUICK ASSETS

Quick Assets	$4,500,000
Minus Current Liabilities	2,500,000
Net Quick Assets	$2,000,000

QUICK ASSETS RATIO

$$\frac{\text{Quick Assets}}{\text{Current Liabilities}} = \frac{\$4,500,000}{\$2,500,000} = \frac{1.8}{1} \text{ or } 1.8 \text{ to } 1$$

In this case there is $1.80 in quick assets for every $1 of current liabilities.

We're also interested in a company's inventory position, so a common question is: "How big should a company's inventory be?" Naturally, that depends on the type of business, the time of the year, and so on. For example, an auto dealer should have a substantial inventory on hand at the *height* of the season. But, at the *end* of the season, the same inventory may be a sign of weakness.

A large inventory position may indicate that the company has on hand a big supply of unsalable goods—and that a drop in prices may cause serious losses. Moreover, inventories tie up working capital and run up interest charges which cannot be easily recovered.

One way to measure the adequacy of inventory is to compare it to the total sales for the year. In the case of the XYZ Company, as you can see from the "Income Statement," sales for the year were $6,500,000 while inventories were shown as $1,500,000 in the "Balance Sheet." Thus, *Inventory Turnover* was a little over four times a year.

Another important thing you can learn from the balance sheet is the book value of the company's securities. The *Book Value* of a bond, a share of preferred stock, or a share of common stock represents the amount of corporate assets backing up each of these securities.

The book value of the company's bonds is determined as follows:

NET BOOK VALUE PER BOND

Bonds	$2,700,000
Preferred Stock	600,000
Common Stock	1,500,000
Accumulated Retained Earnings	2,300,000
Total—Net Book Value of All the Bonds	$7,100,000

We divide $7,100,000 by 2,700, the number of $1,000 bonds outstanding:

$$\frac{\$7,100,000}{2,700} = \$2,629 \text{ Net Book Value for Each Bond}$$

As you can see, there are $2,629 in assets behind each $1,000 bond.

The book value of the preferred stock is obtained by eliminating the par or face value of the bonds and following the same procedure. We add the preferred stock, common stock, and retained earnings together to get a figure of $4,400,000. We divide this by 6,000, the number of shares of preferred stock outstanding, and the net book value per share of preferred stock is $733. Here's the calculation:

NET BOOK VALUE PER SHARE PREFERRED

Preferred Stock	$ 600,000
Common Stock	1,500,000
Accumulated Retained Earnings	2,300,000
Total—Net Book Value of All Preferred Stock	$4,400,000

$$\frac{\$4,400,000}{6,000} = \$733 \quad \text{Net Book Value Per Share of Preferred Stock}$$

The book value of a common share is obtained in the same way, by eliminating the par value of the preferred stock:

NET BOOK VALUE PER SHARE OF COMMON

Common Stock	$1,500,000
Accumulated Retained Earnings	2,300,000
Total—Net Book Value of All Common Stock	$3,800,000

$$\frac{\$3,800,000}{300,000} = \$12.67 \quad \text{Net Book Value Per Share of Common Stock}$$

THE INCOME STATEMENT

The Income Statement is important because it measures the company's operating progress over a period of time. And, for this reason, it serves as a guide as to what the company might do in the future. In its most common form the income statement adds up the sales for the year and all costs and expenses incurred. The result is a *Net Profit* or *Net Loss*.

The overall costs are usually broken down into the following categories: *Cost of Sales* and *Operating Expenses* represent all costs incurred to convert raw materials into finished products. These costs include raw materials, direct labor, and overhead items like basic supervision, rent, electricity, supplies, maintenance, and repairs.

Depreciation is the year's decline in value of all the capital equipment used by the firm. It is a cost of doing business, but is separated out for accounting and managerial reasons.

Selling and administrative expenses are grouped separately, so these items can be evaluated in relation to other costs. Salesmen's salaries and commissions, advertising and promotion, travel, and entertainment are significant items of *Selling Expenses*. Executives' salaries, office expenses, and the like are the important items under Administrative Expenses.

XYZ Manufacturing Company, Inc., and Consolidated Subsidiaries

INCOME STATEMENT—Year 1966

Net Sales		$6,500,000
Cost of Sales and Operating Expenses		
Cost of Goods Sold	$4,400,000	
Depreciation	900,000	
Selling and Administrative Expenses	500,000	5,800,000
Operating Profit		$ 700,000
Other Income		
Dividends and Interest		110,000
Total Income		$ 810,000
Less: Interest on Bonds		135,000
Profit before Provision for Federal Income Tax		$ 675,000
Provision for Federal Income Tax		320,000
Net Profit for the Year		$ 355,000

RETAINED EARNINGS STATEMENT
(Earned Surplus)—Year 1966

Balance January 1, 1966		$1,495,000
Add: Net Profit for the Year		355,000
Total		$1,850,000
Less: Dividends Paid		
On Preferred Stock	$ 30,000	
On Common Stock	120,000	150,000
Balance December 31, 1967		$1,700,000

Interest on Bonds represents the interest paid to bondholders for the use of their money. Interest is a cost of doing business, and is deductible before income taxes are paid. In this case, interest came to $135,000 a year.

Federal Income Taxes were $320,000, leaving a net profit for the year of $355,000. This net profit figure is then blended into the Balance Sheet through a "Retained Earnings Statement" shown at the bottom.

Thus, the previous balance sheet showed retained earnings of $1,495,-000. We add to this the 1966 profit of $355,000, giving a new figure of $1,850,000. From this, we must subtract the preferred and common stock dividends of $150,000, leaving $1,700,000—the figure shown in the present balance sheet.

WHAT THE INCOME STATEMENT TELLS US

The Income Statement—like the balance sheet—tells us a lot more if we're able to make a few comparisons. For example, we may want to know the company's *Margin of Profit* and how it has changed over the years. Our hypothetical XYZ Company had sales for the year of $6,500,000 and profits before taxes of $700,000.

MARGIN OF PROFIT

$$\frac{\text{Operating Profit}}{\text{Sales}} = \frac{\$\ 700,000}{\$6,500,000} = 10.8\%$$

Thus, for each dollar of sales, it realized 10.8¢ in profits before taxes.

Companies are more interested in the *net profit after taxes* since they can't use tax money, although they might be eligible for a refund in case of future losses. To find the net profit, we divide the net operating profit by the sales:

NET PROFIT MARGIN

$$\frac{\text{Net Operating Profit}}{\text{Sales}} = \frac{\$\ 355,000}{\$6,500,000} = 5.5\%$$

In other words the XYZ Company made 5.5 cents in net profit for every $1 of goods sold. We can pretty well judge the company's progress by comparing the net profit margin from year to year and with other companies in the same industry.

Investors are interested in the safety of their investment and the regularity of its income—so, to them, the company's earnings per share are particularly important. When an income statement doesn't give the earnings per share of common stock, it can be calculated as follows:

EARNINGS PER SHARE—COMMON STOCK

Net Income for the Year	$355,000
Less Dividend Requirements on Preferred Stock	30,000
Earnings Available for the Common Stock	$325,000
Number of Shares of Common Outstanding	300,000

$$\frac{\text{Earnings Available}}{\text{Number of Shares}} = \frac{\$325,000}{300,000} = \$1.08 \text{ Per Share}$$

The XYZ dividend rate is 40 cents a share, so it's adequately covered by the company's earnings. However, the company's record over the years is more important than its performance in any single year.

One way to check a company's historical progress is to keep track of the relationship between its earnings and market price over the years. This is called the price-earnings ratio, and it's calculated in this way: Our company earned $1.08 a share. Now, if the XYZ Company's stock were selling at 15, the price-earnings ratio would be about 14.

PRICE-EARNINGS RATIO

$$\frac{\text{Market Price}}{\text{Earnings Per Share}} = \frac{15}{1.08} = 14$$

By keeping an eye on this ratio over a period of years, we can pretty well tell when the company's stock is a better than normal buy. Finally, the Income Statement is useful for deterimning cash flow, which means the company's *net profit* plus *depreciation*.

Net Profit for the Year	$355,000
Depreciation Charges for the Year	900,000
Cash Flow for the Year	$1,255,000

Our net profit was $355,000. But, this was after we deducted depreciation charges of $900,000. Actually, the $900,000 doesn't represent an outlay of cash by the company, but the write-off of our investment in capital equipment during the year. We can regard this depreciation charge as cash generated during the year, and we add it to our profit to give us XYZ's "cash flow" for the year.

CONCLUSION

A company must keep an accurate set of accounting records to guide its own progress, to inform its stockholders, to report to the government, and to furnish the general public with detailed information about its business. A person can learn a great deal about a company's operating results if he takes the time to master the "ABC's" of financial statements.

Discussion Questions

1. What is the significance of depreciation to a company?
2. What items generally are contained in a profit and loss statement? What does the statement show?

3. Identify equipment bonds, mortgage bonds, and debenture bonds.

4. What is meant by equity capital? Debt capital?

5. Define the following terms:

   a. assets
   b. cash
   c. accounts receivable
   d. reserves
   e. prepaid items
   f. liabilities
   g. current liabilities
   h. preferred stock
   i. common stock
   j. surplus
   k. fixed assets

6. How is a corporation regarded in the law?

7. Outline the advantages and disadvantages of corporate organization.

8. List several ways in which a corporation can raise new capital.

9. How is a corporation organized under state law? Under federal law?

10. What do we mean by capital stock?

11. Use the following data to prepare a balance sheet for the Small Atlantic Company. Cash on hand: $50,000; accounts receivable: $25,000; inventory: $35,000; investments: $25,000; machinery, land, and building: $100,000; prepaid items: $5,000; reserves for bad debts: $2,000; reserves for depreciation: $13,000; accounts and notes payable: $40,000; bonds and mortgages payable: $100,-000; preferred stock: 1,000 shares @ $50 par; common stock: 1,000 shares @ $25 par. Calculate the book value of the common stock.

12. Use the following data to prepare a profit and loss statement for the United Imperial Textbook Company. Inventory, January 1, 1965: $50,000; purchases during 1965: $250,000; inventory, December 31, 1965: $60,000; wage bill, 1965: $50,000; depreciation, 1965: $10,000; interest paid, 1965: $5,000; taxes, 1965: $70,000; net sales income, 1965: $600,000.

13. Comment upon this statement: "The balance sheet is a still picture of assets and liabilities, while the profit and loss statement is a moving picture of performance."

14. A corporation is considered a "person by law," with limited liability. What implication does this have for raising venture capital?

15. Compare the yields of five stocks selling for above $100 a share on the New York Stock Exchange.

16. Describe how a short sale is handled by a broker.

17. What is meant by "leveraging the capital structure"?

18. How do corporate income taxes affect retained earnings as a source of capital?

19. In your opinion, have equity funds become scarce in recent years? Support your answer.

20. What are put-and-call options? Straddles? What functions do they serve?

Circle the T or F (True or False) before each statement:

T F 1. Accounts receivables are listed as current assets on a balance sheet.

T F 2. Plant and equipment are carried on a balance sheet at their original cost, less depreciation and amortization.

T F 3. The owners' equity can be found by subtracting the company's liabilities from its assets.

T F 4. A balance sheet doesn't show the taxes paid last year.

T F 5. Common stock and limited liability are characteristics of corporations.

T F 6. A company is better able to pay its bills when its current ratio is low.

T F 7. Depreciation and amortization are costs of doing business.

T F 8. Interest charges are tax deductible.

T F 9. Cash flow includes net income plus depreciation.

T F 10. Inventory turnover figures should be related to gross capital investment.

ANSWERS

10. F	8. T	6. F	4. T	2. T
9. T	7. T	5. T	3. T	1. T

10

THE INTERESTING
STORY OF MONEY
AND BANKING

Money is the most familiar part of the economic system to children
as well as to adults. It has developed many connotations, ranging all the
way from the root of all evil to the most sought after possession. "Lack
of money," "money to burn," "poor people," "the idle rich," "Wall
Street, the money market"—all become scrambled into an indigestible
mass. Soon, what seems to be a familiarity with money turns out to be
a hazy knowledge of its physical appearance, rather than its underlying
principles. So it's important that we "unscramble" this basic economic
tool and show its relationship to the rest of economics.

Today we are accustomed to a special kind of money; but in the past,
many commodities were used as money. Indeed, anything can be used
for money as long as it is acceptable in exchange for goods and services.
But it's not hard to imagine the inconvenience you would experience
if you conducted your daily business by means of barter. Suppose you
went out to dinner, and had to barter with the restaurant owner for
your meal. What would you offer him that would match exactly what
he wanted?

Most people think of money in terms of dollar bills and coins, even
though these are used in only a small percentage of all business transactions. The other side of the picture—checks, credit, and banks—really
facilitates about 90 per cent of all transactions in our economic system.

The United States differs from other large countries because we do
not have a government-owned central bank. We have a system of privately owned banks which are coordinated and controlled by the Federal
government through the Federal Reserve System. Keep these things
in mind as we turn to the very interesting story of money.

THE STORY OF MONEY

Today, money appears in the form of metal (coins of silver, copper, nickel, bronze), as paper governmental notes, certificates, and bank notes, and in some primitive localities in the form of commodities (cattle, tobacco, corn, or fish).

Historically, commodity moneys appeared first. In primitive times people built their own homes, made their own clothes, and hunted and farmed for the things they needed. But as time went on, some families specialized in hunting while others devoted their attention to farming or making tools. And as people specialized, they began to barter. The hunter would trade his meat and hides for items the farmer or toolmaker had to offer. Barter was practical as long as there were not too many items to trade and provided that the goods did not have to be carried long distances. But as economic systems expanded with better transportation, markets became more distant, and this made it necessary to find a more convenient form of money or medium of exchange. At this point, many portable items—such as spices, tobacco, beads, and precious stones—came into use as money. But, as economic activities became increasingly complex, a more universal medium of exchange had to be found. This started the trend toward precious metals, particularly gold and silver.

Precious metals were more acceptable than other forms of money because they were durable, portable, relatively scarce, and easily recognized. Another important advantage was the feasibility of storing a metal, like gold, for future use. So whenever a person accumulated more gold than he needed at the moment, he could store the excess with a goldsmith in his community. As a rule the goldsmith was an individual of public trust, and he kept each depositor's gold separate from that of other depositors. And he made a storage charge for this service. This is quite different from banks that pay interest to encourage deposits.

The early goldsmith gradually developed into a community bank, because it soon became apparent that people seldom took out all their gold at one time. As a result the goldsmith had more gold on hand than he needed to operate under normal circumstances. It didn't take him long to learn that he could lend out the excess gold—that is, the gold he had in reserve—and earn a substantial amount of interest. By doing so he could pay a return to those who deposited the gold with him in the first place.

Improvements in the banking system came about when these early banking establishments began to deal in receipts for gold rather than trying to measure out gold from individual bags, as they had done earlier. The use of receipts for gold in exchange for goods and services and for the payment of debts led to the next stage—the development of checks and paper money.

The final stage came when governments began to issue paper money to represent gold and silver in their mints. In most cases this paper money promised to pay whatever gold and silver was called for in exchange. Thus the money was "convertible," since gold and silver could be had on demand, if the individual wanted it. This was true in the United States until 1933, when gold was made illegal as circulating money, although it was retained by the Federal Reserve System in the form of gold certificates backing up a portion of the currency outstanding. More recently, the promise to redeem in silver has been removed from our paper money—so today we are not on a convertible standard in either gold or silver.

THE FUNCTIONS OF MONEY

There are four basic functions of money. It acts as:

- A medium of exchange
- A measure of value
- A store of value
- A standard of deferred payments

A Medium of Exchange

A most important function of money is to act as a medium of exchange when goods and services are bought and sold.

Think how difficult buying and selling would be if workers were paid in the goods they produced! For example, suppose that the employees of an electric motor plant received their pay in electric motors. To get clothes, food, or housing, they would have to find someone who was willing to accept their motors in return. Then there would be the additional problem of making change.

Money provides generalized purchasing power, something that everyone will accept in exchange for goods or services. Without money we couldn't have our present degree of specialization. As a result, each family or neighborhood unit would have to provide most of its own food, clothes, and shelter. Our standard of living would drop sharply, for we would have few luxuries.

To perform efficiently, money must be "generally acceptable" in exchange. However, the use of a given commodity, once in a while, does not qualify it to be called money. You can trade a fountain pen for a book, yet neither is considered money as such. Money must enable transactions to be deferred or to take place between distant markets, to permit the particular possessor of the money to select the time and the type of transaction, and to lend an impersonal nature to the transaction—separating buyer and seller, maker and user.

A Measuring Stick of Values

Money also acts as a measure of values. In other words, with money we can compare goods and services in about the same way that we measure physical dimensions with a yardstick. Thus, if a fountain pen were traded for a book, we can say that the fountain pen has the value of the book. But what would that mean as far as the relative value of the fountain pen when compared to, say, a typewriter? A society like ours produces and consumes millions of items, so the number of possible combinations is bewildering. To avoid this we measure the value of each commodity in terms of the common denominator—money. Thus the fountain pen might be valued at three dollars, the book at three dollars, and the typewriter at sixty dollars.

A Store of Value

We can save money and use it later to buy goods and services, and for this reason money serves as a store of value. Of course, if prices change, the money may not have exactly the same buying power as when the money was originally earned. Nonetheless, a person may save his money, and this is more convenient than holding on to goods that may deteriorate or lose value over a period of time.

A Standard of Deferred Payments

Finally, money also serves as a standard of deferred payments. More than 90 per cent of our business transactions are conducted by means of credit, which is a current transfer of goods and services in exchange for the promise to pay at a future date. Here again, money measures the nature and extent of the future obligation.

TYPES OF MONEY IN CIRCULATION

There are basically two types of money in circulation:

- Money issued or created by banks
- Money issued by the United States Government

Bank Money

Bank money is made up of demand deposits and of bank notes.

Demand deposits are checking accounts. Checkbook money represents about 80 per cent of the country's total supply of money and is used in about 90 per cent of all business transactions. At mid-1967, checkbook money amounted to about $135 billion. The other 20 per cent of the country's money consisted of paper money and coins.

The main feature of checkbook money is that it can be increased in response to public need. This comes about because banks can increase their deposits whenever they make loans or pay investors for government securities. We'll describe this process later in this chapter.

The most common currency in circulation today consists of notes that are issued by the twelve Federal Reserve banks to their member banks, as the community's needs require more or less currency. There were about $41 billion in Federal Reserve notes in circulation in mid-1967.

Federal Reserve notes are issued in denominations of $1 or more. The face of each note has a small circle with a letter printed inside. This letter designates the district Federal Reserve bank which issued the note. For example, the letter "A" stands for Boston (First Federal Reserve District), and the letter "B" stands for New York (Second District). The other districts are as follows:

C	Philadelphia	H	St. Louis
D	Cleveland	I	Minneapolis
E	Richmond	J	Kansas City
F	Atlanta	K	Dallas
G	Chicago	L	San Francisco

Money Issued by the Federal Government

In the past, the United States Treasury issued paper money, like treasury notes and silver certificates. Some of these are still circulating, but the Treasury is in the process of replacing them with Federal Reserve notes. Today, therefore, coins are the basic money issued by the United States Treasury.

The relative importance of paper money and checks can be seen from the following table, which indicates the kinds of money in circulation in the United States.

Currency in Circulation—May, 1967*

Federal Reserve notes		$ 38.9 billion
Treasury currency		5.5 "
Silver dollars	$ 482 million	
Silver certificates	547 "	
Fractional coins	4,117 "	
United States notes	302 "	
Others	87 "	
Total currency		$ 44.4 billion
Bank demand deposits (checks)		$134.5 billion

* SOURCE: *Federal Reserve Bulletin,* Board of Governors of the Federal Reserve System (July 1967), p. 1187.

As you can see, checking accounts represent the largest portion of our money supply.

Money Standards

When money was first introduced, principally in the form of gold and silver, it was necessary that it have an intrinsic value. There were no governments with a dependable stability exercising the sovereign power of coining money. As stable governments developed, however, they began to change the coinage value attached to a given unit of metal. Thus an element of instability was introduced into the value of the standard measuring unit.

This practice has not been abandoned by governments, even in recent times. For example, at the beginning of World War I, the French government had about 16 billion paper francs redeemable on demand in gold. These paper francs circulated internally as the equivalent of gold. Under the pressure of the war the supply of paper francs was expanded to about 80 billion, and they were no longer convertible into gold. Consequently, the currency—when compared to a standard of gold —dropped in purchasing power from 19.3 cents a franc to 2.8 cents, a drop to less than one-fifth of the former value. In December of 1947 the Russian government called in all the rubles in the hands of the public and issued one new ruble for ten old ones.

Until recent years there was more uniformity among the nations as far as their monetary standards were concerned. Today, the variety has become confusing. In general, standards are usually monometallic, bimetallic, symmetallic, multiple, paper, or some combination of these. Monometallism today usually implies the gold standard, although it may mean silver or any other single commodity. Bimetallism connotes both gold and silver. Paper usually implies an irredeemable and nonconvertible government issue of fiat currency.

Monometallism refers to a monetary standard in which only one metal is the basis for money. Other types of money which may be in use are made convertible, directly or indirectly, into the standard metal. In addition, there are no restrictions placed on the use of the standard metal. It can be melted down and employed in whatever manner its owners desire. It is not necessary, however, that the standard metal be coined so long as other moneys are freely convertible into it. To be a pure gold standard, however, coins of the metal must be in circulation. Monometallism may take the form of the gold standard, the gold bullion standard, the gold exchange standard, the international gold bullion exchange standard, or similar combinations of silver.

Until the World War I monometallism most commonly connoted the "gold coin standard." Under such a standard, gold coins are in circulation, free coinage of gold exists, gold is given unlimited legal tender privileges, other moneys are freely convertible into gold, the standard will consist of an actual weight of gold, and a free market exists, including the right to hoard, melt, import, or export gold.

When such a standard is adopted, the value of the standard unit is defined in terms of a given weight of the metal. Thus, in the United States from 1900 to 1933, the standard was defined as a gold dollar of 23.22 grains of pure gold. This weight then determined the number of dollars necessary to purchase an ounce of pure gold. So $20.67 became the value of an ounce of gold. In 1933, the new dollar was declared to have but 13.71 grains of pure gold (or 15.24 grains of standard gold), and the number of dollars necessary to purchase an ounce of gold rose to $35.

Now, let us turn to the banking system and see how it's organized to increase or decrease the supply of money.

HOW OUR BANKING SYSTEM OPERATES

Banks make most of their profit on the interest they receive from loans and from income on other investments that they may have made. For this reason banks encourage individuals to deposit money with them. They can operate with a comparatively small amount of currency on hand because all of their depositors do not withdraw their money at the same time. A withdrawal of money by one person is usually offset by the deposit of another.

As a rule, neither individuals nor companies keep large amounts of currency on hand. Their money is represented by a checkbook, and they usually write checks to pay their bills. This causes a part of their deposits to be transferred to someone else's account.

The fact that banks make most of their money on loans means that they are anxious to increase their deposits and their lending ability. As more money is deposited in banks, more loans can be made, more checkbook money is created, and the overall supply of money is increased. The banking system plays an important role when business conditions change, because there is a close relationship between the quantity of money in circulation and the general price level. An expansion of bank deposits can contribute to prosperity or inflation, while their contraction can lead to a recession or possible depression.

Banks expand their loans when business looks good because their risks are fewer and new money is being deposited. When business looks bad, banks cut back on their lending operations. Borrowers act in the same way. When business is good, they are eager to borrow. But when business is bad, they want to get out of debt.

With this in mind, we shall now turn to the Federal Reserve System and see how our banking system operates to expand or contract the supply of money.

THE FEDERAL RESERVE BANKING SYSTEM

If a single bank were to set aside, say, 20 per cent of its deposits and lend out the other 80 per cent, it would place itself in a dangerous position. For, if depositors representing more than 20 per cent of its deposits decided to withdraw their money, the bank would not be able to meet their demand for funds.

Before the Federal Reserve System was set up, banks kept their reserves partly in cash and partly on deposit with the larger banks in metropolitan areas. From time to time there would be a financial crisis, and banks all over the country would call for their reserves from these larger banks. At times, the big city banks found it difficult to supply the funds. Congress appointed a commission to see what could be done to straighten out the banking system, and the result was the Federal Reserve System, established in 1913.

Organization of the Federal Reserve System

The Federal Reserve System consists of twelve Federal Reserve District Banks and more than 6,100 member banks.[1] It is headed by a Board of Governors appointed by the President of the United States, with the consent of the Senate.

At the end of 1966 there were 14,274 banks of all types, including 13,770 commercial banks (a bank that must do *checking account* business) and 504 savings banks (banks which may not conduct checking account business). Of the commercial banks, 44 per cent or 6,150 were Federal Reserve members. And of the member banks, 4,811 were national banks, while the remainder were state banks which voluntarily joined the system. The member banks accounted for about 82 per cent of all demand deposits in 1966.

Federal Reserve banks do not accept the deposits of individuals or business firms. They are primarily a bank for banks, and their stock is owned by the banks which are members of the system.

The reserves of the member banks must be deposited with their District Federal Reserve Bank, although a small portion may be held by the individual bank as vault and till cash. Member banks can use these reserves in the same way that you use your checking account.

Powers of the Federal Reserve System

The Federal Reserve has four important powers that affect the supply of money:

---

[1] *Ibid.*, p. 260.

- Fixing the reserve requirements for member banks
- Setting discount rates
- Open market operations
- Selective credit controls

Fixing Reserve Requirements for Member Banks

The Federal Reserve, within the broad limits set by Congress, determines the minimum amount a member bank must keep in reserve. This amount is expressed as a percentage of the bank's deposits. If the reserve requirement is 20 per cent, a bank must keep 20 cents in reserve for every $1 of demand deposits.

By raising reserve requirements, the Federal Reserve can reduce the amount of money the member banks can lend. By lowering the reserve requirement, the Federal Reserve can increase the lending power of its banks and thus increase the money supply.

The importance of this power is better understood when we trace an example of bank credit and deposit expansion. If you went to a bank to borrow money, the chances are that you would not leave the bank with your wallet bulging with dollar bills. You would probably leave the money at the bank in a checking account in your name. In this way bank loans create new deposits and new money.

The following is a simplified account of how bank loans create new money. Suppose that a depositor puts $100 in Bank A. Bank A then becomes liable to the depositor for his $100, but it also has money it can lend. If banks are required to keep 20 per cent of their deposits as reserves, Bank A must send at least $20 of the money to the Federal Reserve Bank. But if it wants to make loans, the other $80 is also sent to the Federal Reserve Bank, where it becomes excess reserves which Bank A can lend out to someone.

Now, suppose Bank A lends someone its $80 of excess reserves. The bank will take a note from the borrower, and set up a deposit for him of $80 against which he can write checks. The note becomes a bank asset, while the deposit is a bank liability. The bank's books balance, as follows:

Assets	Liabilities
$20 Legal reserve	$100 Deposit
$80 Loan	

When the borrower draws on his deposit at Bank A, the party who gets his check will probably deposit it in another bank, say Bank B.

Bank B will credit the depositor with the amount of the check and send it to the Federal Reserve Bank for collection from Bank A. The Federal Reserve will transfer the $80 from Bank A's reserve account to Bank B's reserve account. The $80 will be removed from Bank A's books, and it will appear as reserves on Bank B's books. Since the borrower from Bank A will have spent the $80 deposit, it is no longer a liability of Bank A and will be removed from its books. It appears now as a deposit liability of Bank B. Thus Bank B has deposit liabilities of $80 and reserves of the same amount. Required reserves will be 20 per cent of the $80 deposit—or $16. The remainder of the cash reserves, $64, are excess reserves that the bank may lend.

Assets	Liabilities
$16 Legal reserve $64 Loan	$80 Deposit

Let's say that Bank B lends out the $64, credits the borrower's deposit account with this amount and takes a note, which it adds to its assets. The borrower writes a check on Bank B and the receiver of the check deposits it in Bank C, where he receives a deposit credit of $64. Bank C sends the check on Bank B to the Federal Reserve Bank for collection. The Federal Reserve Bank transfers $64 of excess reserves from Bank B's account to Bank C. Since the borrower has checked out the $64 from Bank B, this no longer appears on Bank B's balance sheet as a liability. Bank C's required reserves have been increased by 20 per cent ($12.80) of the new deposit and its excess reserves by $51.20, which it may lend.

Bank C lends its excess reserves, $51.20, by setting up a deposit credit to the borrower for this amount and by taking a note which it adds to its assets. The borrower writes a check on his account at Bank C, and the recipient of the check deposits it in Bank D, and the process of shifting excess reserves (smaller each time) from bank to bank through the clearing and lending process continues.

Assets	Liabilities
$12.80 Legal reserve $51.20 Loan	$64 Deposit

Now, let's stop here and count up the deposits that have been created from the initial deposit of $100 of currency in Bank A, remembering that the borrower's deposit in each case has been transferred out of the lending bank.

Bank A still has only $100 on deposit. To this must be added the $80 on deposit at Bank B, the $64 at Bank C, the $51.20 at Bank D—a total of $295.20.

Is this the end of the process of deposit creation? No! There are still excess reserves with Bank D. When Bank D transfers this to another bank through the lending process, deposits will continue to grow until all of the excess reserves become required reserves. This is demonstrated in the following table:

Other Banks

	Required Reserves	Excess Reserves	Loans	Deposits
Bank A	$ 20.00	$ 80.00	$ 80.00	$100.00
Bank B	16.00	64.00	64.00	80.00
Bank C	12.80	51.20	51.20	64.00
Bank D	10.24	40.96	40.96	51.20
Bank E	8.19	32.77	32.77	40.96
Bank F	6.55	26.22	26.22	32.77
Bank G	5.24	20.98	20.98	26.22
Bank H	4.20	16.78	16.78	20.98
Bank I	3.36	13.42	13.42	16.78
Bank J	2.68	10.74	10.74	13.42
Bank K	2.15	8.59	8.59	10.74
Bank L	1.72	6.87	6.87	8.59
Bank M	1.37	5.50	5.50	6.87
Bank N	1.10	4.40	4.40	5.50
Remaining Banks	4.40	17.57	17.57	21.97
Total	$100.00	$400.00	$400.00	$500.00

So, if you add up all the required reserves from Bank A through all possible "remaining banks," they total $100. All excess reserves have been used up in the lending process, so loans add up to $400. The deposit liabilities of all banks total $500, and these developed from an initial deposit of $100.

In our example we assumed that each bank lost its deposits to another bank and thus its excess reserves as well. In real life it frequently happens that the recipient of the check banks at the same bank as the borrower. In this case, the bank that creates the deposit loses neither the deposit nor the excess reserves. If this were to happen, it could create additional deposits by lending out its excess reserves.

There is an easier way to figure the maximum amount of loans that can be made and how many deposits can be created. In our example we could have arrived at the potential limits by dividing the amount of the original deposit ($100) by the fraction required to be held as required reserve ($\frac{1}{5}$): $100 ÷ \frac{1}{5} = $100 × 5 = $500. If reserve requirements were raised to ¼, then the lending power would be reduced accordingly: $100 ÷ ¼ = $100 × 4 = $400. So when you change the reserve requirement, you change the lending power and the money supply.

Setting Discount Rates. Discounting at a Federal Reserve Bank works like this. When a member feels that its reserves are getting too low in relation to its deposits, it can ask the Federal Reserve Bank for a loan to increase its own reserves.

The bank pays interest to the Federal Reserve for the loan, and this interest rate is called the "discount rate." The Federal Reserve sets its own discount rate, so it can encourage member banks to borrow by simply reducing the interest rate. This allows banks to make more loans to businesses and individuals, thereby increasing the supply of money.

When discount rates are high, banks are discouraged from borrowing. Fewer bank loans are then made to individuals and businesses, and the money supply is decreased.

Open Market Operations. The Federal Reserve also can increase or decrease the supply of money by buying or selling Federal government securities in the open market. This is known as the Federal Reserve's "open market operations."

The person or bank who sells bonds to the Federal Reserve receives a check in return. When the check is deposited, it forms the basis for a new series of bank loans.

If the Federal Reserve wants to reduce the supply of money, it sells securities on the open market, thus draining off money in the process.

Selective Credit Controls. The Federal Reserve can exercise selective credit controls through its member banks whenever it feels that there is an unhealthy amount of speculation in the trading of securities, real estate, or commodities.

In summary, the Federal Reserve's powers can be listed as follows:

To decrease the flow of money, it can:
- Raise reserve requirements
- Raise the discount rate
- Sell securities on the open market
- Tighten selective credit controls

To increase the flow of money, it can:
- Lower reserve requirements
- Lower the discount rate

- Buy securities on the open market
- Relax selective credit controls

The powers of the Federal Reserve better enable it to curtail inflation than to stimulate business when times are poor. This is true because the Federal Reserve can make credit available but it cannot force borrowers to use it.

The Federal Reserve System is owned by the member banks and not by the Federal government, but there has been a working relationship between the Reserve System and the United States Treasury throughout most of its history. This relationship was somewhat broken early in the 1950s, when the Reserve System asserted its independence. Since that time there has been a good deal of disagreement between the two.

The Reserve System has been more conservative than the Administration on several occasions. This was particularly true in 1965 and 1966, when the Reserve System adopted a policy of tightening money. The Administration was more interested in continuing a monetary policy that it believed would insure an uninterrupted rise in business and an increase in employment—even at the probable risk of inflation. By late 1966 money became "tight" and the two forces were again in accord because of the possibility that a tight money policy might trigger a real downturn in business.

Discussion Questions

1. What is the relative importance of currency in our monetary system?
2. What are the key characteristics of good money?
3. Why are precious metals especially acceptable as money?
4. Why do governments have a monopoly over the issuance of money?
5. Explain the "medium of exchange" function.
6. From your experience, illustrate the fact that money acts as a measure of value.
7. How does money act as a store of value?
8. Describe how money facilitates deferred payments.
9. What is the difference between bank money and government money?
10. What types of money are used in the United States?
11. What kinds of money are issued through the Federal Reserve System?

12. In what Federal Reserve District are you located?

13. What is meant by a monetary stardard?

14. How would you describe a gold standard?

15. Describe the organization of the Federal Reserve System.

16. Explain how our Federal Reserve System operates.

17. What powers can the Federal Reserve System use to fight inflation?

18. Explain how the banking system tends to monetize the federal debt.

19. Show how fractional reserves permit an expansion of the money supply.

20. Describe open market operations and their effects.

Circle the T or F (True or False) before each statement:

T   F   1. Money is a measure of value.

T   F   2. Currency consists of dollar bills and coins.

T   F   3. The Federal Reserve System can reduce the supply of money by selling government bonds to the public.

T   F   4. Checking accounts are the largest part of our money supply.

T   F   5. Bank loans serve as money in our economy.

T   F   6. The U.S. Treasury sets the basic policies for the Federal Reserve System.

T   F   7. When the Federal Reserve raises reserve requirements, banks are encouraged to lend more money.

T   F   8. Banks cannot make loans which exceed the cash they have on hand at the time.

T   F   9. The Federal Reserve should start buying bonds when the economy has hit the top of the business cycle.

T   F   10. Gresham's Law states that good money will drive bad money out of the market.

ANSWERS

1. T	3. T	5. T	7. F	9. F
2. T	4. T	6. F	8. F	10. F

11

FOREIGN TRADE: THE CHALLENGE OF A CHANGING WORLD

Why take the time to study foreign trade? Well, walk into any store. You will find all sorts of foreign-made products on sale in direct competition with American-made goods.

Pick up a newspaper or magazine. You will find our country's leaders discussing the balance of payments, the outflow of gold, our international debts, and tariffs.

A knowledge of foreign trade and international economics is essential if each of us is going to make intelligent decisions as a citizen.

This chapter provides an explanation of:

- Why countries trade with one another
- How international debts are settled
- The difference between balance of *trade* and balance of *payments*
- The meaning and importance of gold outflow
- The reasons for and against protective tariffs

Foreign trade is a very interesting subject. Its study is also personally rewarding because it will give you a better picture of some of the most important problems we face as a nation.

THE IMPORTANCE OF WORLD TRADE

World trade has become increasingly important to the United States in recent years. The economic expansion of Western Europe and Japan, and our economic, scientific, and ideological struggle with worldwide

communism, have placed the United States in an entirely new world position.

Our economic leadership is no longer undisputed. The impact of foreign competition at home and abroad reminds us forcefully that our economy is inevitably bound to the rest of the world.

Today we *export* from 4 to 5 per cent of our total national output, and we *import* 3 to 4 per cent of what we consume as a nation. These percentages seem small when compared to countries like Belgium, the Netherlands, or Venezuela, which generally export between one-third and one-half of their national products. But when stated in dollars and cents, the figures make the United States the most important trading country in the world.

Our key industries depend heavily on foreign trade, either for markets or for essential raw materials and supplies. For example, we export from 15 to 30 per cent of our total output of machine tools, tractors, office equipment, and other types of machinery. We also export from 20 to 50 per cent of our cotton, wheat, tobacco, and other agricultural crops.

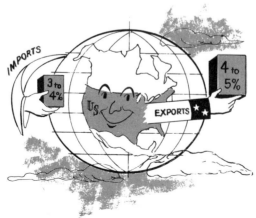

On the *import* side, our dependence on foreign sources is even more striking. We get from abroad 100 per cent of our tin, 85 per cent of our nickel and aluminum, and 73 per cent of our newsprint. All of our coffee and cocoa is imported, along with half of our zinc and wool and about a fourth of our copper and sugar.

Obviously, our standard of living would be lower if we didn't sell goods abroad or buy the materials and foods we receive from other countries.

U.S. ECONOMIC TIES WITH OTHER CONTINENTS

IN MILLIONS OF DOLLARS - 1965

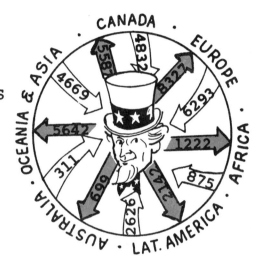

An important principle of foreign trade becomes apparent when we look around the world and pinpoint our main customers and suppliers. The figure above shows that the United States has strong economic ties with every continent. But by countries, our largest volume of business is with Canada, followed by Japan, the United Kingdom, West Germany, Mexico, Italy, and France.

You will notice that most of our best customers and suppliers are countries that are similar to the United States in their economic structure: they are industrialized; they enjoy reasonably high standards of living; and their economies are expanding because of technological change and capital formation.

This is true of international trade in general. The most active traders are the highly developed nations, and they trade primarily among themselves. Thus the pattern of world trade is much more complicated than the commonly held notion of less developed countries trading raw materials for the finished products of more developed countries.

WHY DO COUNTRIES TRADE WITH ONE ANOTHER?

Here are just a few reasons why nations trade with one another:

1. Differences in geographical conditions—climate, natural resources, and land forms—permit countries to specialize in certain products and to trade them for other products.

2. Differences in human capabilities among nations play an important role. This does not mean that some people are inherently more intelligent or harder working than others, but it does mean that history and conditions of environment have led to the development of varying ambitions and skills among nations.

3. Political, economic, and social conditions differ from country to country. People are reluctant to invest their savings in a country that is politically unstable. Moreover, modern technology is slow to take root in a country that has a high rate of illiteracy.

4. Most important of all, countries possess different amounts of productive resources—land, labor, and capital—and they possess these factors in differing proportions. When workers in Southeast Asia carry dirt to a construction site in baskets, this reflects the fact that labor is plentiful and cheap while capital equipment, like steam shovels or graders, is scarce and expensive.

Thus there are many factors that affect a country's ability to make certain products and the cost of making those products.

Labor costs are one of the important factors, but in international trade the advantage does not necessarily go to the countries that pay

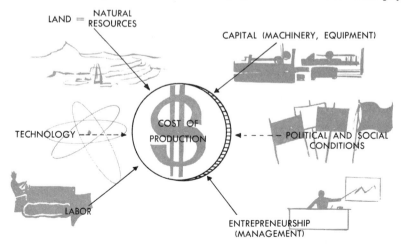

the lowest wages or have the lowest standards of living. Natural resources, an appropriate supply of capital, ambitious and ingenious management, effective economic incentives that persuade people to use their energies and abilities to the fullest, a high level of technological know-how, the wise conduct of economic, political, and social affairs—all of these are important and help make a nation strong in international trade.

The best explanation for the "why" of international trade is provided by the principle of comparative advantage—which simply means that each country produces what it is better at producing than other countries. To illustrate this principle, let us consider two imaginary countries —Country "A" and Country "B."

Each country has the necessary factors of production—materials, labor and capital—to produce sunglasses and razors.

In Country "A," it costs $1.00 to produce a pair of sunglasses, and it also costs $1.00 to produce a razor. Internally, then, one pair of sunglasses has the same basic cost as one razor.

But in Country "B," conditions are different. It costs $1.00 to produce a pair of sunglasses and $2.00 to produce a razor. Country "B," therefore, can make two pairs of sunglasses with the same material, labor, and capital investment needed to produce one razor.

Will it pay these nations to trade with each other?

The answer is "Yes," because it is to their mutual advantage to do so.

If Country "B" can switch some of its razor factories to the making of sunglasses, they could trade the additional sunglasses they produce for Country "A's" less expensive razors. This is true, provided that they give *fewer* than two pairs of sunglasses in trade for one razor. If they have to give two or more pairs of sunglasses for a razor, they may as well make the razors themselves because there would be no trading advantage.

On the other hand, Country "A" would be happy to convert some of its sunglasses facilities over to making more razors, provided it can get more than one pair of Country "B's" sunglasses for each razor. But it has to get better than an even trade, or there is no advantage in doing business with Country "B."

Clearly, then, there is an opportunity for mutual benefit from trade between these two countries. The terms of trade—that is, the ratio at which goods are traded—will lie somewhere between one pair of sunglasses for a razor and two pairs of sunglasses for a razor. Within this range, both countries will benefit from the exchange.

The principle of comparative advantage explains *why* foreign trade takes place. Interestingly enough, however, it isn't necessary for businessmen to know this principle in order to find opportunities in foreign trade. The market mechanism will make these opportunities more or less apparent—and in a free world market, each country will eventually come to produce what it is comparatively best at producing.

SETTLING DEBTS BETWEEN NATIONS

Of course, foreign trade is much more complicated than the example we have used. For when two countries trade, they run up against different laws, different economic objectives and policies, different ways of doing business and—most important of all—different monetary systems.

For example, if businesses in one country want to buy from or invest in another country, they need the money of that country. Whenever there is buying, granting of credit, or giving of money from one country to another, purchasing power is transferred. One country has increased the other country's ability to make purchases. Let us call this purchasing power *foreign exchange.*

We can think of each country as having a pool of international purchasing power—or foreign exchange—to which it adds, or from which it subtracts, with every international transaction. This pool takes different forms. Some of it will be in actual currency, such as dollar bills, pound notes, and so on. But usually, it is in the form of bank accounts not much different from those held by ordinary citizens. For example, in trade between Great Britain and the United States, large American banks have pound sterling accounts in Great Britain, and British banks hold dollar accounts in the United States. When a British importer

FOREIGN EXCHANGE POOLS

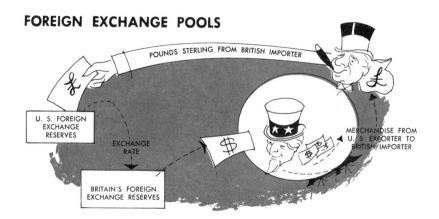

wants to buy something made in the United States, he buys dollars in exchange for pounds sterling.

When he does this, the American pool of foreign exchange—in pounds sterling—has been increased by the amount that the British importer paid in. At the same time, the British pool of exchange—in dollars— is reduced by the amount paid to the American company that manu- factured the product.

The price the British importer pays for dollars, in terms of pounds sterling, is called the *exchange rate.*

Let us go one step further. If the currencies of *all* countries are freely interchangeable, it is no longer important whether Great Britain has dollars in its foreign exchange pool. They may just as well earn German marks, or French francs, and then buy dollars with these. In this manner, international purchasing power is bought and sold among countries through the *international exchange market.* This is not like the stock market, where all the trading is done in one location. Nonethe- less, it is highly organized. Exchange rates are well known at any given moment, and transactions can be carried out quickly and efficiently.

BALANCE OF INTERNATIONAL PAYMENTS

Certain transactions help a country obtain foreign exchange—that is, international purchasing power—while other transactions require it to use or spend its international purchasing power. When we total up all of a country's receipts and spending in the international market for a given period of time, the result gives us that country's balance of inter- national payments.

Below is a simplified statement of the balance of payments for the United States for the year 1965.

In the left-hand column are listed all payments made to foreign coun- tries—that is, all of the transactions that gave foreigners purchasing power in the United States. In the right-hand column are listed the trans- actions by which we gained foreign exchange and obtained purchasing power elsewhere in the world.

Note one very important fact. The first line of each column lists our merchandise imports of $25.5 billion and our merchandise exports of $29.2 billion. The difference is our *balance of trade.* In other words, we sold other countries about $4 billion more in goods than we bought from them. Our balance of trade was favorable, since we took in about $4 billion more than we paid out.

Balance of Payments—1966*

Payments made to foreign countries:	_Billion_	_Receipts from foreign countries:_	_Billion_
Merchandise	$25.5	Merchandise	$29.2
Transportation	2.9	Transportation	2.6
U.S. Travel Abroad	2.6	Foreign Travel in U.S.	1.4
Military Expenditures	3.6	Military Sales	0.9
Income Paid Out on Investments	1.9	Income on Investments (5.6 private, 0.6 government)	6.2
Miscellaneous Services	1.1	Miscellaneous Services	2.6
Imports of Goods and Services	37.6	Exports of Goods and Services	42.9
Private Remittances and Pensions	0.6	Repayment on Government Loans	1.2
Government Pensions and other Transfers	0.4	Foreign Capital other than Change in Liquid Assets	2.2
Government Grants and Capital Outflow	4.6	Receipts from Rest of World	46.3
Private Capital Outflow (net)	3.9		
Unrecorded Transactions	0.6	Short-term Claims and Sale of Gold	1.4
Total payments to rest of world	$47.7	_Total receipts from rest of world_	$47.7

* SOURCE: _Federal Reserve Bulletin,_ April 1967, p. 678.

COMPUTING BALANCE OF PAYMENTS

However, when we total up all of our international transactions to get our balance of payments, we must include such things as maintaining military forces abroad, foreign aid programs, American investments in other countries, foreign investments in our country, grants, loans, services, and so forth. When these items are included, our payments to the rest of the world for all transactions add up to $47.7 billion, while our total receipts come to only $46.3 billion. This means that we made $1.4 billion more in commitments to foreigners than we received from them.

How is the difference made up? We must sell $1.4 billion worth of gold from our gold reserves to buy the international purchasing power we need to pay our bills, or else increase the short-term claims against us. Gold is accepted as the medium for settling international debts. As long as it is accepted—and provided we have some gold to sell—we can make up our balance of payments deficit by selling our gold for foreign exchange.

Obviously, we do not have an unlimited supply of gold. That is why you frequently hear people express concern over our outflow of gold, and the deficit in our balance of payments. There are, of course, many short-term measures that can be taken to correct this deficit. For example, our actual gold losses from international transactions would have been much worse had we not made arrangements with foreign countries to increase our short-term indebtedness to them in place of immediate gold settlements. The long-term answer boils down to the simple fact that no country can consistently spend more than it earns, unless it has a virtually unlimited supply of gold or credit.

No rule as to a "good" or "bad" balance of payments is valid for all economies at all times. Just what constitutes a desirable structure of balance will vary from country to country and from time to time because of different economic characteristics, stages of development, and policies pursued by the government.

TARIFF BARRIERS VS. FREE TRADE

Everything we have said points to the conclusion that there is a strong economic case for free international markets and for the free transfer of international purchasing power. Yet free markets do not exist today. Many problems remain to be solved before manmade barriers to free trade are broken down.

Most countries have devised tariffs that raise the price of certain foreign goods or keep them out altogether. They have regulations that prevent the free flow of credit and investment, and literally dozens of other ways of restricting world trade. Yet we know from our example of sunglasses and razors that, in a free and dynamic market, each country would shift its productive facilities to the items it could best produce —and, comparatively speaking, all countries would benefit. This is the way in which a free market works, and it is the source of the market's strength. Tariffs and subsidies cannot avoid the shift; they can only postpone it, and slow down the natural workings of the market.

It is true, nevertheless, that such shifts involve losses to some investors and unemployment among some workers until the transfer of facilities is completed. Our own country has legislation to assist companies that may be affected—and people who may be displaced—because of changes in our tariff program.

Similar adjustments are constantly taking place wholly within our domestic markets. This dynamic adaptability creates problems, but it gives us the best assurance that our economic system will continue strong in the future.

Let us remember, though, that it is not enough for *one* country to play the game of free international trade. Nations can benefit only when there is widespread participation and acceptance of the rules of the game. The General Agreement on Tariffs and Trade (GATT) is an attempt to set such rules and to insure a fair and equitable system of international trade and competition.

The economic integration of Western Europe into the Common Market, similar movements in Africa and Latin America, and our enactment of the Trade Expansion Act of 1962—all reflect a movement toward freer international markets in the future. Our own stake in this movement is large. Our ability to come to terms with the challenges of a competitive world economy will help maintain our future economic leadership.

Discussion Questions

1. Make a list of the imported items that you have purchased recently.
2. Why do countries trade with each other?

3. Just how important is world trade to the United States?

4. Which major industries depend upon foreign imports?

5. Which industries rely on export sales?

6. How do differences in a country's productive resources give rise to foreign trade?

7. Illustrate the principle of comparative advantage.

8. Outline the major steps in the settlement of debts between nations.

9. What is foreign exchange?

10. How are exchange rates determined?

11. What is meant by balance of trade?

12. What is meant by balance of payments?

13. Describe the major items entering into the U.S. balance of payments account.

14. Why is gold significant in settling international balances?

15. Present the basic arguments for tariffs.

16. What are the arguments for free trade?

17. What trade restrictions exist aside from tariffs?

18. Which U.S. industries would be hurt and which would benefit from freer trade?

19. What is meant by tariff retaliation?

20. What is the current status of our tariff protection system?

Circle the T or F (True or False) before each statement:

T F 1. High tariffs are an effective way to increase the living standards of our people.

T F 2. There are economic gains when all countries buy and sell from each other in great quantities.

T F 3. A tariff acts as a subsidy to some producers.

T F 4. The disadvantages that result from the immobility of resources can be reduced when worldwide trade operates without restrictions or tariffs.

T F 5. A country that runs a deficit in its balance of payments is paying out more to other countries than it is receiving.

T F 6. International trade depends upon the convertibility of one currency into another.

T F 7. Devaluating the dollar would improve our export position in the short run.

T   F   8. The European Common Market is not having the impact on foreign trade we thought it would.

T   F   9. Equalizing the cost of entry of American and foreign goods is a first step toward freer trade.

T   F   10. Free trade would lead to more efficient specialization by most countries.

ANSWERS

10. T	8. F	6. T	4. T	2. T
9. T	7. T	5. T	3. T	1. F

12

YOUR PERSONAL ECONOMICS

It is quite fitting that a chapter of this book be devoted to personal economics. Economics itself was once described as the art of household management, and few of us are so affluent that we need not concern ourselves with how we spend our money. Indeed, about 42 per cent of our nation's families end up each year in debt or with no addition to their savings. It is important, then, that the typical consumer learns how to "stretch" his dollars and maximize each dollar that he spends.

Personal economics is a matter of psychology as well as of money because of differences in abilities and capacities, goals and expectations, size of family, and income and job security.

From the economic point of view, personal financial planning is concerned with *income* and *spending,* and with changes in *net worth* over the years. It tries to meet the present and foresee the future needs of an individual or his family.

Generally, a person's income depends upon his ability, education, and willingness to work for what he and his family would like to have. No amount of planning can make up for the unusually low or irregular income brought on by lack of skill or ambition. Moreover, when a person lacks initiative, he may develop the very personality traits that prevent sound financial planning.

The spending side of the problem involves a great deal of psychology. Some people just have to have everything they want, even if this means going deeply into debt. They live from day to day and depend on every dollar of income. They seldom plan for the future or have anything to carry them through the "rainy days."

Other people resign themselves to constant money problems, even though they may earn $250,000 or more during their lifetimes. Yet, if they could save $40 a month regularly, they would have over $14,500 in savings and interest in just twenty years. Actually, a person's income

has little to do with his need for financial planning. Several years ago, a national survey showed that most people believed their money problems could be solved by a 10 per cent increase in pay. Surprisingly enough, some of those interviewed were making $25,000 a year or more.

It is easy to see why even people with high incomes have financial problems. When a person's income increases, he may develop an "easy come, easy go" attitude. He spends more on services and commercial forms of entertainment. His family expects more and spends more on nonessentials, so it is not long before the family gets bogged down with money problems.

Regardless of our level of income, personal economic planning is essential if we are going to:

- Control family *spending* by consciously choosing between what is necessary or what is not essential
- Add to the family's future *net worth* by systematic savings
- Prepare for a happy *retirement,* free from financial problems
- Plan the distribution of our *estate* in the event of death

With these objectives in mind, let us turn to the problem of controlling family spending.

HOW TO CONTROL FAMILY SPENDING

The first step in controlling family spending is the preparation of a detailed budget that lists all monthly income and operating expenses. You must put accurate figures on paper, or it will be impossible to plan ahead and cut family expenses.

However, personal economics involves far more than the preparation of a budget. Budgeting is a wonderful thing, provided you stick to it and don't make it a mechanical tool with purely limited objectives. But for many of us it is like a trick diet: it works for a while, then all too soon we are back overeating.

The big problem in financial planning is to change the basic spending patterns we have developed during our lifetimes. This means cutting out impulsive buying, developing greater self-control, and planning far ahead into the future. These, in turn, require will power and the application of several practical yardsticks whenever we intend to make a purchase:

- Do we really need the item or service?
- Can we afford it?
- Is it worth the price?
- Can we do something better with our money?

Simple as these questions are, few people use them consistently when they do their shopping.

THE NEVER-ENDING SEARCH FOR VALUE

To begin with, never take at face value the statement that "you get what you pay for." The chances are that you'll probably "get what you shop for."

Some people always find bargains. They shop around, take advantage of sales, and have an incredible ability for stretching a dollar. Others never get their money's worth because they don't take the time nor do they have the patience to look for bargains. They buy at stores because of convenience or available credit. They spend first and rarely save later. They buy for sheer price rather than quality. And they are constantly in debt with charge accounts.

There are many ways to save money if you'll take the time and make

the effort. Most home owners know the value of "doing things yourself." If you're handy around the house, you can save hundreds or thousands of dollars which can be used for other purposes. But know where to draw the line, or you may endanger your family by defective wiring or faulty plumbing.

For most of us, public transportation is cheaper than driving to work. This is particularly true in city locations where parking is expensive.

Whenever possible, eliminate the small "leaks and losses" which add up to sizable amounts at the end of the year. Here are a few examples:

- An extra pack of cigarettes a day may build up to more than $100 a year.
- An extra newspaper a day may cost $35 a year.
- A couple of hard drinks a day can add up to more than $250 a year.
- Extra coffee, tea, or soft drinks each day may run $50 a year.

Moderation in these areas can really pay off for you and your family.

INSTALLMENT BUYING

Installment buying is an accepted part of our economy, and without it most families would find it very hard to manage over the years. We should know, however, how much installment debt a family can bear exclusive of a mortgage on its home. The national average runs between 15 and 20 per cent of take-home pay, but the best level for each family depends on available savings, family obligations, stability of employment, and the purpose of the loan.

For example, when a person borrows to improve his home, he uses the money to acquire an asset that has value. But when he borrows to take a vacation, he merely faces a liability when he returns. It may still be smart to borrow for the vacation—to maintain a good cash position—but it is better to borrow to acquire an asset that adds to your net worth.

A washing machine is well bought on the installment plan since it pays for itself during its lifetime. So does a house, which gives a family its basic comfort and sense of security. House ownership forces us to save regularly—and because of the size of the investment, most of us have to pay for it over a period of years. Large items, like an automobile, usually are paid for in installments because a full cash payment may deplete the family's emergency funds.

The main point is this: Don't over-borrow! *Use credit when you need it, and for those items which pay for themselves as they are used.* Don't let installment buying become an uncontrollable habit.

The next point is to borrow sensibly and keep your interest charges at a minimum. Many people think that the cost of borrowing is the same regardless of where they get the money. But the charges vary a great deal depending on who lends the money, for how long, and under what circumstances. Make sure that you borrow money under the most favorable conditions. Here are three general rules to guide you:

- You will pay more in interest if the loan is made on a purely personal basis.
- You will pay more if the amount borrowed is small and is repaid in monthly installments.
- You will borrow at lower rates of interest if you can offer some worthwhile security for the loan.

Be sure you read very carefully the papers you are asked to sign. Have someone in authority explain all the terms of the loan to you before you complete the loan.

TAKE ADVANTAGE OF COMMUNITY SERVICES

Everyone should take advantage of the many services offered by a community at no "out-of-pocket" expense to a family. Almost every community offers free courses in mathematics, history, English, public speaking, art, music, economics, politics, sales, and job trades. They are well advertised, yet they often have a hard time getting people to attend. There are other educational, social, and character-building activities available free, or at low cost, through the Scouts, the YMCA, Junior Achievement, and civic organizations. In most cities there are swimming pools, libraries, concerts, parks and playgrounds, and church groups in which the family can participate.

DON'T CUT EXPENSES IN THE WRONG PLACES

Some people splurge on nonessentials and then cut costs in the wrong places. For example, they try to save money by not sending their children to the dentist. They delay medical checkups, thus creating problems that may trouble their families for years to come. Or they settle for much less than a comfortable home in a desirable neighborhood.

Moreover, no one should overlook the value of a sound education. A college education is worth more than $100,000 in earnings over a person's lifetime beyond what he might have earned as a high school graduate. This is a return of $25,000 or more for each year spent in school. Over and above the economic value are the personal and social benefits that go along with a better education. Some people plan far ahead for their children's education because they rightly believe this investment will make them more successful and independent. Others keep putting it off until it's too late.

Even if it appears too late, it is worthwhile to look into the college-loan programs. Most schools are permitted to lend money to worthy or needy students; and upon graduation, the student has quite a few years to repay the money at a comparatively low rate of interest. And don't overlook your own bank. You may be able to raise the required money and repay it in monthly installments.

HOW TO INCREASE YOUR FAMILY'S NET WORTH

How much your family will be worth over the years depends, in part, on your level of income. That is why all of us should try hard to improve our income by making ourselves more valuable as time goes on. Of course, a person's net worth to his family does not depend entirely on his income. He may earn a large salary and still end up with much less for his family than a person with less income but a better insurance program.

It is not hard for a young man to build up an immediate estate by systematic premium payments made out of his regular earnings. He may not have much cash in the bank, but he can safeguard his family from his premature death or disability. Will his children go to college? Will they have a comfortable home? Will his wife get along after he's gone? He can say "yes" to these questions if he is covered with adequate insurance. And the growing cash values can be used to provide additional income for his retirement.

No one can tell you, without a detailed examination of your family position, what kind or how much insurance you should have. But here are a few general pointers.

• *If yours is a growing family, buy protection rather than cash value.*

A family man of 30 years of age can buy any one of the following policies for an annual premium of about $300:

Face value in dollars	Type of policy	Sample annual premium
6,000	20-year endowment	$297.00
14,000	30-payment life	369.82
16,000	Ordinary life	330.54
60,000	Term insurance	363.90

Where maximum protection is the immediate need, term insurance or ordinary life may be preferable to the others. Term insurance gives protection only. No cash values are built up over the years.

Today, some of the most popular insurance policies are designed to meet a family's long-term need for income. These family income plans combine large amounts of reducing term insurance with level term policies or ordinary life. For example, one company insures a man of 30 for $300 a year on a family income plan that guarantees his wife and two children $200 a month for 30 years, plus a cash payment of $10,000. The overall coverage is $60,000, with the coverage highest during the early years of the contract, when the children are young.

• *Insure yourself high enough on personal liability policies.*

Personal injuries to others can lead to very large claims over your lifetime. It is foolish to underinsure yourself, since liability policies are very cheap for the amount of protection they provide.

• *Keep your insurance program flexible and up-to-date.*

Consider inflation, additions to your family, or other changes that may raise or lower your insurance requirements. It is also a good idea to schedule your premium payments so that they come due at different times during the year.

If your insurance program is tied in with your company's insurance and pension plans, social security, and other probable benefits, you can build a much better security base for yourself and your family. Thus, as you do your planning, check these items and possible benefits:

• Verify the settlement options and the cash values of your present policies.

• Make sure that your beneficiary clauses are correct.

• Get the facts about your company's insurance and pension programs.

• Verify your present status under Social Security by obtaining a card from your local office and mailing it to the Social Security Administration, Baltimore, Maryland. They will return a card showing the wages credited to your account.

- Recent revisions in the Social Security Law have liberalized benefits and have extended coverage to many new groups of people. Find out how these changes affect you.
- Veterans and their families are entitled to special benefits—like medical care, home and business loans, educational assistance, and aid to widows and dependent children. See your Veterans Administration office about these benefits.

DEVELOP THE SAVING HABIT

Everyone should save regularly from his income. The best rule is to save first and spend later.

Pay-roll deductions for government bonds, or regular amounts placed in banks or building and loan associations, accumulate into very substantial amounts. If you save $40 a month and invest it at 4 per cent or more, it will add up to a minimum of $2,658.59 in 5 short years.

NO ESTATE IS TOO SMALL

As a person builds up his net worth by systematic savings, he accumulates assets that he can depend upon in case he becomes sick, unemployed, or temporarily disabled. At the same time he creates an estate problem.

Many people think that only the rich have inheritance problems. Actually, the smaller the estate, the more important it is to do everything possible for the protection of the family. When we list the things we possess—house, insurance, cash, stocks and bonds, and other personal property—it is easy to see that there are many things we want to leave to certain heirs. Most of us can do this best with a well-prepared will. If a person dies without leaving a valid will (dies intestate), an administrator is appointed by the courts and the individual's real and personal property are distributed according to the laws of the state in which he resides. In many cases, the court's distribution is contrary to the individual's wishes, and the probate charges are quite high.

There is a common belief that you do not need a will when property or other valuables are held jointly by a man and his wife. Unfortunately, joint ownership is often a poor way to hold or to convey assets, so it is wise to consult your attorney about a will and the best manner in which to hold your family's assets. It is also a good idea to make a list of your assets and liabilities. Place this list in a safety deposit box or in some safe but easy-to-find location.

Discussion Questions

1. Prepare a brief version of your personal income statement and balance sheet.
2. Cite several examples of your personal economic prudence.
3. List the main factors upon which a person's income generally depends.
4. Why does personal spending involve a great deal of psychology?
5. Give specific examples of how personal financial planning can increase an individual's living standard.
6. Present a brief outline of your personal economic plans.
7. Indicate several major ways by which family spending can be controlled.
8. Discuss the statement: "You get what you pay for."
9. When is a bargain a very expensive purchase?
10. Describe how "small leaks and losses" eat up a family's income.
11. How important is installment buying to the average family? When should it be used?
12. What types of installment buying have you used?
13. How does your state regulate consumer credit?
14. Describe how you would check the interest rate on an installment loan.
15. What community services are available to help you stretch a dollar?
16. What is the function of the New York Stock Exchange?
17. Mention several ways in which a family can increase its net worth.
18. Discuss the pro's and con's of the different types of life insurance.
19. Discuss this statement: "No estate is too small as far as estate planning is concerned."
20. Present your views on the value of stock investments to a middle income family.

Circle the T or F (True or False) before each statement:

T   F   1. It's safer to spread your stock investments over several companies in different industries.

T   F   2. A stock with a par value of $25 generally sells for $25 on the stock exchange.

T   F   3. When an insurance policy has less cash value, its insurance coverage is closer to the face value of the policy.

T   F   4. An endowment policy provides more insurance protection for each dollar of premium than renewable term insurance.

T   F   5. Bondholders are usually affected more by inflation than common stockholders.

T   F   6. Limited payment policies insure a person for life, after premiums have been paid for a given number of years.

T   F   7. Mutual funds are a good way to diversify a small investment.

T   F   8. A bear expects the market to go down.

T   F   9. A bull expects the market to go down.

T   F   10. A flat rate interest charge on the original balance is the best way to finance a car.

ANSWERS

10. F	8. T	6. T	4. F	2. F
9. F	7. T	5. T	3. T	1. T

PART TWO

Economic problems and policies

13

THE GROSS NATIONAL PRODUCT

In recent years economists have become increasingly concerned with the nature, formation, and composition of the nation's annual flow of goods and services—what is called the Gross National Product. This concern is part of the macro-approach to economics, which stresses aggregates like national income, the volume of employment, gross investment, the general price level, government spending and revenue, foreign trade, and the allocation of productive resources.

Few quantitative measures are as widely used as GNP. Its frequent use, however, should not cloud the fact that there are many conceptual and accounting problems involved in the calculating of the GNP. Therefore, it may be well to describe in detail the *nature* and *measurement* of *GNP*.

MEASURING THE PERFORMANCE OF OUR ECONOMIC SYSTEM

Gross National Product is a measure of the flow of goods and services produced by a nation during a specific period of time, usually one year. In its crudest form GNP would consist of a long tabulation of goods and services—such as typewriters, machinery, candy, pig iron, shoe shines, medical care, and so on—accounting for everything that had been produced. This kind of record is known as the nation's output in physical product, but it is useless, because we cannot add together pounds of meat, carats of diamonds, pairs of shoes, tons of sand, yards of cloth, units of housing, or hours of teaching. The tabulation can be made functional by using money as a common denominator. Instead of listing goods and services in units, we take their market values as represented by their sales prices. We then add up the dollar figures to arrive at the *monetary value* of the nation's *physical product*.

147

Changing physical product into monetary terms helps us compare the national production of different years. We must remember, however, that the price of an article or service reflects its conditions of demand and supply as well as the value of the monetary unit in which the price is stated. For example, if our GNP increased from $700 billion to $770 billion, we cannot tell whether the real national product has increased, decreased, or has remained the same until we can determine what changes, if any, have taken place in the value of the dollar. Thus, if GNP has risen from $700 billion to $770 billion while the general level of prices has advanced from 100 to 110, the real national product has not changed because both measures have gone up 10 per cent. If prices had advanced to only 105, this would mean an increase in the real national product, while a rise in prices to 120 would indicate a decline in real product.

THE CYCLE OF INCOME

Now, let us see how a nation's income is generated.

Individuals regularly spend a part of their incomes on goods and services of all kinds. These transactions transfer to producers a definite portion of the nation's money income. Businessmen, in turn, make expenditures. Thus producers and consumers generate the money incomes which are diffused throughout our economy.

Business expenditures are of two types: first, outlays are made for using the factors of production—land, labor, capital, and entrepreneurship—often called *factor costs;* second, payments are made for raw materials—transportation, power, and the like. These costs represent payments made to other businesses for items or services purchased from them rather than paid directly to the owners of the productive factors. They are called *user costs.*

For example, an entrepreneur will have a user cost when he spends $1,000 for raw material. His supplier, however must use a part of the $1,000 to pay for the labor, capital, and land that he hired to produce the raw material. These would be factor costs to him. In this manner all user costs ultimately become factor costs.

As we follow business activities to their ultimate conclusion, the money income originally spent on goods and services becomes a series of income streams flowing to the owners of the productive factors at various levels, until the entire national income is divided into distributive shares. The total money income to be distributed depends, in the first instance, on the total value of the goods and services sold on the markets.

This, then, is how the income cycle is generated. It flows into the hands of producers as receipts from their sales, and these producers then pass on the income to others as they make business expenditures.

THE NATURE OF THE GROSS NATIONAL PRODUCT

The GNP includes the value of the products or services of government-owned as well as privately owned industry. So we include the value of the services performed by a civil service employee as well as the value of the steel fabricated by a privately owned company or the services of an advertising agency.

The goods and services which make up the GNP may be purchased by private individuals as consumer goods, by private industry or business as producer goods, by foreign buyers, or by the government. Included are expenditures for such diverse items as radios, food, clothing, entertainment, office buildings, factory equipment, capital facilities, war materiel, and general supplies for the government.

The Problems of Measurement

Computing the monetary value of the GNP poses a number of practical and theoretical problems. For example, if an automobile manufacturer sells a car for $2,000, we know that $2,000 worth of production has taken place, that receipts of $2,000 have flowed to the producer, and that expenditures of $2,000 have been made by the buyers. Thus it is possible to measure national product in terms of the value of the goods and services produced, the income to owners of the factors from this

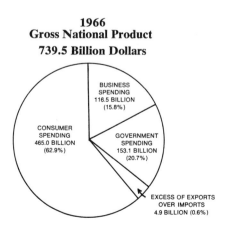

1966
Gross National Product
739.5 Billion Dollars

BUSINESS SPENDING 116.5 BILLION (15.8%)

CONSUMER SPENDING 465.0 BILLION (62.9%)

GOVERNMENT SPENDING 153.1 BILLION (20.7%)

EXCESS OF EXPORTS OVER IMPORTS 4.9 BILLION (0.6%)

production when it is sold, or the expenditures made by buyers when the production is purchased. These approaches to the measurement of national product are called the *product, income,* and *expenditures* approaches.

Our understanding of the statistical data concerning Gross National Product can be improved by indicating the items which are included and excluded.

Items Excluded for Theoretical Reasons

Generally, we exclude from GNP all transactions that do not affect the flow of goods and services. For example, if you receive funds which augment your income—like the proceeds of a loan, the sale of a personal asset, or a gift—there is a transfer of income but no increase or decrease in the flow of goods and services. These are not counted as part of the GNP because they are merely *private transfer payments* that represent a redistribution of income.

There may also be a flow of income from the government to the public—like social security payments, relief disbursements, or veterans' benefits. These are *government transfer payments,* and they are distinguished from government expenditures for goods and services. Interest payments on the national debt are considered a transfer payment, because government accounting methods do not break the debt down according to the purpose of the expenditures.

A capital gain that results from the sale of an asset for a price higher than its purchase price is considered a private transfer payment, if no work was done by the owner to bring about the increase. Thus, if you buy a house for $25,000 and then sell it in its original condition for $30,000, the extra $5,000 is a capital gain and is excluded from the GNP since no contribution was made to the national output. If the increased value resulted from improvements to the house, the $5,000, or some portion of it, would be included as part of the GNP.

Items Excluded Because of Accounting Difficulties

The GNP is limited to goods and services for which a market price exists, so goods and services are not included unless they are sold on the market. For example, the work done by a housewife, the produce raised in a private garden, or other types of imputed income are not included.

We exclude, too, goods and services that are sold through illegal marketing activities, like the services of a gambler or the value of dope sold by a dope peddler.

Double Counting and Value Added

When figuring GNP, we must avoid double or multiple counting. For example, take the case of a generator. Raw materials, semi-finished goods, and parts make up the final product. If the values of these items are counted separately, and also included in the value of the finished generator, production will be counted more than once and the size of the Gross National Product will be artificially increased.

Moreover, some services are counted as part of the value of the product that they help to produce. Thus the value of the services of a worker in a coal mine is included in the value of the coal, and the value of a carpenter's services is included in the overall value of the house when it is sold. We don't list these separately when calculating the GNP.

On the other hand, the services of a physician, barber, or attorney are not associated with the production of a commodity, so they are listed as a separate component of the GNP.

Capital Consumption

Gross National Product measures the total flow of goods and services, and so no allowance is made for capital equipment that may be consumed in the process of producing this flow. There is no deduction for depreciation or any other conditions that would diminish the nation's capital account.

The Size of the Gross National Product

The statistics on the size, structure, and composition of the Gross National Product come, for the most part, from the United States Department of Commerce, which reported a GNP of $739.5 billion for 1966, broken down as follows:

Personal consumption goods or expenditures	$465.0 billion
Gross private domestic investment	116.5 billion
Government purchases of goods and services	153.1 billion
Net excess of exports over imports	4.9 billion
Total value of goods and services	$739.5 billion

Personal consumption expenditures consist of the market value of the purchases of consumer goods and services by individuals and nonprofit institutions. Of the $465.0 billion, 44 per cent was for nondurable consumer goods, 15 per cent for durables, and 41 per cent for services.[1]

"Gross private domestic investment" means the value of newly produced goods acquired by private business, as well as the value of any changes in the worth of inventories held by them. It also includes the value of new dwellings, whether owner- or tenant-occupied. With the exception of owner-occupied new homes, this gives us a measure of the flow of producer goods, the expenditures for producer goods, and the income of the producer-goods industries. Not included in this category, however, are producer goods destined for government or foreign purchasing.

In 1966, gross private domestic investment consisted of: $51.4 billion for producer durable equipment, $27.9 billion for producer purchase of structures, $25.8 billion for residential structures, and $11.4 billion for changes in inventories.

Government purchases of goods and services cover the outlays of all units of government, which consist mainly of government employee salaries and purchases from industry. In 1966 the Federal government accounted for about half (77.0 billion out of 153.1 billion, the rest being state and local) of all governmental outlays. And of the Federal government totals, about 78 per cent was associated with national defense.

The excess of exports over imports measures the change in status of our international *balance of trade,* and dropped in 1966 to $4.9 billion, from a high of $8.5 billion in 1964. This is not much above the $4.0 billion of 1960, which is the low thus far for the 1960's.

A Comparison with Other Years

When comparing the GNP of 1966 with some other year, we must take into account the changes in the purchasing power of the dollar. The following table shows what happens to the GNP when it is stated in current dollars and then in constant dollars.

In current dollars, the Gross National Product increased more than 600 per cent between 1929 and 1966; but in constant dollars, using 1958 as the base, the real increase was about 220 per cent.

---

[1] *Economic Report of the President,* U.S. Department of Commerce, 1967, pp. 213, 224.

Year	In Current Dollars	In Constant Dollars[2] (1958)
1929	$103.1 billion	$203.6 billion
1933	55.6	141.5
1937	90.4	203.2
1939	90.5	209.4
1940	99.7	227.2
1950	284.8	355.3
1955	398.0	438.0
1958	447.3	447.3
1960	503.8	487.7
1961	520.1	497.2
1962	560.3	529.8
1963	590.5	551.0
1964	631.7	580.0
1965	681.2	614.4
1966	739.5	647.7

NET NATIONAL PRODUCT

The Gross National Product exaggerates a given year's production to the extent that current production causes wear and tear of the plant and equipment in existence at the beginning of the period. To this extent, current production embodies a part of the production of the past.

It is necessary to subtract these depreciation charges—what are called capital consumption allowances—from the value of the GNP to get a true picture of the net contribution to annual production. This then gives us the Net National Product.

In 1966 depreciation charges came to $63.1 billion, so we had a Net National Product of $676.4 billion.[3]

NATIONAL INCOME

We have been considering the flow of goods and services for the economy as a whole. But, we're also interested in seeing how this income is distributed among the productive factors of land, labor, capital, and entrepreneurship.

We know, for example, that many indirect business taxes are included in the market prices that make up the value of the national product, so the gross receipts of business are increased by these taxes. This income

[2] *Ibid.,* p. 214.
[3] *Ibid.,* p. 227.

is siphoned off by the government before the productive factors receive their income in the forms of rent, interest, wages, or profits and losses. These taxes are kept separate from direct taxes, such as income taxes, which are levied after the distributive shares have been received.

When we subtract indirect business taxes from the net national product, we have our first approximation of the national income going to the factors of production. However, a few adjustments still remain to be made. These include the excess of subsidies paid out by the government over profits earned on government-owned enterprises, certain business transfer payments that have to be deducted from factor earnings—like bad debts or charitable contributions—and any statistical discrepancies which might occur because of the accounting calculations involved. When these final adjustments are completed, we come up with the national income.

In this sense, the national income may be viewed as that portion of the net national product that flows to the factors of production.

In 1966 we had a net national product of $676.4 billion, and after subtracting indirect business taxes ($65.5 billion) and other adjustments of $1.2 billion (total of $66.7 billion), we had a national income of $609.7 billion.[4]

The Department of Commerce divides the recipients of the national income into five categories, as shown in the following table:

1966 National Income by Distributive Shares
(in billions)[5]

Compensation of employees	$433.2
Rental income of persons	18.9
Net interest	20.0
Income of unincorporated enterprises, including farms and inventory valuation adjustments	57.8
Corporate profits and inventory valuation adjustments	79.8
National Income	$609.7

PERSONAL INCOME

Up to this point our analysis of national income has been in terms of the total amount of income flowing to the productive factors. But we are interested, too, in the amount of income available to individuals. This measure is called "Personal Income" and is defined as the current income received by persons from all sources.

---

4 *Ibid.*
5 *Ibid.*

Personal income will be less than national income, because the latter includes taxes on corporate profits and some corporate profits that are not paid out to individuals. Then, too, contributions for social insurance by employers and employees will be deducted from national income because these amounts do not reach the pockets of individuals.

On the other hand individuals may receive income from sources other than their employment. There may be transfer income from government and business—like interest paid by the Federal government, veterans' bonuses, subsidies, prizes, disability payments, dividends, and so on.

The final adjustments gave us a personal income of $580.4 billion in 1966.[6]

To get this figure from the national income ($609.7 billion) we subtract $117.6 billion ($79.8 billion for corporate profits and inventory valuation adjustments and $37.8 billion for contributions for social insurance), but we add back $88.2 billion ($41.9 for government transfer payments, $22.8 for interest paid by governments and by consumers, $20.9 for dividends, and $2.6 for other business transfer payments). Thus, we subtract a net of $29.4 billion and arrive at personal income of $580.4, which is slightly different from $580.3 because of rounding the decimals.

DISPOSABLE PERSONAL INCOME

Now we come to a measure of the amount of income that individuals have available for their own use—what we call Disposable Personal Income.

This measures the amount of income that remains after people pay their personal taxes and make non-tax payments to the different government bodies. These payments include all tax and non-tax liabilities levied against individuals, their income and their property, and which are not deductible as business expenses.

In 1966, the $580.4 billion of personal income is reduced by $75.1 billion for personal tax and non-tax payments, leaving $505.3 billion as disposable personal income.[7] This in turn was divided into the following:

Personal consumption expenditures	$465.0 billion
Interest paid by consumers	12.7
Personal transfer payments to foreigners	.7
Personal saving	26.9
Total Disposable Income	$505.3 billion

[6] *Ibid.*, p. 228.
[7] *Ibid.*, p. 229.

FACTORS INFLUENCING THE LEVEL OF NATIONAL PRODUCTION

The two most important forces which determine the level of national production at any given time are the *volume of consumption* and the *volume of investment.*

The Propensity to Consume

The relationship between total consumption expenditures and total disposable income is called the *propensity to consume.* The propensity to consume may be high or low, depending upon a number of factors that influence the individual. General habits of consumption may change over a period of years. Or, an individual may change his attitude about the future and become optimistic or pessimistic.

There also may be objective factors that affect the propensity to consume, like changes in taxes, changes in prices, or changes in future income expectations.

The desire of people to spend has a direct influence on the volume of national output. If their propensity to consume goes down, without a corresponding increase in the volume of investment, the nation's output will be reduced. On the other hand, a rising propensity to consume stimulates business expansion and investment. As consumers demand more goods, consumer goods industries increase their inventories and buy more machinery and equipment from producer goods industries. This has the effect of increasing employment and the flow of income. Because the future looks brighter, consumers are encouraged to consume a greater percentage of their income. In fact, many will go in debt to finance current purchases.

In 1966, personal outlays accounted for 94.7 per cent of disposable income (personal consumption expenditures accounted for 92 per cent and interest paid by consumers came to 2.7 per cent). This allowed 5.3 per cent for personal saving. Thus, we have an average propensity to consume of 92 or 95 per cent, depending on how we consider interest paid by consumers. Since 1950, the highest percentage for personal consumption alone has been 92.7 and the lowest has been 90.9, thus showing a remarkable stability of consumption on a relative basis.[8]

---

[8] *Ibid.*

The Propensity to Save

The portion of an individual's income that is not used for consumption is available for savings, and, the ratio between savings and income is called the *propensity to save*.

The propensity to save plus the propensity to consume always equals 100 because all income is either spent or saved. So, if the propensity to consume is 90 per cent, the propensity to save is 10 per cent.

The propensity to save will depend, first, on the size of the income, because savings will go up more rapidly than consumption, as income increases.

Savings become investments when they are used to buy production facilities.

Producers tend to invest when they expect an increase in their future profits. Decisions to invest in new buildings and equipment, in the accumulation of inventories, or in the expansion of capital facilities will mean an increase in employment. This, in turn, increases the disposable income that flows into the economy, so consumers will continue to buy increasing amounts of the product in the next period. Moreover, as each firm makes its investments, it will buy materials from other firms and these firms, too, will begin to expand their employment. Again, additional sources of expanded consumer income are set into flow.

Not all savings, however, find their way into the formation of new capital. Some savings end up in financial or other markets in the form of speculation, or they may be kept as idle or hoarded funds. Savings must be converted into investment to have an effect on the level of national production and income.

As a rule investments will be encouraged when the return on capital exceeds the rate of interest, that is, the cost of capital. So in making decisions about investing, the businessman tries to anticipate the future. He tries to forecast what the price level will be when his production is ready for the market, the effective demand at that time, the degree of competition he will face, and the probable return on capital that he can expect.

Just as consumption on a relative basis has not varied much over the years—so, too, personal saving has been reasonably stable. In 1966 personal saving accounted for 5.3 per cent of disposable income. In the 1960's the range has been from 4.9 per cent to 5.8 per cent. Nonetheless, marginal variations are important in influencing business activity at any given time. For example, a one percentage point change in personal savings means a plus or minus variation of about $5 billion.

SUMMARY

It may be helpful to the reader if we summarize the main Gross National Product accounts as follows:

GNP − Capital Consumption Allowances = Net National Product

NNP − Indirect Business Taxes = National Income

National Income − (Corporate Retained Earnings + Corporate Income Taxes) + Transfer Payments = Personal Income

Personal Income − Personal Tax Payments = Disposable Personal Income

Disposable Personal Income = Savings + Consumption

The reader should be cautioned that the foregoing covers the major items, but that there are a few others that have not been included, for sake of simplicity.

Discussion Questions

1. What economic areas are included under macro-economics?
2. Define GNP.
3. Why is it more convenient to discuss monetary rather than physical GNP?
4. How do changes in the price level affect the measurement of GNP?
5. Explain the cycle of income.
6. What are factor costs? Give examples.
7. What measurement problems are involved in calculating GNP?
8. Indicate the relative sizes of the main components of the current GNP.
9. Describe and give examples of transfer payments.
10. How is multiple counting avoided in calculating GNP?
11. Illustrate what is meant by "value added."
12. Explain the nature of capital consumption.
13. Describe net national product.
14. Explain how national income is calculated.
15. Why is national income called "factor income"?
16. Explain how personal income is measured.
17. What is included in personal income?

18. Explain what is meant by the propensity to consume.

19. If I have $5000 of income and consume $4000, what is my average propensity to consume?

20. What is disposable personal income?

Circle the T or F (True or False) before each statement:

T F 1. The Gross National Product is calculated in about the same way in most countries.

T F 2. The Gross National Product includes the amount of national depreciation of buildings, plant, and equipment.

T F 3. The real Gross National Product takes into account the effects of inflation.

T F 4. Per capita real Gross National Product is a good measure of economic progress.

T F 5. Gross National Product is more closely related to economic growth than to economic progress.

T F 6. National income gives us a better idea of the distributive shares going to various groups.

T F 7. Our real Gross National Product increases, on the average, about 5 per cent a year.

T F 8. Economic progress and leisure time are interrelated.

T F 9. Living standards are affected by the size of the real Gross National Product.

T F 10. Government activities and defense depend largely on the size of the real Gross National Product.

ANSWERS

10. T	8. T	6. T	4. T	2. T
9. T	7. F	5. T	3. T	1. F

14

THE UPS AND DOWNS
OF BUSINESS

A HISTORICAL REVIEW

The greeting "How's business?" is synonymous for "How are you?" There is an unconscious coupling of the idea that if business is good, a person's health can be taken for granted. We probably can say, in a humorous way, that the condition of a businessman's ulcers is related to the state of his business. When things look good, everyone feels better, and, as a rule, we experience a high rate of employment, active buying, business expansion, and an optimistic attitude toward the future. On the other hand, bad times suggest just the opposite. With this in mind, let us take a closer look at business fluctuation over the years.

Some people believe that the business cycle is peculiar to capitalism, yet good and bad times were a matter of historical record long before capitalism came into being. Until the nineteenth century, discussions about the business cycle were largely in terms of physical causes. Agriculture was the most important economic activity, so catastrophes like floods, earthquakes, fires, and famines were extremely important. The change in emphasis from physical to price factors came about because of the Industrial Revolution. Business then became complicated by many factors—the differences between management and labor, the specialization of labor, the development and expansion of bank credit, and the growth in size of national markets because of improved transportation and communication.

SOME ASPECTS OF UPS AND DOWNS IN BUSINESS ACTIVITY

In modern times economic activity has been characterized by business fluctuations rather than by business stability. Such fluctuations may be *secular, seasonal, random,* or *cyclical.* Even though all four are interwoven, we will try to examine their influences separately.

We could study, for example, a series of statistical data showing how automobile production has changed over a period of fifty years. If we did this, we would have a secular or long-term trend reflected in the data. This trend relates to circumstances that change rather slowly, like population trends and basic changes in consumer taste. Such changes are not easily perceived in short-term periods, so secular movements tend to reflect the growth or decay of the industry involved. Statisticians have several techniques for isolating or eliminating this factor when desirable.

Suppose that a series of data shows that there has been a long-term growth factor of 2 per cent a year compounded, and we begin with a starting base of 100 for a given year. If the growth rate is maintained we should have an index level of about 110.40 five years later. If the level is less than this, we can say that the industry has not maintained its historical growth pattern.

We can also study data to find out whether changes occur periodically, such as seasonally, monthly, or weekly. For example, agricultural production is different in September from December, and department store sales vary substantially between December and May. Oil and gas sales are higher in the colder months. So, statisticians have devised ways to isolate, measure, and eliminate these influences.

Further, our data may contain movements of a random or irregular nature. These are changes that do not recur regularly, such as floods, fires, wars, or earthquakes.

If our statistical techniques have been applied correctly, the remaining data will contain only the movements resulting from the cyclical ups and downs in business.

A MORE PRECISE VIEW OF THE BUSINESS CYCLE

The business cycle refers to the ups and downs in business activity, but for a precise description, we must analyze the entire cycle from one period until a similar period reappears. Thus we may begin with a period of prosperity and expansion, then experience periods of recession, depression, recovery, and prosperity once again, and then go through a second cycle. We must examine each of these periods to better understand their nature and to see what takes place and why.

Prosperity

What is prosperity and when is it present?

Some writers call a period prosperous if the index being used happens to be above 100. Others include only the peak period and the area before and after the turning point. Thus, if an index moved from 100 to 116 and then back down to 98, prosperity would be designated as the period from around 110 to 116 and back to 110.

Typical economic changes take place during a period of prosperity. As a rule, selling prices go up faster than production costs, and profits rise at an increasing rate. This is partly because costs like utilities, taxes, and interest remain relatively fixed, while others, like maintenance, move up rather slowly. In anticipation of greater profits, businessmen borrow more heavily, and inventories are accumulated to take advantage of future higher prices. Additional capital is invested in new plant capacity.

Costs eventually increase. Wages and raw materials go up, and less efficient factors of production are put to work. The larger supplies on the market no longer move with ease, and the threat of a market glut becomes apparent. Banks, whose reserves are low, become reluctant to extend credit, so they begin to call in outstanding loans.

Meanwhile, the cost of living goes up and labor demands more pay. Management becomes cautious. The new plants, provided earlier in the cycle, begin to pour out more goods. Banks increase interest rates and other loan requirements, and the accompanying liquidation on the security market adds another pessimistic tone, as a downturn begins in the cycle.

Recession

The downward spiral from a period of prosperity brings with it recession or crisis. The maladjustments that were hardly evident during the period of prosperity become apparent. Production begins to outrun consumption. The disparity between profits, rents, wages, and interest increases. Other dislocations may occur between farm and industrial prices or between the prices of raw material and finished goods. Cash positions are squeezed, and businessmen become uneasy about their inventory positions and unload to meet their liabilities.

Houses and durables purchased on the installment plan may be sacrificed, as foreclosures and bankruptcies increase. Security margins are tightened. Factories lay off workers, and some close completely. This cuts purchasing power, further reducing aggregate demand.

The international economic situation—gold and other money problems—usually adds its critical influence.

Recession or Depression

After continued liquidation, business seems to hit a stable level, even if at a low rate of activity. Prices are lower, employment is up, inventories are down, security prices are depressed, money costs are low, profits are at a minimum, plant operations are below capacity, bank reserves are up, and pessimism prevails.

Businessmen are unwilling to make commitments, labor unions have a hard time bargaining, and consumer buying is at a low ebb.

Recovery or Revival

After a more-or-less prolonged period, business starts on the upswing again. Inventories are replenished as demand slowly increases. Replacement demand increases. Postponed repairs have to be made. Profits reappear. Plant expansion or improvement may be encouraged because of lower costs.

Various stimuli may be introduced to accelerate the upward spiral. Banks with large reserves tend to relax their credit restrictions, and this encourages business activity and expansion. Optimism begins to return, especially if the security markets show rising tendencies. Many high-cost firms may have been eliminated during the depression, and so the more efficient firms may be able to take advantage of a favorable cost and price situation.

This upward trend ultimately leads again to the prosperity phase, and the business cycle is completed.

Obviously, this is a very oversimplified picture of a classic business cycle. Actually, each cycle has its own characteristics based on the times. For example, some revivals may not lead to recovery but may

164 · ECONOMIC PROBLEMS AND POLICIES

revert to recession or depression. There is no reason, either, why every period of prosperity must lead to a decline within a short period. We may experience long periods of relatively uninterrupted prosperity. Indeed, since the end of World War II, we have not experienced a depression, and our recessions have been relatively short-lived.

THE ACCELERATOR AND THE MULTIPLIER

When discussing ups and downs in business, we usually think in terms of two principles—the *accelerator* and the *multiplier*.

The acceleration principle deals with the effects of an increase in the demand for consumer goods on the demand for investment goods.

For example, suppose we start with a company capable of supplying 100 consumer goods units annually, a consumer demand for 100 units, 10 machines with a 10-year life, and we assume that one worn-out machine is replaced each year. This means that each machine can produce 10 units and that the company will buy 1 machine a year, thereby creating a producer demand of 1 machine annually.

Now, let us say that there is an increase in consumer demand to 110 units. To meet this increased demand of 10 units requires an additional machine, so that producer demand for that year will rise from 1 to 2 machines. Thus, a 10 per cent increase in consumer demand has generated a 100 per cent increase in producer-goods demand—an accelerated effect.

Later, if consumer demand drops back to 100, this represents a decline of about 9 per cent. However, the company now will purchase only 1 new machine instead of 2. This means a 50 per cent decline in the producer-goods industry—which is an acceleration downward.

It follows, then, that changes in the demand for consumer goods have proportionally larger effects on the demand for producer goods. This is aggravated by the fact that an increased demand for consumer goods cannot be met immediately. A seeming scarcity exists until new plant capacity is producing goods. Each producer who experiences this inflated demand may undertake expansion programs. So, overexpansion may easily result.

When this greater capacity is completed and its production enters the market, the enlarged capacity requires that consumer demand remain stable or increase; otherwise serious changes will take place in investment demand as capacity remains unused.

The multiplier principle deals with the effects on consumer demand of increased spending for producer goods by private industry or by the government, as on public works or for defense.

Let us say that $10,000 is spent for capital goods. This may actually create $30,000 of total purchasing power—depending upon the velocity of circulation of the original $10,000 and the amount of that sum which is drawn off for savings, foreign purchases, or hoarding. This is the basic theory behind government deficit spending during recession or depression years.

Government spending on public works will provide purchasing power for those employed. These workers, in turn, will spend their money for more consumer goods, thus increasing the demand for consumer goods several times more than the original expenditure on the public works.

To estimate the size of the multiplier, we have to know what is called the *marginal propensity to consume* (MPC). This measures the percentage of one's added income devoted to consumption. For example, an individual who earns $8,000 a year, consumes $7,500, and saves $500, has an average propensity to consume of about 94 per cent. If then he receives a wage increase of $1,000, his annual income is now $9,000. If with the extra $1,000 he divides it into $600 for consumption and $400 for savings, his MPC becomes 60 per cent.

The MPC influences the size of the multiplier. Thus, if a community's income is increased by $100,000 due to the construction of a new plant and recipients of this added income divide it into $80,000 of consumption and $20,000 of saving, we have an MPC of 80 per cent. If the recipients of the $80,000 divided their income on a $\frac{4}{5}$, $\frac{1}{5}$ basis, they would generate $64,000 of income for the next stage ($80,000 × $\frac{4}{5}$). If this process continued, a total income of $500,000 would be generated as a result of the initial $100,000. The multiplier, in this case, would be 5.

In the United States, today, the average multiplier is estimated at about $2\frac{1}{2}$.

INVESTMENT AND SAVINGS

The terms "investment," "savings," and "spending" sprinkle business-cycle literature, so let us give some attention to their meaning.

National savings are the national income less consumption. The important point here is that savings need not be equal to investment, which really means the amount of national income devoted to further production. Investment may exceed savings through the processes of debt accumulation.

Gross investment is total investment for capital goods (new investment plus replacement).

Net investment refers to gross investment minus replacement investment.

To achieve long-term growth and stability, an economic system must keep its over-all net investment on the rise. This means keeping its national savings fully invested in the production facilities of the future, so that its real national income in goods and services is on the rise over the secular trend. When this occurs, the principles of-the multiplier and accelerator, working together, may generate full employment of the factors of production.

CONCLUSION

There have been as many explanations of business cycles as there are writers in this field. And their explanations range all the way from physical changes in the atmosphere to intricate maladjustments in the economy. Fortunately, the dogmatism of the past has given way to a more balanced explanation. This is realistic, because the cycle is far too complicated to be explained by a single set of factors.

The "human factor" explanation of the business cycle appeals to many people, but technical students of the cycle tend to regard this as a case of circular reasoning. Does optimism cause the cycle, or does some other force cause the optimism which fortifies the original force? The query is valid, but the human theory does help explain the course of the cycle once it has begun, regardless of the originating force. Optimism and pessimism are contagious, especially with the many paper profits and losses now in existence.

The confidence theory received a great deal of attention during the depression of the 1930's. Presidential candidates argued about who could best restore business confidence. Governmental policies and enactments were hailed or condemned as furthering or retarding national confidence.

Other theories of the cycle are based on the circumstances surrounding modern technology—like large-scale, roundabout production. The time-consuming process of modern production is blamed for many of the problems arising out of consumption, production, spending, saving, and investment. Moreover, the technological characteristics of modern production—inventions, discoveries, innovations, and changes in consumer demand—are other impelling forces affecting the cycle.

Another group of theorists explains cyclical reactions in terms of our exchange economy. They see the causes in the profit motive of industrial capitalism, speculation, and market errors arising from an apparently unplanned national production.

Still another group sees the key relationships involving the quantity of money and credit, and the resulting price level. Basically, this group feels that recessions take place when the quantity of money does not expand as rapidly as business. In this case, credit is conceived of as the impetus-giving force. Many of those who follow this theory admit that other factors are involved, but they believe the major cyclical swings are the result of the expansion and contraction of money and of central bank credits.

Another group talks about the inadequacy of aggregate demand. They insist that the purchasing power of the economy is inadequate to buy the flow of goods. This causes unemployment and a further decline in effective demand. Their solution is to increase purchasing power, using government spending whenever necessary. They regard any cut in wages or prices as dangerous, because they believe that this will simply reduce aggregate demand.

All of these theories lead to one conclusion: the business cycle is a complex phenomenon that cannot be explained by a single set of factors. Today, therefore, most writers are pluralistic in their analysis, even though they may emphasize some particular aspect in their approach.

Discussion Questions

1. Discuss this conclusion: "The business cycle is unique to capitalism."
2. Describe the factors that contribute to the business cycle.
3. Distinguish among secular, seasonal, random, and cyclical changes.
4. What seasonal factors affect the firms in your community?
5. Describe the prosperity phase of a classic business cycle.
6. How would you characterize a recession?
7. Describe the recovery phase of a typical cycle.
8. Illustrate the accelerator principle.
9. Describe how the multiplier works.
10. What is the multiplier when the marginal propensity to consume is $\frac{4}{5}$ and there is an additional investment of $10,000? How much total income might be generated?
11. Distinguish investment from saving.
12. Distinguish gross and net investment.

13. Distinguish real and financial saving.

14. Describe the confidence theory of the business cycle.

15. How does technology affect the business cycle?

16. How does aggregate demand affect the business cycle?

17. How do the patterns of consumption affect the propensity to consume?

18. Relate aggregate demand to the Gross National Product.

19. Discuss this statement: "Monetary and fiscal policies have little effect on the business cycle."

20. Discuss this conclusion: "The Gross National Product can increase while business activity is slowing down."

Circle the T or F (True or False) before each statement:

T F 1. The multiplier and acceleration principles are always inflationary in their effects.

T F 2. The multiplier and acceleration principles are related to economic growth.

T F 3. Advancing technology tends to revitalize a stagnant economy.

T F 4. The "consumption function" deals primarily with capital investments.

T F 5. Savings and investments are really different names for the same thing.

T F 6. The multiplier varies between prosperities and depressions.

T F 7. The multiplier has been quite effective in the United States in recent years.

T F 8. The marginal propensity to consume is of greater significance to national income economics than the average propensity.

T F 9. The propensity to save has little to do with the business cycle.

T F 10. The propensity to consume can be measured mathematically.

ANSWERS

2. T	4. F	6. T	8. T	10. T
1. F	3. T	5. F	7. T	9. F

15

UNEMPLOYMENT AND FULL EMPLOYMENT

Unemployment is a serious economic problem, and the fear of job loss is one of the greatest personal uncertainties. The word "unemployment" implies idle manpower, but it applies as well to land and capital.

Naturally, the problems of unemployment have become more complex as our economy has become more interdependent. The specialization of labor increases the dependence of workers on our market-place system. Disturbances in market equilibrium can lead to ups and downs in the demand for labor, and that is why economists pay close attention to changes in the rate of unemployment.

WHAT IS UNEMPLOYMENT?

To begin with, we need a better definition of unemployment. Generally, a person is considered unemployed if he has no job, is able to work, is seeking employment, and cannot find work. We include new entrants into the labor force, the people who are returning to the labor market after having left it voluntarily, and those who have lost their jobs.

We leave out those who do not have a job because they are not actively looking for work. We exclude, too, those who are unemployable because of disabilities or inadequacies, even though they may be looking for work.

THE CAUSES OF UNEMPLOYMENT

There is little agreement on the causes of particular cases of joblessness, but there is reasonable agreement on the causes of general unemployment. We can lump these causes under three broad categories:

- Those resting with the unemployed person
- Those relating to the actions of employers
- Those arising from economic conditions, local or national

The causes that arise from the employee's situation are usually limiting factors, like physical and mental handicaps. These people are excluded from the labor force because it is difficult to find jobs for them even under the most favorable economic conditions. Nonetheless, modern rehabilitation programs prepare many so-called unemployables to fill existing job openings.

Some workers prefer to remain unemployed for personal reasons, and they are excluded from the unemployment figures because they have freely decided not to work. We should, however, distinguish two groups of the voluntarily unemployed. There are some who could find a job at satisfactory rates of pay, but they choose to remain unemployed. These are truly voluntarily unemployed, because the person could find a job if he wanted to. Other people however choose not to work because the rate of pay is below what they consider adequate. There is some argument as to whether these people should be classified as voluntarily unemployed. Classical economics contends that, when more people are willing to work than employers are willing to hire, the resulting unemployment can be reduced by a drop in real wages. This could be achieved by a cut in wage rates to restore a position of equilibrium—the way supply and demand would operate in any market situation. This approach was criticized by Keynes and by his followers. They argued that a change in the level of employment could come about only through an increase in effective over-all demand. Keynesians, therefore, would classify these people as involuntarily unemployed.

Meanwhile, others find themselves unemployed because of inadequate or improper education. This is an ever-increasing problem, especially for the middle-aged unemployed. Technological advances increase this problem since skills become obsolete with the introduction of new machinery and methods. Existing workers may be too old to be given effective training, or workers may resist the effort required to gain new skills. So, while there may be a shortage of workers with the new skills, there may be unemployment among older workers who have obsolete skills no longer in demand.

Other workers may be unemployed because they are not sufficiently mobile. New job opportunities may be available in areas distant from a worker's home, but personal reasons may cause him to hold on to his present job longer than is prudent for the area.

Unemployment may arise, too, from conditions attributable to the employer—like his lack of managerial skills, the poor profitability of his business, or the relative size of his operation. Bad production planning may contribute to unemployment, creating peaks and valleys in his employment level. During the off-seasons workers may be reluctant to move because of the hope of returning to their jobs and the uncertainty about what a new location might offer.

Marginal concerns may find themselves in an unfavorable competitive position, so they are prone to lay off workers as a cost-saving device.

In the long run social and economic forces are the most important causes of unemployment. The causes stemming from employee or employer characteristics usually correct themselves with a minimum of public interference. But those arising from the operation of the economic system or the organization of society do not correct themselves easily or readily. They are, more often, beyond the ability of employees or employers to combat.

MAJOR CLASSIFICATIONS OF UNEMPLOYMENT

Seasonal Unemployment

Many firms find that the demand for their products varies with the seasons of the year. Such variations may reflect physical conditions—like the inability of some farmers to have more than one harvest season; or custom—like the time of the year when new automobiles are introduced; or social behavior—such as particular holidays like Christmas or Easter; or changes in the labor market—like large numbers of students seeking summer employment.

Some companies may meet their seasonal peaks by using overtime or incentive systems to encourage more production from a given labor force. In other cases, there is a seasonal influx of workers who drop out of the labor market when the peak period is over.

Labor differs from other commodities because it can be varied in quantity only with great difficulty. Thus, it takes a number of years for a child to mature into an adult member of the labor market, with proper skill qualifications. But once attached to the labor force, a worker may find it hard to remove himself because of the need to provide for his family.

Until recently, very little was known about the labor market. Studies by the United States Bureau of Employment Security have increased our knowledge of the labor market, but individual workers have imperfect knowledge about it and are not generally able to make effective adjustments. For example, a worker who loses a job because of technological change may be qualified for another job with minimum retraining, but he may have no knowledge of the similarities between the different jobs in different industries. Improvements in job analyses are helping reduce this kind of labor-market imperfection.

Even during periods of high employment there will be some unemployment because of so-called frictions in the labor market. Basically, frictional unemployment arises because some workers are not at the right place, at the right time, for the right job.

For example, a metal firm in the state of Washington may need machinists who happen to be available elsewhere, but many of the unemployed machinists may not want to move to the West Coast. They may have deep roots in homes and social ties, and have children in school. At other times they may not know of the new job opportunity.

Frictional unemployment is an inevitable by-product of our economic system, because we permit a high degree of personal freedom in the decision-making process. There is a constant stream of new job seekers who have little knowledge about the labor market and who may thus not make their presence felt at the places where job openings exist.

Frictional unemployment is also related to the speed with which the economy adjusts to seasonal, cyclical, secular, structural, and technological changes. This type of unemployment will be present regardless of the size of the labor force, the demand for workers, and the numbers of people employed. Even during World War II, unemployment was greater than 1 per cent of the labor force.[1]

A great deal of frictional unemployment balances itself out in the overall labor market. From 1 to 2 million workers may quit their jobs voluntarily during a given month, but most of these will find new jobs. In fact, they may have a new job at the time they quit their old one.

Frictional unemployment tends to represent an irreducible amount of unemployment—and as such, it involves the idea of a labor reserve, which is a phenomenon of the competitive nature of our economy. The labor reserve is estimated at between .75 and 1.5 million workers. But these workers are not always unemployed, so they do not really constitute an equivalent amount of unemployment. Part of this reserve could be eliminated by increasing the overall mobility of workers. This might involve a re-evaluation of union policies as well as fringe-benefit plans, that are customarily tied to employment in a given firm. Perhaps the most effective way to reduce the labor reserve, as well as frictional unemployment, is by a better organization of the labor market. This

---

[1] *Economic Report of the President,* U.S. Department of Commerce, 1966, p. 232.

involves more effective worker counseling, improved worker education, more efficient employment services, activities designed to increase the mobility of labor, more vocational training and retraining, and a wider dissemination of labor market information.

Structural Unemployment

Changes in consumer demand have far-reaching effects on employment because they affect the demand for workers and the total volume of unemployment. Workers in industries that experience declining demand may lose their jobs. Obvious examples are the horse and buggy, vaudeville, and high-button shoes. When such changes are gradual, employers may adjust in a manner that minimizes unemployment. Also, the rising demands of new industries may cushion the unemployment in declining industries. Such changes are described as structural, and they cover a considerable amount of unemployment not explained by other causes. Frictional unemployment implies a maladjustment between a worker and the demand for his skills, while structural unemployment is a mass phenomenon involving groups of workers, industries, geographic regions, or even the total economy.

Structural causes of unemployment are associated with over-all demand, labor supply, shifting demand, international trade, the location of industry, and other dynamic conditions of an economic system. Structural changes may have differing effects on geographic regions, even though the national effect balances out. For example, when the textile industry shifted from New England to the South, a great deal of structural unemployment occurred in New England. But the South gained in employment, so that the national figures were not seriously affected.

Structural unemployment includes much of the "hard-core" unemployed—those who remain out of work for long periods despite improved economic conditions and labor shortages. These people usually have the wrong skills, live in the wrong area, or are attached to declining industries.

Changes in the labor force may contribute to structural unemployment. The labor force at a given time contains varying percentages of older workers, women, younger workers, unskilled laborers, or nonwhites. Thus the amount of unemployment will vary with the demand for these particular workers. A change in the composition of the labor force, even without a change in labor demand, could bring on structural unemployment.

Structural unemployment depends, too, on the growth rates of the economy. When economic growth is rapid, there are forces offsetting structural unemployment. New industries absorb workers who lose their jobs in declining industries. On the other hand, slow growth rates lead to increases in structural unemployment.

When a given person is unemployed, it is difficult to know whether the cause is structural, frictional, seasonal, or cyclical. A structural change may account for the initial loss of his job, but frictional factors may cause its continuance. And adverse business conditions may aggravate the problem.

Technological Unemployment

Labor-saving devices or processes give rise to a special type of structural unemployment called "technological unemployment." Economists have debated whether there really is technological unemployment, or whether the loss of jobs is due to lack of labor mobility rather than to new capital equipment. But the distinction is unimportant to the worker who is displaced by a better production method. What concerns him is that he has lost his job. Public policy, however, dictates that we know the real cause because policy will differ with the cause of unemployment.

Most technological advancements are labor-saving, but it is possible for an improvement to be capital-saving. This is particularly true when a new product takes the place of an old one. Output per man-hour is usually raised because of savings of both labor and capital. Labor-saving improvements may cause unemployment for workers immediately affected by inventions, innovations, and research and development. However, most economists believe there is a net gain in employment in the longer run. Otherwise our unemployment rate would be far greater than it is today, since technological advances in the recent past have been tremendous.

Generally, better production processes will permit a firm to reduce its prices, leading to an increase in the demand for that product. This will require more production, which means that some of the displaced workers may be rehired. Other workers will be employed in manufacturing the new equipment. Still others will find employment in operating or maintaining the new machinery. If there is no drop in the price of the product, the improved profitability of the firm may encourage it to expand production and to add more workers.

Obviously, the welfare of a nation depends upon technological progress. For example, England experienced the sad results of the underdevelopment of its coal mines during the 1920's. Labor was fearful of capital improvements, and management was satisfied to keep capital costs low. As a result, the British coal industry became a high-cost operation, and after World War II, it was cheaper to import coal than to mine it domestically. In the long run, both labor and management lost out.

Inadequate Effective Demand

A basic factor behind structural unemployment is the inadequacy of effective demand. Unemployment may persist at an unsatisfactory rate despite a high GNP. This problem was considered by the Council of Economic Advisers, in 1961. The Council was concerned about slack in the economy, which to them represented a gap between what the economy was capable of producing and what it actually did produce. The GNP was about $560 billion in 1962,[2] while full employment would have required a GNP of between $600 and $610 billion.

The rate of growth is increased when all buying sectors increase their effective demand. This includes businessmen, the government, and the consumers who really do about two-thirds of all the spending. In the long run, increases in the economic growth will take care of much of the unemployment problem because an increase in effective demand will increase employment enough to offset the drop-off of jobs in declining sectors. But when the growth rate stabilizes or declines, the economy no longer provides sufficient new job opportunities.

Cyclical Unemployment

The most serious type of unemployment is that associated with unfavorable business conditions. For example, cyclical unemployment accounted for most of the unemployment of the 1930's, when unemployment exceeded 10 million persons a year for most of that period.[3]

After World War II, there were several periods of business decline, but there were no depressions or even serious recessions. The production index declined, yet the GNP continued to rise.

Cyclical forces are closely related to conditions of ineffective demand and growth rates. But it is possible to distinguish cyclical unemployment from inadequate demand, since cyclical unemployment tends to

---

[2] *Federal Reserve Bulletin,* November 1966, p. 1706.
[3] *Economic Report of the President, loc. cit.*

disappear with improved business conditions, while unemployment due to inadequate demand will continue even though the upswing is in full momentum.

FULL EMPLOYMENT AND UNEMPLOYMENT

There is a close relationship between GNP and the level of employment. In general, employment increases with the GNP, although the rates of advance may be dissimilar. In its broadest sense, full employment refers to the employment of all factors of production—land and capital as well as labor. About 40 per cent of our population is in the labor force, so anything less than full employment is serious. Each unemployed worker affects two to three people who are dependent on him for family income.

There is no unanimity of opinion as to what constitutes full employment. Nobody argues that every member of the labor force must be employed to achieve full employment. But there is argument over how much unemployment is acceptable. Some economists argue that an unemployment rate as high as 5 per cent is acceptable at times, while others prefer 3 per cent or less. Actually, a 2-point difference means about 1.5 million workers. When this figure is multiplied by 2½, the number of individuals indirectly affected is approximately 4 million. Once an acceptable level of unemployment is agreed upon, public policy tries to achieve this level by increasing the volume of national spending.

There are three main groups of buyers—private consumers, private industry, and governments. If spending by consumers and producers is not sufficient to maintain full employment, then governmental spending is used to achieve full employment. Likewise, when there is more employment than the full employment level, governmental outlays should be reduced to lessen inflationary pressures. This action is called fiscal policy—and it involves broad changes in the volume of public spending and changes in tax rates to influence private spending.

Another approach looks at the problem through monetary aspects, and argues that the cost of money will discourage or encourage private business activity.

The Employment Act of 1946 declared that it was public policy to maximize employment, production, and purchasing power. Thus, a degree of employment may have to be sacrificed in the interest of price stability. The Act established the Council of Economic Advisers to study, analyze, and recommend national economic policies to the President.

FUTURE EMPLOYMENT

As we look to the future we can be sure of two things:

1. Our technology of production will become more complex as time goes on.
2. The rate of technological change will increase because of research and development, automation, and the need to adjust to changing markets at home and abroad.

These factors will force individuals to adapt, and they will require business firms to change their hiring policies as well as their ideas about the people they want on the pay roll.

We can sharpen our approach to employment problems by asking a few key questions:

1. What do these trends mean with regard to the employment of individuals?
2. Will employment opportunities rise or fall during the remaining years of the 1960's? The 1970's?
3. Which areas of our economy will most likely be affected by these trends?
4. Will the "service" areas or the "production" areas grow faster? Why?
5. What about the employment outlook in manufacturing in view of foreign competition?

Overall, we can conclude that the service areas will probably continue to expand, while mass production industries will not grow as fast with regard to employment. Moreover, the employment mix will change toward higher job requirements on the part of workers.

As we move toward a service economy, there will be a greater need for teachers, scientists, accountants, lawyers, dentists, doctors, and government workers. New specialties, like telemetry, oceanography, astronomy, recreational services, and so on, will be looking for all the talent they can get.

There will be less expansion of job opportunities in mass production industries, because minor skills will be replaced by new ways of doing things through computer-directed and electronically controlled production lines. *This change is fundamental, because an individual will be hired for his basic knowledge rather than for a particular skill that remains useful over his lifetime.*

The need for knowledge and flexibility will increase as product cycles get shorter and as research develops new and better ways of doing things. Old patterns of production will change, perhaps dramatically, and those with rigid skills will be seriously affected. There is no doubt that the emphasis will be on the quality of personnel rather than on quantity. The mass employment of unskilled or semiskilled labor is a thing of the past. In the future, the key ingredient will be broad-gauged talent. So, for his own security the average individual must acquire more flexibility and a willingness to improve and change as circumstances require. What does all this mean in the employment of those who become redundant because of all these changes?

The big problem will be the individual's qualifications. Complex mechanisms and the trend toward automation will place a premium on the person who has the knowledge and is flexible, from a training point of view. Static or conventional skills may not be as important as they have been in the past. Actually, the number of job opportunities will rise as technology changes. The trouble may be that those who are most affected by the change may be the ones who are least able to make the switch.

Today, we are faced with two pressing problems. First, we have to retrain or readapt *older workers* to the rapid changes taking place. Unfortunately, retraining is not as simple as some people seem to think. For example, if you intend to make a computer programmer out of a person who does not have the mathematical and theoretical background, you cannot employ him until he is properly qualified, regardless of how much you would like to see him on the new job. This kind of unemployment and retraining falls hardest and longest among people who do not have employable skills or capabilities, or who lack sufficient education. As a result, they find themselves unemployed later in life, when they are not readily hirable. These people tend to be the ones who do not have the right educational background for the new jobs. On top of that, many of them are reluctant to start doing something new after earning high wages and working for years in a given industry.

The second group we have to worry about is *the very young*—those who are just finishing high school or dropping out without graduating. During the 1960's there will be about 7 million young men and women who will lack an adequate education at the very time when our economy can least afford to hire them because of its increasingly complex technology.

We can still do something about this group because most of them are young enough to get the education and training they need. As a rule, they have no pressing family obligations. And, for many of them, their trouble is largely a case of motivation and guidance on the part of teachers and parents. Recent studies emphasize that, despite tight labor markets, we have a million youngsters wasting away their lives because they have not adequately prepared to earn a decent livelihood.

There are, however, many favorable aspects of the picture. According to present estimates, most sectors of the country will experience a growth in aggregate demand, although the rate of growth will vary from area to area. As a result, industry will make heavy capital investments to meet its future market requirements. This willingness of companies to invest in new and better equipment will insure more and better job opportunities and the economic growth of our nation.

All in all, we can look ahead to a future of growing opportunities, although one in which companies will compete for their survival and individuals will compete for their future on the basis of qualifications and demonstrated merit.

Discussion Questions

1. Why have unemployment problems persisted as the economy has grown in output and complexity?
2. Give a good definition of unemployment.
3. What is meant by the labor force?
4. Trace the major causes of unemployment.
5. How would you distinguish the voluntarily from the involuntarily unemployed?
6. What effect does education have on the level of unemployment?
7. Discuss this statement: "Advancing technology is a major cause of unemployment."
8. What is meant by the labor market?
9. How does custom affect the volume and types of unemployment?
10. Describe frictional unemployment.
11. What factors are included under structural unemployment?
12. What type of unemployment was most prevalent during the 1960's?
13. Is there such a thing as "technological" unemployment?
14. How does aggregate demand affect overall employment?
15. Why is cyclical unemployment serious? What causes it to exist?
16. What is meant by full employment? How is it measured?

17. How is economic progress related to employment?
18. How does movement toward a "service" economy affect the level and type of employment?
19. Discuss this statement: "Employment in private industry has been growing at too slow a pace for our population."
20. Describe why employment in the public sector has been rising sharply since 1962.

Circle the T or F (True or False) before each statement:

T F 1. Lack of education and unemployment are not as closely related as people think.

T F 2. Older workers can be easily retrained for the labor force.

T F 3. The most important thing to give an unemployed worker is continued income.

T F 4. Birth rates affect the volume of employment and the degree of unemployment.

T F 5. Worker attitudes have a substantial effect on their employability.

T F 6. Cultural and personal factors affect unemployment.

T F 7. Companies can do very little about seasonal unemployment.

T F 8. Technological unemployment affects different industries in about the same way.

T F 9. Skill and talent are the best safeguard against unemployment.

T F 10. There is no such thing as "hard core" unemployment.

ANSWERS

10. F	8. F	6. T	4. T	2. F
9. T	7. F	5. T	3. F	1. F

16

THE IMPACT OF AUTOMATION AND TECHNOLOGICAL CHANGE

Some people think of automation and technological change as threats to jobs, purchasing power, and future progress. Others see automation as mankind's greatest blessing. To them automation makes possible rapid improvements in man's well-being—like higher living standards, better medical services, increased leisure time, challenging work, and more and better education. As they see it, man can be freed for a better life only when machines are available to take over physical work.

Who is right? Will automation and advancing technology wipe out millions of job opportunities for young people entering the labor force? Or will it bring in an era of economic progress and provide millions of new and better jobs for years to come? This chapter discusses automation and technological change, and describes the basic factors behind our country's economic progress. The facts it presents may help to sort out these notions about the effects of automation.

THE ROOTS OF ECONOMIC PROGRESS

Today the United States enjoys the highest standard of living the world has ever known. In less than two hundred years we have risen from a desolate wilderness to become the most productive nation on earth, with the highest living standards known to Man. How has our economy grown from virtually nothing to this pre-eminent position in such a short span of history?

Some people believe we got to the top because of an abundance of natural resources. Perhaps, to some extent. But the Indians camped on these same resources for years without developing them. When oil bubbled out of the ground, they used it to paint their faces. England, on the other hand, has been described as a lump of coal surrounded by fish. Almost everything else had to be imported. Yet the Industrial Revolution started there and only later spread to the United States and Europe. If economic progress depended only upon rich natural resources, then Asia, Africa, and South America would be the leading industrial areas of the world. It appears, then, that natural resources alone do not insure economic progress.

Is favorable climate the answer? There is no doubt that the great civilizations of Egypt, Greece, and Rome had their start in areas where the climate was mild. But in modern times the areas of greatest economic growth—England, northern Europe, and northeastern United States—have not been blessed with good weather.

Perhaps Americans are more industrious, possess more knowledge, or have more brain power? This, however, is doubtful. Most of our ancestors came from other countries—and, when you trace the origin of physical, chemical, electronic, and atomic discoveries, you begin to realize that other areas of the world produce proportionately as many first-rate minds as we do. Moreover, where knowledge is concerned, there are few secrets today. The scientific journals go everywhere, so, for all practical purposes, all countries have access to the same information. Furthermore, people work harder and longer in the poorest countries. We have even reduced the work day, shortened the work week, extended vacations, and provided for earlier retirement. So hard work and long hours alone are not the mainsprings of economic progress.

None of these reasons really tells us why we in the United States work shorter hours with less physical effort and still produce more than any other country on earth. What accounts, then, for our economic abundance? Besides our competitive, private, free, incentive approach to economic organization, the American worker has better technology and more machinery, plant, and equipment—what we call capital goods—to work with than anyone else in the world. These, in turn, make our economy the most productive in the history of mankind. It will be helpful to examine briefly the history of industrial development.

When the steam engine was invented in the seventeenth century, it enabled man to convert the energy of coal into industrial power. The Industrial Revolution got under way as soon as this new source of power was applied to tools like the spinning machine. Interestingly enough, some people predicted that the new spinning machines would wipe out most of the 40,000 jobs in the textile industry. But from 1760 to 1835, employment rose from 40,000 to 135,000, because better and cheaper textiles led to new markets not possible by hand methods.

Some years later the electric generator began converting the energy of water into electricity that could be carried hundreds of miles by power lines to areas where power was needed.

Perhaps the most revolutionary development was the gasoline engine. This gave us portable power that could be carried into farm fields, over highways, and to any location, however remote. Portable power led to new industries which now employ millions of people and turn out the consumer products that are in great demand. Farm implements, automobiles, appliances, airplanes, even steel and other metals, owe their basic growth to this new source of portable power. Thus the development of more and better tools has done much to increase our productivity and to raise our living standards.

A few examples will illustrate the direct relationship. A coal miner working with hand tools can produce about 3 tons of coal a day; with mechanized equipment he produces 70 tons a day or more. By hand, a man can clean about a pound of cotton fiber a day; with equipment, his production rises to more than 1,000 pounds a day. With animal power and simple tools, a farmer takes about 58 hours to plant and harvest 20 bushels of wheat; with mechanical equipment he can plant and harvest more than 25 bushels of wheat in less than 2 hours.

In all of these ways capital equipment makes it possible for us to harness the power of nature and to put it to work through the tools of production.

Thus capital equipment makes possible the leisure time and the growing volume of consumer goods that have raised our standard of living and have created millions of new and better job opportunities.

AUTOMATION AND JOB OPPORTUNITIES

Despite these facts, we hear a great deal about automation and the so-called undesirable effects of technological change on job opportunities. Automation and advanced technology do mean change—and, for that reason, they are feared. But is this fear justified? Here are the opinions of outstanding individuals in different fields of endeavor.

Dr. Arthur F. Burns, President of the National Bureau of Economic Research, and formerly Chairman of President Eisenhower's Council of Economic Advisers, states:

Automation and technological progress are essential to the general welfare, the economic strength, and the defense of the nation.

Dr. Seymour L. Wolfbein, Special Assistant to the Secretary of Labor for Economic Affairs, has this to say:

Thousands of people whose jobs are replaced by machines . . . get better, upgraded jobs. . . . Automation has come in for an unnecessarily large amount of blame for unemployment. . . . Many jobs have been created by technological advancement.

Former Senator Paul Douglas, Democrat of Illinois, and at one time Professor of Economics at the University of Chicago, in an issue of the *American Federalist* stated:

Not only are new opportunities for employment built up to an equal degree . . . for every man laid off a new job is created somewhere. . . .

The fact is that we are creating more than *three* new jobs for every *two* being destroyed from all causes. We are actually adding about 1¼ million new jobs to the labor force each year. The need to provide even more jobs comes about because our population has increased and not because of harmful effects from technological change.

Moreover, automation is only one factor that affects employment. Scientific inventions, changes in production methods, new product development, just to mention a few, also have their effects.

Some of these changes save labor. Others require more of it. Most of

them create impacts which are felt in more than one area. For example, twenty years ago the occupation of computer programmer was unknown. Today, about 75,000 people are employed in this job classification and 200,000 more will be needed by 1975.

Office-clerical employment is also rising sharply. More than 600,000 new jobs are added annually in this field—and this is largely the result of new uses to which automatic data-processing equipment is being put by banks, insurance companies, and other businesses.

Another example is the light bulb. It is wrong to regard the electric light as simply replacing gas lights and candles. It replaced these all right, but it also replaced unlighted streets and did away with going to bed early. In addition, the electric light led to a whole generation of new electrical products, all of which have made modern life easier and more comfortable.

Likewise, the automobile did far more than replace the horse and buggy. It put an end to the need for staying at home, and is now in process of creating new cities and towns. While the buggy industry employed thousands, the automobile industry employs millions of people, directly and indirectly.

The point is . . . automation and advancing technology create many new jobs as well as destroying some old ones. The new jobs are more challenging, the pay is higher, and the working conditions are far better than ever before. We can point to many instances where employment in a company or industry increased following mechanization or automation.

For example, dial equipment was introduced in the telephone industry in the 1920s. Today, more than 96 per cent of all the phone calls in the United States are completed without the help of an operator, yet employment in the Bell System has increased from about 200,000 in 1920 to more than 750,000. At the same time, transcontinental telephone rates for a three-minute call have gone down from $16.50 to $1.00. Today's long-distance calls are made routinely, efficiently, and economically because of mechanical and electronic advances.

The oil industry started using continuous-flow refining methods around 1920, yet employment has more than doubled since that time.

Naturally we cannot say that these increases were all due to auto-

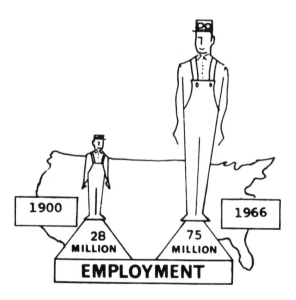

1900   1966

28 MILLION   75 MILLION

EMPLOYMENT

mation, because these particular industries were experiencing an expansion in their own right; but, on the other hand, we cannot say that automation wiped out employment within them. Far from it; employment showed a healthy growth.

We can further illustrate this point by nation-wide statistics. In 1900, the United States had about 28 million persons employed. Sixty-six years later we have 75 million employed, even though this period has witnessed the greatest amount of technological change. In other words we have created 47 million new jobs despite all the labor-saving changes made in American industry.

Foreign countries are certainly not concerned about unemployment due to automation. The European Common Market invests heavily in automation. Instead of automation unemployment, they have had an acute labor shortage. For its part, the Soviet Union added thousands of individuals to its Automation Institute to improve its economic impact at home and abroad.

The facts are these:

- Foreign countries are automating as fast as we are.
- Their low production costs are making them tough competitors in the world's markets.
- We must improve our productivity and lower our production costs, or we cannot compete effectively.

The real question is not whether to automate, but how to automate so that human problems are kept to a minimum while long-term benefits are realized for the nation as a whole.

We can get a better perspective on automation by stressing three key points:

- Automation and technological change are essential if we expect to combine more leisure time with higher living standards, adequate defense, and improved medical and other services. We must produce more with less effort, or we shall not be able to attain these goals

- The figures show that overall job opportunities have increased in the long run as automation and mechanical improvements have been made.

- Some employees and some industries are definitely affected in the short run, so there is a need for retraining people and switching production resources into areas of future growth.

Many of those displaced by automation are unskilled or semiskilled workers who do not meet the entrance requirements of the new jobs that automation makes possible. Naturally we should do all we can to make the transition easy and effective.

The undesirable effects of automation and technological change can be reduced by more and better training for new job opportunities, by increasing the mobility of the work force, and by income payments to those affected during periods of unemployment.

Finally, we should stress an obvious point which is sometimes overlooked. *We cannot have economic progress without change!* Where would we be as a nation if we had not developed from a simple farm

economy to a modern industrial nation? What would our standard of living be if we had stayed with the horse and buggy, the hand plow, the scrub board, the ice box, or the kerosene lamp?

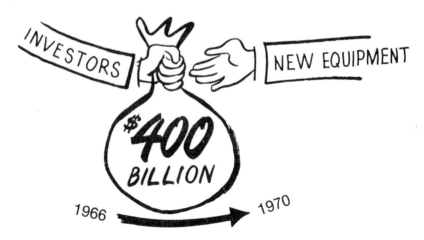

The secret of our country's phenomenal progress is technological change for the better—change that raises productivity, expands and improves products and services, and increases leisure time.

All of these depend on machines and tools that do jobs more quickly, more easily, and better—leaving men free to seek new frontiers of the mind and to dream dreams of a glorious future yet to come.

THE ROUNDUP

The disturbing notes often sounded about automation and technological change parallel the dismal theories that the early English economists developed when the factory system first came into existence. According to them, wages were determined by the supply of labor, which in turn was determined by population. And as they saw it, population could only be held down by starvation, disease, or war.

They maintained that workers were condemned to a bare existence— and nothing more. Higher wages would lead to increased population. A bigger population would create a larger labor supply. As a result, wages would again move back to the bare existence level.

It is clear that these dismal theories do not fit our American economy. Actually, about 70 per cent of our entire national income is paid out in wages and salaries and supplements. And the percentage rises considerably if we include independent farmers, small unincorporated businesses, and professional people who receive pay for their services.

Most people, therefore, have shared in our country's economic progress. We have made improvements in our standard of living, and we have largely realized what the Communists say they hope to accomplish—an economy of plenty in a classless society.

But knowing this is not enough, because we must go on from here. The future will be more competitive and more difficult than the past. To prepare for it we must:

- Continue and expand the improvements in productivity that automation and technological progress make possible.

- Provide basic incentives for people to take chances, to accept changes, and to make improvements.

- Insure an operating business climate that encourages risk-takers to invest larger sums in the machines and tools of private business firms.

Technology, incentives, and risk-taking can assure a future which will be far better than the past for consumers, workers, and stockholders.

Discussion Questions

1. Discuss this statement: "Automation and technological change are synonymous terms."

2. Discuss this statement: "Automation is mankind's greatest blessing."

3. Discuss this statement: "Automation makes it very difficult for the younger generation to advance."

4. How is automation related to economic progress?

5. Which is more important—automation or an abundance of natural resources?

6. How are competition and free enterprise related to a changing technology?

7. Give several examples of technological progress.

8. Discuss this statement: "The people who are replaced by machines get new jobs."

9. Cite several examples of workers unemployed because of changing technology.

10. What new jobs have been created by automation?

11. How is automation related to foreign competition?

12. How does automation contribute to leisure?

13. How do the short-run and long-run effects of automation differ?

14. How is capital investment in new equipment related to technology?

15. Is an increasing population a blessing or a hindrance? Discuss.

16. Discuss this statement: "An economy of plenty in a classless society is the goal of the United States."

17. Show how risk-taking is related to progress.

18. What are the major future tasks of the American economy?

19. How is productivity related to automation and to progress?

20. Relate productivity changes to our economic potential.

Circle the T or F (True or False) before each statement:

T   F   1. The nation suffers when its production facilities expand rapidly.

T   F   2. Expenditures for recreation adversely affect our economic potential.

T   F   3. Everyone shares in the benefits of technological progress.

T   F   4. Mass consumption is needed to purchase the output of our business firms.

T   F   5. Employees cannot greatly increase the per cent of the national income they receive, but the amount they receive can be enlarged by increasing productivity.

T   F   6. The conservation of natural resources is important to the improvement of our economic potential.

T   F   7. The worldwide increase in population has important economic implications.

T   F   8. The growth in the real income of workers is due to our natural resources.

T   F   9. As consumers, people are quite favorable to technological progress.

T   F   10. As producers, people are generally opposed to technological changes.

ANSWERS

10. T	8. F	6. T	4. T	2. F
9. T	7. T	5. T	3. T	1. F

17

A LOOK AT
ECONOMIC GROWTH

Macro-economics is the study of the overall economy, and in such a study you are tempted to ask: "How is the economy doing?" "Is it advancing or declining?" "Is it growing?"

Economic growth is a characteristic of most modern economies. But with economic growth, other phenomena appear, like increased population, expanded production, growing money supply, advancing levels of consumer demands, rising price levels, and instability in economic activity. As a result, many economists question whether we can have economic growth and full employment without inflationary price rises and increasing population.

There are problems, too, when you try to measure economic growth and predict future trends. You get different answers, depending upon when you begin and end your series of data. It is important that, when rates of growth are used for policy making, the measures you use should be consistent and reliable.

Public concern with economic growth is not new. The early mercantilists believed that an increase in the supply of gold was the main process by which a nation could become wealthy. Adam Smith sought the increase by specializing labor, while John Maynard Keynes believed that the government's participation would be a counter-cyclical and growth force.

In recent years, an important force influencing economic growth has been our increasing population explosion—and more specifically, our population mix, which has important implications for future needs and job opportunities.

It will be helpful to keep these theories in mind as we turn to a discussion of what economic growth is and how it may be achieved.

WHAT ECONOMIC GROWTH REALLY MEANS

Economists define "economic growth" as an increase in Gross National Product, when measured in constant dollars. For this reason, the measure of economic growth is expressed in terms of physical output, as measured by the "Real Gross National Product." It is measured in constant dollars to remove the effects caused by changes in prices.

In 1966, the GNP was about $740 billion, measured in 1966 prices. But if the 1966 GNP were stated in 1958 dollars, it would drop to $648 billion on a real basis.

When we discuss economic growth, we are talking about expanding the production of all marketable goods and services—that is, the goods and services that people buy, including changes in inventories. The term "production" includes marketing and all the other processes required to provide goods and services where and when they may be desired.

Another point to remember is the difference between potential and actual production. When talking about economic growth, some people think of the country's potential production—its overall capacity to produce goods and services. But economists prefer to discuss economic growth in terms of actual production. In the long run, of course, the GNP is governed by both factors. But in the short run it is better to use actual production figures rather than potential capacity.

A third point to keep in mind is that economic growth is not the same as economic progress or economic welfare. For example, economic growth does not take into account greater leisure time, changes in income, or the uses to which the larger national product is put.

There is a fourth point about economic growth—and that's the question of size. Very small percentage changes in national output, year after year, add up to very large increases over a period of fifteen or twenty years. This is important to remember, since many people have the impression that an increase in the rate of growth of, say, from 3 to 4 per cent a year is a relatively small change. Actually, this is a very large change, and it requires substantial increases in production resources.

As a simple example, a 4 per cent rate of growth is just one percentage point more than a 3 per cent rate—but in reality, it is 33⅓ per cent larger. A growth rate of 33⅓ per cent larger requires a "one-third" increase in production resources over and above a 3 per cent rate. This could mean four new workers instead of three, four new machines instead of three, one-third more education and training, or a combination of all of these.

There is a further complication regarding growth rates: our population, which is expected to increase from 199 million to about 250 million by 1980. This is an average rate of increase of about 1.7 per cent a year.

A more significant measure of the economic progress of a nation is its per capita growth in GNP. We obtain these data by dividing the total GNP by the total population. Measured in this way, increases in population tend to offset increases in GNP. Thus, a 3 per cent real growth rate in GNP and a 1.7 per cent increase in population turns out to be a 1.3 per cent real growth rate as measured by "per capita national product." On the other hand, a 4 per cent growth rate would mean a 2.3 per cent real growth rate per capita. Since 2.3 is 80 per cent higher than 1.3, a 4 per cent rate would require us to increase per capita national product at a rate 80 per cent greater than would be necessary at the 3 per cent rate.

As you can see, then, very small percentage changes mean big differences in the production resources needed to obtain the additional growth. So, when people say that our growth rate should be increased from 3 to 4 or 5 per cent, as though this is minor, remember that one or two percentage points are really big changes.

Now, much of our concern is with the wide variation in growth rates among the nations of the world. In some countries the growth rate is estimated at 6, 8, or even 10 per cent a year. Naturally, this distresses some people because the United States is growing at a long-term rate of less than 3 per cent a year. Usually, however, the countries with the highest growth rates are the most underdeveloped in their present state of industrial and agricultural technology. As a result, improvements in their methods of production, advances in technical knowledge, or increases in their capital invested per worker automatically add larger percentages to their worker productivity. The United States has a substantial technological and capital structure, so that marginal additions to capital stock or knowledge are not reflected in larger output to the same extent.

In any event, keep these points in mind:

- Economic growth is an increase in Gross National Product, measured in constant dollars and best expressed in per capita terms.

- Economic growth measures actual production rather than productive capacity.

' Small percentage increases in the growth rate have large effects over the years.

• Growth is far more difficult for mature economies because they have an established technology and capital base.

WHY WE NEED ECONOMIC GROWTH

Now let's consider the reasons why we need economic growth. Let's approach this inquiry by seeing how many reasons we can come up with to explain the critical need for economic growth. Here are several important reasons that stand out:

1. Economic growth is required if we're going to pay for the ultra-modern, complex, and expensive national defense which is essential to our survival.

2. Adequate growth is needed to raise our overall standard of living, to provide the schools, roads, hospitals, churches, and public services required by our growing population.

3. Economic growth is essential if we are going to provide job opportunities for our expanding labor force.

4. We also need economic growth because the nonproductive segments of our population are increasing year after year.

This means that our employed workers will have to be more productive to care for the young, the disabled, the sick, the retired, and those in government and defense work—all those who do not make direct contributions to consumer goods or services.

Today, we have about 80 million people in the labor force out of a population of 199 million people. In other words, almost 120 million people are not in the labor force, yet their goods and services must be provided by those who are. A closer look at the population estimates of the future emphasizes why growth is essential.

Population Increase
(*In millions*)

	1966	1980
Total population	199	250
Labor force	80	101
School population	43	66
Households	58	76
Persons 65 and older	19	23

Our population is rising rapidly even though the rate of increase has slowed some since 1964. The low estimate is that our population will grow to 228,000,000 by 1980—an increase of 31 million people, or 16 per cent more than we have today. The high estimate places our 1980 population at 250 million people. For 1985, the high and low projections are 275 million and 242 million respectively.[1]

The labor force will rise from about 80 million to approximately 101 million—a 26 per cent increase.

Our school population will go up from approximately 43 to 66 million—a rise of about one half.

The number of households will jump from 58 million to 76 million—a jump of over 30 per cent.

People 65 years of age and older will increase from about 19 to 23 million—or more than one fifth in fourteen short years.

Many people regard this population explosion as a guarantee of prosperity. All they see are more houses, bigger and better cars, color television sets, longer vacations, shorter workweeks, and more leisure time. But those who study population growth realize that jobs must come first if our economy is to enjoy the beneficial effects of increased purchases and expanding markets. Even during the record prosperity of the 1960's, we have had a difficult time finding jobs for the tremendous crop of young people pouring out of our schools. The jobs are often there, but many of those entering the labor force are not qualified to take them.

Naturally, our increased population means more marriages, and so there will be a large number of new houses being built. These, in turn, will generate problems of zoning, sewage, roads, traffic, and public transportation. The unusually large proportion of young and old people will require schools, recreational facilities, and special medical installations. This will require that a great deal of money be spent on the "non-producing ends" of the population curve. Other problems also may increase in intensity. The most serious are international crises and limited wars that force us to produce conventional weapons and to develop complicated and expensive armaments—guided missiles, atomic submarines, satellites, space stations, and all the rest.

As a result of this increased load at all levels of government, public spending will be much greater than it is today. The Federal government alone will spend well over a *trillion and a quarter* dollars—$1,250 billion—during the next ten years. And when you include the increased spending by our state and local governments, all levels of government may spend as much as $2.5 trillion. This is an average of $250 billion a

---

[1] *Economic Report of the President* 1967, p. 235.

year—which, by the way, is more than two and one-half times the entire national income for the year 1940.

Even if we try to control spending, we will need a much larger GNP to carry the heavy load. In other words, if we can produce more goods and services, the "nonproductive" load of government may become a static or smaller proportion of our total production. For example, if the GNP is $700 billion and governmental expenditures are $150 billion, the percentage for the public sector is 21.4. But, if the GNP is increased to $1 trillion and governmental outlays advance to $200 billion, the percentage for the public sector declines to 20 per cent even though there has been an increase of a third in aggregate expenditures.

For all of these reasons our Gross National Product will have to increase well in excess of $900 billion by 1970. If it does not, the tax load will increase sharply, or we will have to cut many services that may be regarded as essential.

HOW DO WE ACHIEVE ECONOMIC GROWTH?

The question, of course, is "How Do We Get Economic Growth?"

The answers are not simple, and there is considerable disagreement among economists as to the importance and priority of suggested answers. They do agree, however, that the following factors have a decided influence on the direction and pace of a country's economic growth:

1. The number of people working and the number of hours they work.

2. The quality of the labor force—its level of education and the multiplicity and quality of its skills.

3. The increase in the amount and quality of capital equipment over the years.

4. Advances in general, scientific, and technical knowledge—which, in turn, lead to greater efficiency and better ways of doing things.

5. Research and development, public and private.

6. Economies of operation brought about by increases in company size or in the scale of company operations.

7. The business climate—taxes, regulations and controls, collective bargaining, and so forth.

8. The profitability of business and its effects on investment and innovation.

Economic growth depends on this variety of complicated factors, and, since it is not easy to make quick changes in these factors, high rates of economic growth cannot be generated in a hurry.

To increase capital equipment, we would have to change the spending-savings patterns of millions of people.

To increase general and scientific knowledge would require a continuing program of education for the entire population.

To change the quality of the labor force implies broad technical training and development programs.

To improve the business climate means dealing with sociological, political, and economic factors that are not easy to influence and which are not often regarded as part of a firm's business.

So, although it is easy to agree on the need for economic growth, it is hard to agree on how this growth can be best achieved. We can make one observation, however. If we want to achieve economic growth within the framework of our free enterprise system, we must find ways of stimulating personal and corporate incentives.

Perhaps the most pressing requirements for economic growth is the maintenance of the profitable operating rate of business firms—one of our economy's key incentives.

A LOOK AT THE FUTURE

Let us assume that our rates of economic growth in the next ten years will not differ materially from those of the past. Perhaps the main factor in this trend will be our population, which will continue to increase at a rate of between 2½ to 3 million a year. This increasing population will create demand pressures for consumer goods and services—in food, education, medical services, housing, clothing, and so on. Here, then, is a built-in force that must be considered.

Demand pressures also continue because of governmental outlays, particularly Federal government expenditures for defense. It is not likely that the world's economic and political picture will suddenly improve, and so the demand pressure from defense spending no doubt will continue. At the present time, the largest part of the Federal government's outlays are for wars, their aftermath, or their probabilities. And as long as some $60 billion or more is spent for national defense, there will be a continued demand pressure on prices and on long-term interest rates as well.

All indications, therefore, point to a substantial increase in the GNP, probably to a level of as much as $900 billion by 1970. All components of the GNP have shared in its past growth, which has been about 50 per cent in each ten-year period, in constant dollars. Thus, consumer disposable income has more than doubled since 1939, and should continue to advance. Here, then, is another force picking up momentum as growth continues.

The gains from economic growth have manifested themselves in many ways—in more work being performed per hour, fewer hours of work exerted by each worker, greater productivity of resources, and more leisure time.

Finally, as we have said, to continue to achieve economic growth within the framework of our free enterprise system, we must improve incentives, particularly the profit incentive. For if we improve profit incentives, more money will be invested in private industry and this investment will assure our economic growth and growing job opportunities.

Technological change will demand an improvement in the individual's basic knowledge and flexibility, so the individual's ability will be the basic ingredient in his success.

Personal incentives will be particularly important with older workers who may find themselves unemployed, and with younger workers who may not be employed at all because of lack of knowledge or skill.

Increased investments and improvements in personal qualifications imply the freedom on the part of companies and individuals to profit on the one hand and to improve on the other. They also imply freedom in hiring and in moving people along within an organization.

Discussion Questions

1. Is the American economy advancing or declining at the present time? On what factors do you base your conclusion?
2. Discuss this statement: "Economic growth is a characteristic of most economies."
3. What are the criteria of economic growth?
4. How does the selection of base years affect the calculation of economic growth rates?
5. What is the difference between current and constant dollars?
6. What is the difference between potential and actual production?
7. Is economic growth the same as economic progress? Discuss.

8. Explain this statement: "Small increases in the rate of economic growth have important, long-term implications."

9. Describe the nature and significance of per capita economic growth.

10. Why do the underdeveloped countries generally have the highest growth rates?

11. Discuss this statement: "Growth can best be measured by a nation's productive capacity."

12. Why is economic growth essential to the United States?

13. Give the highlights of our population mix.

14. How does a changing age structure affect economic growth?

15. How do the Federal government outlays affect economic growth?

16. What are the major contributors to economic progress?

17. How do research and development contribute to economic progress?

18. Describe the future potentials for economic progress as you see them.

19. How do the incentives of a free enterprise system contribute to economic progress?

20. Describe the interrelationships of profits and economic growth in the private sector.

Circle the T or F (True or False) before each statement:

T   F   1. The developing countries have a faster rate of growth than the United States.

T   F   2. The United States leads the world in economic growth on an absolute basis.

T   F   3. Population changes affect economic needs and the rate of economic growth.

T   F   4. The growth in population has not really increased the need for public services and facilities.

T   F   5. The free market system has really retarded economic progress.

T   F   6. Services are not as important as goods where economic growth is concerned.

T   F   7. Fiscal and monetary policy contribute little to economic growth.

T   F   8. The capital invested per person in the labor force is a key factor in economic progress.

T F 9. Economic progress is better measured by increases in the real net national product per person.

T F 10. Economic growth rises regularly year after year.

ANSWERS

10. F	8. T	6. F	4. F	2. T
9. T	7. F	5. F	3. T	1. T

18

THE PROBLEM OF
INFLATION

There are different types of inflation, but the most dangerous is hyper-inflation of the monetary system. This situation may be defined as one in which the government issues paper money without restraint and the economy loses confidence in the monetary system. Ultimately, the money so issued loses value, as was the case with Germany after World War I, when a bushel of money would not buy even a pound of meat.

Over the years, our American economy has witnessed a gradual rise in prices, while personal income has risen more rapidly. Real income has improved for most persons, but others on fixed incomes have suffered during this persistent inflationary trend. In recent years inflation has become a national problem of growing proportions. The American economy boomed to record heights, stimulated by increased military spending, higher consumer incomes, and record capital outlays by business. The result has been a tightening in many markets—particularly labor, raw materials, and money.

An Opinion Research Corporation survey found that more than 80 per cent of the people were convinced that we were in an inflationary period. Yet only about 40 per cent of them were greatly concerned about inflation, and a slightly smaller number were somewhat concerned.

THE CONSUMER PRICE INDEX

If someone suggested that you take half of your money and start a bonfire you would consider him a little more than crazy. Yet, since 1940, the dollar has lost about 60 per cent of its buying power because of steadily rising prices.

How has this steady decline in the value of the dollar affected you?

The economy as a whole? What is inflation? What causes it? What can we do to keep it from getting out of hand in the future? These are the questions that we will explore in this chapter.

There is a feeling that inflation is not bad provided that a person's income keeps up with increases in his cost of living. Unfortunately, this concept leaves out completely the effect of inflation on assets that do not change with increases in prices.

For example, consider the predicament of a person who makes $8,000 a year and has $8,000 in savings or in insurance of one kind or another. An increase of 3 per cent in the price level along with an increase of 3 per cent in his wage or salary level would have the following effects:

Item	Effect of price increase of 3%	Effect of wage or salary increase of 3%	Net effect
$8,000 Savings	−$240	—	−$240
8,000 Salary	−240	+ $240	0
	−$480	+ $240	−$240

Notice that the increase in net income has offset the price increase, but there has been a definite erosion of the man's *savings* dollars. There is no way of offsetting this penalty on assets unless wages rise faster than the cost of living, or unless assets grow at least as fast as the cost of living goes up.

Fundamentally, then, inflation hurts everyone who works and saves, but it hurts most those who are on fixed incomes—and specifically those whose income is derived from a fixed amount of assets saved in the past.

The value of money is determined by the goods and services it can buy at any given time. If prices are low, our money is more valuable

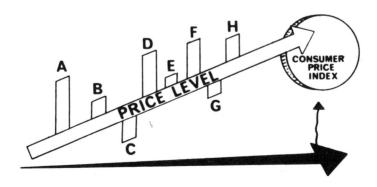

because it will buy a great deal. On the other hand, when we have inflation, the value of money is going down because the overall price level of the goods and services we buy is going up.

When we say prices are going up, we mean that *average* prices are increasing. It is possible for prices of some items to rise while others

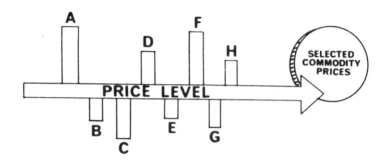

fall, and yet the overall level of prices remains about the same. This is not inflation; inflation takes place when the *overall* level of prices is going up.

The Bureau of Labor Statistics of the U. S Department of Labor measures the amount of inflation by means of Consumer Price Index. Many people call it the "Cost-of-Living Index." The index is based on the average price of a market basket of more than 300 goods and services that the typical consumer buys. This index has been adjusted from time to time to take into account the impact of services like medical, funeral, recreational, and educational expenses.

When an index is used, a base year is selected so that all prices can be compared to a given point in time. Today the 1957–1959 period is used as the base, and the Consumer Price Index at the beginning of 1967 was 115. This means that, using the average of 1957 to 1959 as a base of 100, prices have gone up about 15 per cent since that time, and it now takes about $1.15 to buy what $1.00 would have bought during the base period.

All indexes pose problems, and for that reason, they are "weighted." For example, if we construct an index of food prices, we must take into account the fact that people buy more bread than parsnips. Thus a change in the price of bread is more important than a similar change in the price of parsnips. We must find out how much more bread we buy than parsnips, and then "weight" the index accordingly.

Using the Consumer Price Index shown on the next page, you can trace what has happened to prices since 1915.

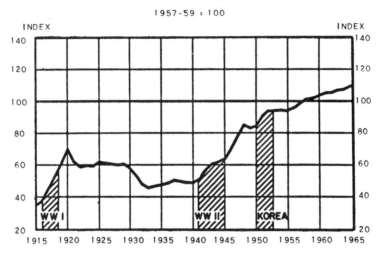

CONSUMER PRICE INDEX

1957-59 : 100

As you can see, prices rose sharply at the beginning of World War II, at which time the government enacted price controls. From 1946 through 1948, prices rose sharply again, and then fell during the recession of 1949. They started another sharp climb, and then in 1952 they began a slow, steady rise. Today they are climbing again.

INFLATION AND PERSONAL PROBLEMS

If the prices of all goods and services moved up and down by the same amount and if our incomes moved in the same way, our power to purchase from income would not change, although savings would be affected. But prices and incomes do not behave in this neat fashion.

For example, the price of medical care has risen by about one-third in the last ten years, while the price of wearing apparel has gone up much less. A family which dresses as nicely as possible and devotes a high portion of its income to apparel would find that prices have risen a little more than a tenth. On the other hand, a family that keeps up a lovely home would find that the cost of overall household operations has gone up about 15 per cent in the same period. If the two families had started out even ten years ago, and had received the same incomes, the family that spent its money on clothing would find itself relatively better off. Clothing money goes further than money spent for services.

Location is also important. If one family lived in Boston and another in Atlanta, they would have been affected quite differently. In 1955, prices in Boston were about 2 per cent lower than in Atlanta. By 1966, however, they were about 5 per cent higher.

So, price changes affect people differently, depending upon *what* and *how much* they buy and *where* they live.

Higher prices also create a serious problem for those who live on fixed incomes. Some of us can look forward to rising incomes as we increase our skills and move to better and higher-paying jobs. However, others are on relatively fixed incomes that do not change. Most of us will be on such incomes when we retire, or if we become widowed or are permanently disabled. People living on pensions, on insurance payments, or on income from savings do not see their incomes change very much over the years. When prices rise, these people lose purchasing power and find it harder to make ends meet.

Thus inflation tends to redistribute a country's wealth. Those with incomes rising faster than prices become relatively wealthier than those whose incomes rise more slowly or not at all. The effect on personal savings and future obligations is even worse.

Consider your own situation. You may be planning the future welfare of your family. That is why you set money aside for your children's education. That is why you buy life insurance to protect your family should something happen to you. Moreover, you depend upon a retirement plan to tide you over the golden years. You plan these things in terms of today's prices, but inflation makes it very hard for you to meet your future needs with any degree of accuracy. If inflation continues:

- A college education 15 years from now may cost 30 to 40 per cent more more than it does today.

- A $7,500 life insurance policy, which matures in 20 years, may buy only as much as $4,300 will today.

- A pension of $150 a month, 25 years from now, may provide only the same standard of living that $79 a month will buy today.

Few of us can afford this kind of reduction in the value of our assets.

THE SQUEEZE ON BUSINESS

Business firms face the same problems, but the businessman may have additional difficulties. Consumers can change their buying habits to help counteract price changes. If the prices of certain meats go up, people can eat other cuts of meat, fish, or poultry. But businessmen cannot easily change their buying habits.

If a company uses a substantial amount of machinery to turn out its products, it is acutely aware that the price of machinery has gone up about 20 per cent in the last ten years. Meanwhile, the price of crude rubber has dropped by about 6 per cent, but crude rubber cannot be substituted for machinery.

Management works hard to keep manufacturing costs as low as possible, but when the prices of production resources go up, the company is usually faced with higher costs of doing business.

- Wages and salaries tend to increase year after year.
- The cost of machinery and equipment keeps going up.
- The costs of supplies and essential services continue to spiral.

These rising costs must be met by increased productivity—that is, the company must turn out more units of output for each dollar of cost, or it must try to get the higher costs back by trying to raise the market prices of its products. The trouble is that it is not easy to cover increased costs. Higher prices are always resisted in competitive situations by the amount which customers are willing to pay. A price increase may simply mean that some customers will stop buying the company's products, and will turn to lower priced products offered by foreign competitors or by substitute suppliers in more favorable cost positions. As a result, many companies find themselves caught in the squeeze between rising costs and competitive prices.

Competitive pressures create another problem for the businessman. If he does not raise his prices, profits begin to disappear—yet it is profit that keeps him in business. If he does raise prices, sales may drop and the cost-price squeeze gets worse.

Most companies need high output to achieve low production costs. But high prices cause sales and output to fall, and then the average cost of output rises, adding to the cost-price squeeze.

These are some of the reasons why conventional producers in basic industries often have a hard time even during inflationary periods.

GOVERNMENT SERVICES AND INFLATION

Even the government runs into real problems because inflation plays havoc with the costs of public improvements, like schools, bridges, hospitals, defense, welfare, and all the rest.

Take a simple service like mailing a post card. The rates have gone up three times, from 1¢ to 4¢ in the last 18 years, a rise of 300 per cent. Meanwhile, during the same period, the mail delivery to private houses has been cut in half. Periodically, new increases are proposed to meet rising costs of delivering the mail.

The main point is that no one really gains from inflation. Everyone—individuals, business firms, and the government—must pay *more* and *more* and *more* for the goods and services they want.

GOV'T COMPANIES CONSUMER

WHAT CAUSES INFLATION?

We have talked about what inflation is and how it affects us. Now let us see what causes it.

Generally, there are two types of inflation. First, inflation may result when consumers increase their spending on consumer goods. Consumers' willingness to spend can increase faster than the productive capacity of our economy. Buyers then find themselves bidding against one another for the goods and services available, and prices go up. This is called "demand-pull" inflation. Second, inflation may occur when producers decide to expand their output because the future looks bright. They may bid up the prices of items they need to expand their plants or operations. Furthermore, workers see these expansional plans as an opportunity to demand higher wages. Raw materials, plants, and wages represent costs to a producer, so this kind of inflation is known as "cost-push."

Either type of inflation tends to breed more inflation. When prices are rising, labor unions fight for wage increases to keep their incomes rising faster than prices. Some of the large unions like to lead the parade of higher wages, and in doing so, they reinforce the inflationary process.

It is fruitless to argue whether cost or demand is the major factor in any given inflationary period. Cost-push and demand-pull forces can be seen in every inflation. However, both have one important element in common—money. Rising prices simply mean that the supply of money is getting larger in relation to the supply of goods. Basically, our supply of money—and money includes credit—is controlled by the banking system and the national government. When a banker decides to increase the amount of credit his bank is willing to give to its customers, he provides his customers with purchasing power—that is, money.

Earlier we learned how our banking system is more or less controlled by the Federal Reserve Banking System, which can limit the amount of credit the banking system can offer.

Our government also has a powerful influence over the supply of money in the economic system. If government spending is increased by government borrowing (deficit spending), the total supply of money in the country will be increased. Then, unless production keeps pace with increases in the money supply, prices will start to rise. On the other hand, we can have a leveling-off of the economy, or even a recession, if the supply of money is sharply curtailed.

A PRESCRIPTION FOR INFLATION

We can summarize the main points about inflation as follows:

- Inflation disrupts an economic system's stability and causes uncertainty and unexpected behavior.
- There is always the danger that creeping inflation will turn into hyper-inflation, that destroys all fixed values.
- Inflation results in a decline in the purchasing power of money, and less fortunate segments of our population are caused great suffering.
- Inflation causes an excessive transfer of income from current savings to spending for capital goods and other fixed assets—and this, in turn, diverts resources into these areas and raises their prices.
- Inflation introduces irresponsibility into the economic system, because thrift and conservative financial management are pushed into the background.

Fortunately, inflation is not like the weather. We can do something about it, but doing something is not easy.

Education is the first step! The nature of inflation and its causes must be understood. This means that people must be educated about the causes of inflation and its bad effects.

Action is the second step! Everyone must be willing to play his part.

- *Consumers* must exercise restraint—and resist the temptation to pay higher-than-reasonable prices or to buy more than they can realistically afford.
- *Labor* must be far-sighted in its demands, seeking its fair share of progress but always remembering that the increased costs of doing business must come out of productivity increases if inflation is to be avoided.

- *Government* at all levels must adjust its operations to live within its income. It must be willing to use its controls over credit to oppose inflation rather than to encourage it.
- *Companies,* wherever possible, must reduce costs, increase output, and try to keep their prices at a level where they can compete.

The more we learn about the effects and causes of inflation and then take action to control them, the better we can control the destructive inflation fire that is literally "burning up" our future purchasing power, day by day, week by week, and year by year.

Discussion Questions

1. Describe several different types of inflation.
2. Which is the most serious type—and why?
3. What does the Consumer Price Index really measure?
4. How is the Consumer Price Index constructed?
5. Who suffers from inflation?
6. What determines the real value of money? Document your answer.
7. Discuss the prevailing price level and the purchasing power of the dollar.
8. What is the value of today's dollar? Use any base year you prefer.
9. Describe how inflation aggravates personal financial problems.
10. Show how inflation affects the cost of government services.
11. How can inflation cause a squeeze on business profits?
12. Discuss this statement: "Businessmen prefer inflation."
13. What are the implications of continually rising wage levels?
14. Show how the government's fiscal and monetary policies are related to inflation.
15. How are consumers responsible for inflation?
16. Which, in your opinion, is more important in causing inflation: *rising costs* or *increasing demand?*
17. What can the government do about inflation?
18. How can each of these groups act to deter inflation?
    a. Consumers
    b. Labor
    c. Business

19. How does economic knowledge help to ease the personal effects of inflation?

20. What has caused our more recent inflationary trends in the United States?

Circle the T or F (True or False) before each statement:

T   F   1. Inflation at the rate of 3 per cent a year is a healthy thing for our economic system.

T   F   2. Most people are adversely affected by inflation.

T   F   3. Anti-inflationary measures would include a reduction in government expenditures.

T   F   4. Tax increases tend to reduce inflation.

T   F   5. Inflation is related to the monetization of the national debt.

T   F   6. The Consumer Price Index gives a good measure of how wholesale prices are changing.

T   F   7. An increase in government spending will cause a proportionate drop in private spending.

T   F   8. The best policy against inflation is to reduce government spending and keep the money supply from expanding.

T   F   9. Monetary measures become more crucial when fiscal measures are not prudent.

T   F   10. Inflation means that the value of money is falling because the general price level is rising.

ANSWERS

10. T	8. T	6. F	4. T	2. T
9. T	7. F	5. T	3. T	1. F

19

THE WEB OF TAXES

The government influences the level of national income through *monetary* and fiscal policies. Fiscal policy tries to affect the level of business activity by increasing or reducing the Federal government's expenditures and/or tax revenues. This chapter discusses the web of taxes and its effect on the economic system.

It has been said many times that the two certain events are death and taxes. Today, with miracle drugs and dramatic surgery, there is some question about the certainty of death—but about taxes, there is no doubt. Taxes have proliferated to the point where income, real property, personal property, sales inventories, and virtually all of our daily economic activities are taxable.

Public expenditures at all levels of government have continually increased, and no one is so naïve as to predict a downturn in the foreseeable future, bearing in mind our population, metropolitan problems, national defense, and all the rest. For these reasons, fiscal policies—public spending and tax policies—will continue to be crucial for years to come.

Fiscal policy—that is, trying to influence the country's economic activity by manipulating the Federal government's budget—is not new. During the 1930's, the idea of increasing government spending to offset the drop in private spending was quite popular. And, of course, it has been used ever since, and with increasing vigor.

The advocates of fiscal policy contend that the Federal government has two tools—*government expenditures* and *taxes*—to affect directly the level of economic activity. By increasing expenditures, it can pour purchasing power into the economy and thus stimulate aggregate demand. By reducing government spending, it can have the opposite effect. Likewise, by cutting taxes, economic activity can be stimulated because consumers and businessmen are left with more money to spend. Tax increases, on the other hand, have the opposite effect.

During the early 1960's, for example, unemployment affected more than 5 per cent of the labor force,[1] despite record levels in our Gross National Product. Economic advisers argued that increased government spending, and particularly tax cuts, were advisable to stimulate aggregate demand. In 1964, personal and corporate income taxes were cut while federal expenditures were maintained. The resulting stimulus to economic activity is history. In fact, many argue that 1964 was the wrong time to insert this stimulus—that the economy was at prosperous levels and that the "furnace was being overheated." By 1966, the Administration had expressed a new concern, that there might be too much expansion and that inflation was a threat.

Then, in early 1967, they became concerned again about the possibility of recession and decided to reinstate the investment tax credit which had been removed.

Should this type of counter-cyclical approach be used in this manner? How far can we go in this direction? These are questions with no easy answers, but they must be answered by each person in the economy.

THE INDIVIDUAL AND THE STATE

The American way of life rests largely on a competitive market system that operates through free and private enterprise. Ours is an economy of incentives, built around the basic ideal that an individual's progress should be determined by his ability, initiative, and effort. Historically, the United States has tried to protect the individual by limiting government activity to essential services and to areas of demonstrated public need.

Taxes affect these fundamental features because they determine how much income we can keep, how much property we can accumulate, and what we can pass on to our heirs. The problem is not merely one of money, for taxes really indicate the degree to which government initiative is growing and individual or corporate discretion is declining. Taxes are really a dollar measure of how individuals, farms, and business firms are caught in a web of government regulations and claims on income and property.

Some things must be done publicly—like national defense, public education, police and fire protection, streets and highways, postal service, and aid to the destitute. On the other hand, difficulties arise when less essential government services are demanded, leading to higher taxes, greater government debt, and inflation. As government activity

---

[1] *Federal Reserve Bulletin,* November 1966, p. 1702.

increases, private affairs become public affairs, personal freedom gives way to control, and regulations and subsidies invade our competitive market system.

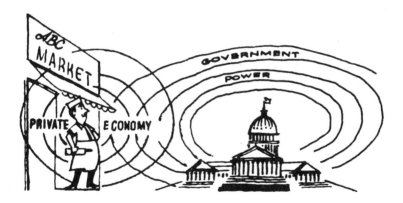

We must decide, then, whether government activity, spending, and taxes have reached the point where economic freedom, economic growth, and ability to compete are adversely affected. This, in turn, depends on our answers to two basic questions. First, what do we want government to do? And second, who will pay the bill?

WHAT DO WE WANT GOVERNMENT TO DO?

In our society people are expected to make their own economic decisions, and we rely on competition and incentives to direct their efforts toward useful and productive goals. Under these circumstances, government has two important functions:

1. It provides essential public services that cannot be provided by private agencies or business firms.
2. It sets the broad operating rules for our economy, and sees to it that everyone competes fairly and respects the rights of others.

During the past 30 years government power and spending have increased far beyond these functions. This rapid growth is reflected in the trend of taxes. In 1929, for example, all taxes—local, state, and federal—came to about 9 per cent of the national output. By 1966, they had risen to well over 25 per cent. The sharp rise in the cost of government has contributed to inflation as well as to a loss of economic freedom. Big government means big spending. Increased spending leads to deficit financing, which is a root cause of inflation.

During the thirties we were concerned when banks failed and depositors lost their savings. Yet the loss in purchasing power of life insurance policies, savings deposits, and government bonds since 1940 is estimated to be about seventy-five times greater than the entire loss suffered by all bank depositors from 1921 to 1933.

Government spending, taxes, and debt are at record levels. In 1966 we paid approximately $143 billion in taxes to the Federal government. State and local governments collected an additional $70 billion. The Federal collections consisted of:

Personal taxes	$ 61.9 billion
Corporate profits taxes	31.5
Individual business taxes	16.0
Contributions for social insurance	33.0
	$142.4 billion

This is more than the entire national income for any year up to and including 1941.

Despite this record spending, however, all levels of government plan to *spend more money, increase taxes,* and *raise the public debt.* The

Federal debt is now approximately $335 billion—more than $1,615 for every man, woman, and child in the country—or about $5,650 a family. The debt ceiling was raised to $336 billion early in 1967. And, when the present Federal debt is added to that of our local and state governments, we come up with the staggering sum of approximately $440 billion in public debt.

We also run into a very real dilemma. On the one hand, our public needs are mushrooming because of a rapidly growing population and sharply increased expenditures for national defense. On the other hand, individuals, special interest groups, and local and state governments are still looking to the Federal government for more subsidies, welfare benefits, and grants-in-aid.

We must begin to realize that the theoretical needs for government money are unlimited, but our resources are not. We can always find supporters or good reasons for more schools, roads, hospitals, welfare benefits, subsidies, and all the rest. Sensible budgeting, however, requires that we "weigh, judge, and select." Population growth will force us to do a lot more budgeting in the future, for, as we said earlier, by 1980:

1. More families will generate more housing, zoning, sewage, traffic, and transportation problems.
2. There will be a sharp increase in juvenile delinquency, murders, robberies, and other crimes.
3. The large number of young people will create the need for more schools, teachers, and recreational facilities.

In addition to these problems, we may be faced with a step-up in the Cold War. This may make it necessary for us to speed the development and production of complex and expensive devices and weapons—like guided missiles, atomic submarines, satellites, and space stations. No one can foretell how much these will cost, but we can estimate that the amount will be staggering. Even so, we cannot afford anything less than the very best in defense.

All in all, the Federal government may spend *$1¼ trillion,* $1,250 billion or $1,250,000,000,000 during the next 10 years. On top of that, local and state governments will increase their spending because of growing needs and problems. Thus, it is quite possible that $2½ trillion will be spent by all levels of government. This represents about $12,000 for every man, woman, and child in the United States.

If this money is not raised from taxes, government debt will be increased, which in turn will bring on inflation. But inflation is really a tax since it raises the price of everything we buy and reduces the real value of savings, insurance, and pensions.

The problem, therefore, is how to meet our growing public needs and still provide the services, benefits and subsidies that individuals and groups are demanding from their local, state, and Federal government. Unfortunately, some people believe that government benefits and subsidies are free and that they do not affect our freedom of choice. These people try to correct all the ills of society by simply having the government do more things and spend more money. But if we want "responsible" government that leaves us free, we must shoulder the major share of our individual responsibilities.

There are four yardsticks we can use to help us decide whether a function should be performed by government:

1. *Is the function one that we can and should perform ourselves? That is, will it affect initiative and self-reliance?*

The government can easily erode self-reliance by giving the impression that it will help those who are not self-reliant. Each year, about 50 million people receive government checks for one reason or another. And at every session, Congress is faced with proposals to increase benefits to one group or another.

2. *Is the function one that private enterprise or existing social agencies can perform? Will it reduce competition within our economic system?*

The Hoover Commission found 2,500 commercial-type facilities in the Department of Defense, employing over 600,000 persons and representing a capital investment of about $15 billion. Many of these activities—like the serving of food in commissaries—can be as effectively performed by private enterprise.

3. *Will the functions safeguard personal freedom, or will they encourage the use of local or state authority?*

4. *Do we know the real cost of the government function after the program is fully grown? Can it be carried out on the basis of sound fiscal policies?*

All four of these questions point to one conclusion. If we want to meet the critical needs of the future and keep taxes or inflation from getting out of hand, we must decide what we want government to do. If we can reduce the scope of government and cut out waste, extra taxes may not be needed because nonessential activities will not be undertaken. On the other hand, free men and free institutions are threatened when the government is regarded as the main provider of men's needs.

Our real challenge is to guard the individual against hazards over which he has no control, and to do so within the framework of our competitive economy. After all, our economic system has produced an avalanche of goods and services while making use of automatic regulators in the market place.

So much for the role of government. Now, let us see how much we have been spending and who will pay the bill.

WHO WILL PAY THE BILL?

The Federal government's budget for fiscal year, 1967–1968, is estimated at $135 billion, which is about $8 billion more than will be collected in taxes. The budget shown below is an estimate of expenditures for the 1967–1968 fiscal year:

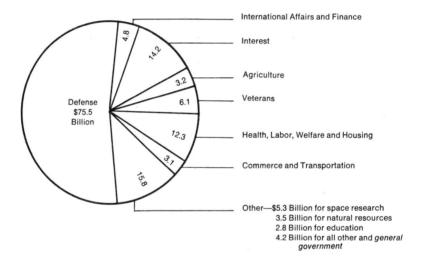

International Affairs and Finance

Interest

Agriculture

Veterans

Health, Labor, Welfare and Housing

Commerce and Transportation

Other—$5.3 Billion for space research
3.5 Billion for natural resources
2.8 Billion for education
4.2 Billion for all other and *general government*

National defense dominates the budget, for it takes almost 55 per cent of our Federal tax dollars. Even so, nondefense items, like farm parity payments, veterans' benefits, welfare programs, and housing, add up to about $25 billion, or about $450 for each family and unattached individual in the United States.

Let us move on to local and state government. Local taxes are levied largely on real estate, while state revenues come mostly from sales, excise, and franchise taxes. State and local spending has risen from $18 billion in 1948 to $87 billion in 1965. Some of this spending was financed by increased public debt, but state and local taxes (which have tripled since 1945) come to more than $51 billion, an average of almost $1,000 for each family and unattached individual. When this $51 billion is added to the Federal government's tax bill of over $100 billion, we have a total in excess of $150 billion. This comes to more than $2,800 for each family and unattached individual—more than most families spend for their food and clothing combined.

Of course, tax payments are not divided equally, but it is no longer realistic to believe that the rich pay taxes while the others benefit. Not long ago a survey showed that the 23,000 people who earned more than $100,000 a year contributed only 6 per cent of the total income tax revenues, even though they paid out as much as 91 per cent of their income in taxes. Today, one-third of our taxes comes from tax-payers who earn less than $5,000 a year.

Pay-roll deductions keep us from realizing the mountainous taxes we do pay. At the same time, other taxes have become so hidden that it is impossible to relate them to the actual cost of government. Tax Foundation, a leading organization devoted to tax matters, compiled some interesting examples of the taxes we do pay. For example, we pay literally hundreds of hidden taxes whenever we buy a loaf of bread, a dozen eggs, or a suit of clothes.

The total tax bite per worker is dramatic when it is measured on the basis of a working day. On the average, we work 2 hours and 16 minutes out of each 8-hour day to pay our taxes. Only 1 hour and 28 minutes of work are needed to provide for our family's food.

Several years ago the Commerce Clearing House came up with several other revealing estimates.

A man of 29 who makes $5,200 a year and has a wife and two children paid $5.05 in taxes each working day, at the time of the study. Over 36 years, he would have paid an estimated $47,221 in taxes, which amounted to $25.23 a week or $1,311.70 a year. At the then existing rates, his income taxes would come to $20,870, but this represents only 44 per cent of his total tax bill. He would pay about $7,248 in Social Security taxes, $7,710 in real estate taxes, and $720 in personal property taxes. Taxes on automobiles, tires, gasoline, and other items would come to another $4,237. And his everyday purchases would require sales taxes of $6,436.

These figures are conservative, because they do not assume any increases in tax rates or changes in his personal income. Companies also face a similar situation:

1. A major steel company earned $4.90 a share, but its tax bill came to $3.83 a share.

2. A chemical company paid out enough taxes in one year to build the long George Washington Bridge in New York, or the five-mile Mackinac Straits Bridge—or even the Pentagon, one of the world's largest buildings.

With corporate taxes averaging almost 44 per cent, many companies work the first 5 months of each year for the government and the remaining time for their stockholders. And, even after all corporate taxes have been paid, the dividends paid to stockholders are taxed again as personal income.

If we are going to prosper as a free nation devoted to private enterprise, we must:

- Provide a fair return to those who risk their savings in business enterprises.
- Have depreciation-tax policies that encourage the replacement of machinery and equipment.
- Become competitive in production costs.

An ever-expanding economy is essential if we want to promote the greatest good for the greatest number. Therefore, every phase of our national policy, particularly spending and taxes, must be examined in terms of its effect on our economic system.

WHAT CAN WE DO ABOUT GOVERNMENT SPENDING AND TAXES?

Economic growth is essential if we are going to provide adequate national defense, higher living standards, and necessary public services without raising taxes or bringing about ruinous inflation. However, high taxes have a dampening effect on economic growth. What, then, can we do about government spending and taxes?

1. We can review government spending programs, and reduce or eliminate those which are not essential.
2. We can support efforts to improve the efficiency of government.
3. We can return more responsibility to state and local governments, where taxpayers can better compare spending programs with their tax costs.
4. We can improve our personal and corporate income tax laws.
5. We can use the force of public opinion, which is still the determining force in public affairs.

We should let our public officials know how we feel and where we stand.

Discussion Questions

1. Show how the Federal government influences the level of the national income.

2. Estimate the probable government expenditures during the next three years.

3. What is fiscal policy and how is it used?

4. Is monetary policy a new technique of government?

5. Discuss this statement: "Taxes encourage evasive forms of economic activity."

6. How are taxes related to the basic relationship between the individual and the state?

7. Give several yardsticks for answering the question: "What do we want government to do?"

8. Discuss several key functions of government in our economic system.

9. How effective is a ceiling on the Federal government debt?

10. What are the approximate sizes of our Federal, state, and local government debts?

11. How does our changing population mix affect the amount and type of governmental spending and debt?

12. What yardsticks can we use to measure the effectiveness of government activity?

13. How have the major expenditures of government changed over the years?

14. Discuss the various features of inheritance taxes, as you see them.

15. Give several examples of hidden taxes.

16. Make a detailed list of the type and amount of taxes you pay.

17. What can the typical citizen do about government spending and taxes?

18. Discuss this statement: "In a democracy, government spending really represents the will of the people."

19. In your opinion, when are taxes too high?

20. Give the advantages and disadvantages of the following taxes, as you see them:
    a. Income taxes, personal and corporate
    b. Real property taxes
    c. Personal property taxes

Circle the T or F (True or False) before each statement:

T   F   1. Government expenditures—Federal, state, and local—represent about 20 per cent of the national income.

T   F   2. Taxes are a part of the fiscal policies of government.

T   F   3. Taxes come under the broad area of monetary policies.

T   F   4. Income taxes are regressive in nature.

T   F   5. Rising government expenditures are straining the existing tax structure of the United States.

T   F   6. Indirect taxes are being used more extensively.

T   F   7. Sales taxes and excise taxes are one and the same.

T   F   8. A tariff on imports is a tax.

T   F   9. Taxes do not affect personal incentives or risk-taking by business firms.

T   F   10. Taxes on cigarettes and gasoline are regressive in nature.

ANSWERS

10. T	8. T	6. T	4. F	2. T
9. F	7. T	5. T	3. F	1. F

20

BUSINESS AND GOVERN-
MENT RELATIONS

In recent years, there have been recurrent clashes between business and government, and to some extent this is unfortunate. The American economy is based on a constitutional form of government that recognizes and provides a significant role for government. Indeed, few business transactions could take place without the help of public law. Most businessmen do not oppose government per se. What they object to is the arbitrary use of power by those in government office. They are deeply concerned when government intervention impairs property rights and management's right to manage the enterprise.

Certainly the implied scope of government has expanded sharply since the 1930's, and particularly after World War II. Actually, the laws that set the parameters for business action today were the political platforms of reform parties several decades ago. That is why Norman Thomas pointed out recently that we have realized in the United States most of what his Socialist party stood for thirty years ago.

The daily papers and public affairs magazines contain numerous articles dealing with government regulation· of business—such as the President's demand that the aluminum and copper industries roll back price increases, the Department of Justice's antitrust suits, or the Federal Trade Commission's objections to a proposed merger, to name just a few of the many instances of government intervention in the private sector of the economy.

Nonetheless, few businessmen want to see all government regulation abolished, or have us return to the kind of competition that flourished in the 1870's. In the absence of desirable regulation, what would happen to our standards of weights and measures, the sanctity of patent and license rights, or the interstate control of drugs and narcotics? In these, and many other areas, government regulation has proven beneficial.

It is apparent, too, that every businessman must take into account many factors that affect public affairs. For example, if his employment record is unstable, he is likely to encounter labor trouble. If he fails to eliminate unpleasant odors, excessive noise, polluted water, or industrial eyesores, the community may discourage employment at his plant or pass ordinances against him. If he arbitrarily raises prices in a vital industry, he may be hailed before a Congressional Committee, receive a call from the White House, or find himself in difficulty with antitrust administrators.

Responsible executives recognize these facts and their obligations. Therefore, they do consider the community, their employees, and the general public along with their investors. In many ways, too, business is involved with government as a partner—in atomic energy, space exploration, public transportation, and housing.

So the central issue is not whether we should have government regulation, but how much regulation we should have. And, in the final analysis, this is something that the general public must decide, because government regulations are often the result of public pressure.

PUBLIC OPINION AND GOVERNMENT ACTION

Most businessmen know from first-hand experience that the government has a tremendous influence on their companies, yet many of them are hesitant to play an active role in reshaping public policies. Many businessmen still feel that if they mind their own business and do a good production and selling job, the business climate will take care of itself. Unfortunately, this just isn't so.

We can compare the business climate to a strong head wind into which business is proceeding into the future. The two components of this head wind are:

1. The character of public opinion, which is based mainly on the public's understanding of economic and political issues
2. The specific policies of government, which are determined by those in government office

An unfavorable combination of public opinion and government power will create a stiff head wind that will make it extremely difficult for a company to reach its future goals.

It does not take any imagination to see that the government is playing a crucial role in everything that concerns business: wages, pricing, tariffs, taxes, labor relations, mergers, fair-trade practices, packaging, and so on. Beyond this, the government advises and admonishes labor, industry, agriculture, education, and society in general. It is the biggest spender, the largest lender, and the most prolific borrower in the nation.

Government is also the *key rulemaker*—and really judge and jury. So government officials have untold powers to regulate business and to set the climate within which companies are to operate.

THE SHARP GROWTH IN GOVERNMENT POWER

There is widespread disagreement as to how far the various levels of government can intervene in our private economy without disrupting the basic freedoms which have made it what it is today. It is generally acknowledged, though, that the power and influence of government have continually increased. Today the local, state, and Federal governments employ over 12 million persons. This means that about 1 out of every 6 employed people, including the armed services, is on a government pay roll. Indirectly, another 10 per cent, or between 6.5 to 7.5 million jobs in the private sector, depend upon government purchases of goods and services.

In the field of agriculture, government expenditures have increased from $1.2 billion in 1939 to about $5 billion today. The support of farm prices has been coupled with limitations on farm production—and both have been implemented by complex rules and regulations.

In 1930, about 6 per cent of all generating capacity was publicly owned. Today, about 25 per cent of all power capacity is government-owned.

Our system of government is responsive to these changes, but it cannot respond unless we interpret our problems and bring them to the attention of our elected representatives in a reasonable and positive manner.

Other general areas in which government and business are both concerned are:

- Tax proposals
- Tariffs
- Antitrust legislation
- Labor relations
- Monetary and fiscal policies

Tax Proposals

For a long time American industry has been working under complex tax rules and double taxation. Corporate income is taxed at rates that take away almost half of a company's income, yet the dividends paid to shareholders are taxed again at personal income tax rates, which rise sharply with income. This means that income is taxed twice—first as company profits and then as dividends paid to shareholders.

Tariffs

Another area of growing concern is the whole question of tariffs and trade restrictions. Almost all economists favor free trade between countries as being the best way in the long run of conducting world trade. Discriminatory arrangements that favor certain countries are not consistent with free trade proposals. Equal costs of entry of American goods are sought by many industries.

Antitrust Legislation and Administration

Our antitrust laws are designed to prevent monopoly, and the most important of these are the Sherman Act, the Clayton Act, and the Federal Trade Commission Act.[1]

Their purpose is to forbid monopoly or combinations in restraint of trade—or to prevent a corporation from acquiring the voting stock or assets of another corporation if the effect will substantially lessen competition.

However, no one really knows what administrative bodies mean by a "substantial lessening of competition." It depends on the views held by people in the Department of Justice who are charged with antitrust enforcement, and ultimately on the justices who make up the Federal courts at the time. It is not clear, for example, what the Department or the courts will even consider the market to be. It may be the entire country or just a part of it. It may be the market for a single well-defined product or for a family of related products all used for the

---

[1] *See* Ernest Dale and L. C. Michelon, *Modern Management Methods* (Cleveland: The World Publishing Company, 1966), p. 97.

same purpose—for example, flexible packaging materials instead of one particular type like cellophane, as the courts decided in one case.

Dozens of books have been written on the subject, and they arrive at the same conclusion—our antitrust laws are so confused that no businessman can interpret them, much less be sure that he is acting in a legal manner. The intent of Congress may have been one thing when the laws were passed, but broad congressional legislation has been applied by administrators or interpreted by the courts or by independent regulatory agencies. So almost anything can happen, depending upon the outlook of the judge, administrator, or commissioner involved.

Judicial interpretation of the Sherman Act and other antitrust laws also has been a source of trouble for American business. From 1890 to 1911, the Supreme Court made no distinction between a restraint incidental to the main purpose of the contract and the main contract itself. Accordingly, all contracts in restraint of trade were illegal.

The Rule of Reason was introduced in the case of *Standard Oil Company of New Jersey* v. *United States* in 1911. This common-law interpretation, or more liberal treatment of business, reached its heights in 1920 in the *United States* v. *United States Steel Corporation*. In this case the Court decided that monopoly power was not itself illegal provided that the corporation had not used its power to oppress labor or its competitors.

Then there was a swing away from this view, beginning in the 1930's. As a result the Rule of Reason is again being ignored in many cases. The assumption is being made that anyone with apparent monopoly power will use it illegally. So, in effect, all monopolies are illegal unless they are provided for by law.

Maintaining competition should be the primary concern of antitrust policy, but we should improve the legal interpretations of what constitutes competition. The statutes themselves make for inconsistencies as they look at different degrees of competition as being lawful and unlawful.

Labor Relations

There was really no national labor policy before the thirties. The Clayton Act exempted unions from antitrust action, but the courts did not see much that was new in its provisions.

The union movement grew under President Wilson's Administration, and then declined from a membership of over 5 million in 1920 to

3,500,000 by 1929. So, by 1930, the union movement had not advanced much beyond its position in 1880.

In 1932, the Norris-LaGuardia Act limited the use of injunctions in labor disputes and outlawed what were called "yellow-dog contracts." Section 7a of the National Industrial Recovery Act of 1933 also gave positive support to the union movement and to collective bargaining.

The Wagner Act (National Labor Relations Act of 1935) really gave labor a tremendous boost from 1935 to 1947. It provided for a National Labor Relations Board and outlined "unfair" labor practices by employers. It said that collective bargaining was desirable, that you could not have this without strong unions, and that a worker could join a union without fear of employers. A wave of state laws or "little Wagner Acts" followed, and, as a result, membership increased rapidly to over 18 million.

Efforts to amend the Wagner Act began at once, particularly after that Act was upheld by the Supreme Court. A number of states began to amend their laws during the forties to bring about greater union control, but the movement was curtailed by World War II.

In 1947 the Taft-Hartley Act was passed by Congress, but it was vetoed by President Truman on the grounds that it would:

1. Increase strikes.
2. Decide issues that should be left to bargaining.
3. Expose employees to numerous hazards.
4. Deprive workers of vital protection.
5. Contain unworkable provisions.
6. Discriminate against employees.
7. Run counter to beliefs held by labor and management.
8. Raise serious questions of public policies.

The Act was passed over the President's veto by a vote of 331 to 83 in the House and by 68 to 25 in the Senate.

Besides legislation and court interpretations, labor and management are both aware of the changing interpretations of labor laws by the National Labor Relations Board. When members of the Board are changed, the decisions of previous boards are often reversed or modified. For example, the original Labor-Management Act was designed to permit employees to organize and to bargain collectively. Therefore the law made it an unfair labor practice for employers to coerce employees in their choice of a union. But what constitutes coercion? The original "administrative law" developed by the National Labor Relations Board took the position that practically anything an employer might say constituted coercion. The employer was barred from explaining, in even the mildest terms, why he did not want his employees to unionize or why he considered one union preferable to another. This was an obvious violation of the freedom of speech guaranteed by the First Amendment to the Constitution.

Over and above these examples of direct control over industrial relations, there are other laws that affect business and labor directly— like wages and hours legislation—and still others which have an indirect effect on wages, costs, and incentives. For example, the government influences wage rates and employment practices by built-in requirements in government contracts.

Monetary and Fiscal Policies

The Federal government exercises control over business through its monetary and fiscal policies.

The purpose of money is to facilitate the exchange of goods and services, and it has come to be regarded as a measure of value, a store of value, and as a standard for deferred payments. But it doesn't serve these purposes equally well, when inflation and deflation upset the usefulness of money.

The Founding Fathers gave Congress the right to coin money and to fix its content in the same spirit that they allowed Congress to fix weights and measures. Unfortunately, in Article I, Section 7, they used the word "value." Congress should not try to fix the value of money because the value of money consists of what can be purchased for it, and this should be determined in the market place. However, since its value is influenced by the amount of money in circulation, credit policies, and consumer demand, the government can easily influence the magnitude of these by its monetary and fiscal policies.

An example of government action is President Franklin D. Roosevelt's changing of the gold content of money as a means of raising depression prices. His authority stemmed from a rider to the Agricultural Adjustment Act of 1933, which gave him four alternative powers:

1. To restore bimetallism
2. To order the Federal Reserve System to buy $3 billion worth of government bonds
3. To print $3 billion in "greenbacks"
4. To reduce the gold content of the dollar by as much as half

He reduced the value of the dollar by 40.96 per cent; but to do so, the gold in circulation was nationalized. This meant that it became impossible to satisfy contracts which called for the payment of gold. Seemingly, today and in the future we are to conduct business on the basis of a dollar determined by what the Congress decides to call a dollar.

The Employment Act of 1946

Probably no single piece of federal legislation has given the national government as much potential power to affect the level of national economic activity as the Employment Act of 1946. This law gives the Federal government the responsibility of providing for the maximization of a package—employment, production, and purchasing power. Under this law the Federal government acted in 1964 to cut taxes to stimulate economic activity. Then, in 1966, it acted to tighten credit to slow down the rate of economic growth. All in all, this is a great responsibility for government planners to assume, if they decide to take the place of normal market forces.

A PHILOSOPHY OF
BUSINESS AND GOVERNMENT

Picture a heavily loaded wagon drawn by two horses. Their success depends upon cooperation and coordination. Both must pull at the same time. Both must seek to go forward. Both must respond to the same order from the driver. You don't need imagination to realize what would happen if there were two drivers—one directing his efforts to one horse while the other seeks to control the other horse—one yelling "whoa" and the other hollering "giddap." Or imagine one driver with two self-willed horses that will not team up—one wanting to stop when the other felt like moving, one deciding to go back when the other pulled forward. Apply the illustration to business and government. Think of business as one horse, government as the other, the general public as the driver, and the courts as the evener among them.

As driver, the public has a twofold nature—he is a political citizen and he is an economic entity. So he is not a very consistent driver. As a worker, the typical citizen wants higher wages, but as a consumer, he wants lower prices. As a tenant he prefers low rents, but as a citizen he wants more government services. As a taxpayer he wants lower taxes all the time.

It is apparent, too, that business and government have not always pulled together. Business blames government, and government spokesmen blame business.

In order to clarify this confusing situation we must ask ourselves three questions:

1. How has the present arrangement between business and government come about?
2. How have the courts behaved as the evener between the two?
3. How can business management best deal with government in the future?

The French phrase "laissez faire" implies that an entrepreneur should be allowed to make what things he likes, that government should allow all trades to be open to everybody, that government should not prescribe to manufacturers "the fashions of their cloth," and that persons and goods should be permitted to travel freely from one place to another without being subject to tolls and unnecessary regulations. "Laissez faire" penetrated the American colonies because the colonists were far removed from their mother country and they had to be self-reliant. As a result, they gradually evolved our present capitalist system, which is peculiarly American and not at all synonymous with the capitalism of other countries.

Two significant events occurred in 1776. On July 4 there was the Declaration of Independence; and in December there appeared *An Inquiry into the Nature and Causes of the Wealth of Nations* by Adam Smith. The two events were closely related—and in a sense, they became the basis of our American political economy. The United States Constitution became effective in 1789. The framers, as the document states, sought "to form a more perfect Union, [to] establish Justice, [to] insure domestic Tranquility, [to] provide for the common defence, [to] promote the general Welfare, and [to] secure the Blessings of Liberty."

Observers point out that the welfare clause has been pushed into prominence in recent years, and they point out that the Constitution did not promise anything except that government would keep the path to attainment open to everyone and then leave it to the individual to make the grade.

SOURCES OF GOVERNMENTAL POWERS

From where does the government derive its power to legislate on a particular subject of concern to business? What plan underlies the law? And what is the resulting economic policy?

The main source of federal power is in Article 1, Section 8 of the Constitution, which has been called its most important section. It states the expressed powers of Congress. Among these are the powers to lay and collect taxes, borrow money on the credit of the United States, regulate interstate and international commerce, establish bankruptcy laws, coin money, fix standards of weights and measures, establish post offices and post roads, grant patents and copyrights, and so on. In addition, Congress is given the authority to make laws that are necessary to carry out the above-stated powers. These are known as "implied powers." Accordingly, it is within the power of Congress to establish a Government Printing Office to print stamps which are necessary to the existence of the Post Office provided for in the Constitution. As a result, the Constitution, which can be read in twenty minutes, has been expanded into thousands of volumes of laws that cannot be mastered even in a lifetime.

Let us take a simple example of how a statement in the Constitution grows. The power to regulate commerce first implied that commerce is traffic, buying, and selling. Gradually, it was broadened to include the conditions surrounding the manufacture, production, or processing of goods which enter commerce, including anything that affects the flow of commerce. So at this point, the distinction between interstate and intrastate activities becomes hopelessly blurred.

BUSINESS AND GOVERNMENT ADMINISTRATION

Our period of American history has been called "the age of administration." We hear of business administration, public administration, hospital administration, and the like. The reason is that we have many jobs to get done.

The distinguishing feature of a public administrative agency is the power to determine, either by rule or by decision, private rights and obligations.

Today we have a multitude of administrative agencies. They sometimes have the name "administration," as in Veterans Administration, Public Housing Administration, or Federal Housing Administration. Sometimes they are called "offices"—for example, Office of Education, Office of Civil Defense. We also meet them as "bureaus": Bureau of International Labor Affairs, Bureau of Internal Revenue Service, Bureau of the Census, Federal Bureau of Investigation, Bureau of International Commerce. Others are called "agencies": United States Information Agency, Central Intelligence Agency, Housing and Home Finance Agency. We see them as "corporations" in the Federal Deposit Insurance Corporation, Virgin Islands Corporation, Commodity Credit Corporation, Federal Crop Insurance Corporation, and Inland Waterways Corporation. We have them in the form of "commissions," such as the Federal Trade Commission, Interstate Commerce Commission, Securities and Exchange Commission, Federal Power Commission, Atomic Energy Commission, Federal Communications Commission, United States Tariff Commission, and the Civil Service Commission. They can appear as "authorities," as in the Tennessee Valley Authority, Commodity Exchange Authority, National Capital Housing Authority. Finally, we meet them as "boards": National Labor Relations Board, Federal Reserve Board, Civil Aeronautics Board, Renegotiation Board, Railroad Retirement Board, National Mediation Board, and Unemployment Compensation Board.

This is not an exhaustive list, but it bears out that we live in an age of administration, whatever we might call the agencies.

Unfortunately business comes up against so many administrative agencies that the businessman often gets the impression that the right hand of government doesn't always know what its left hand is doing. A banker, for example, is affected by the orders, instructions, and decisions of the Comptroller of Currency, the Federal Deposit Insurance Corporation, the Board of Governors of the Federal Reserve, the Housing Administration, and a number of others, including state and municipal agencies.

Moreover the relation of business and government is not confined to the domestic scene. Much of what we face domestically is the result of international forces—for in many respects, international commitments force a certain amount of national planning and preparedness.

CONCLUSION

We must develop a better and more consistent philosophy about business and government relations.

The American team of business and government has carried the economy farther ahead than any other team in recorded history. We should see to it that the future exceeds the past in cooperation and mutual respect. Equally important, the market place and free choice should be preserved wherever possible.

Discussion Questions

1. Cite several recent instances of "clashes" between business and government.

2. Comment on this statement: "The United States is going socialistic."

3. What government and public affairs factors affect the profit prospects of large business firms?

4. Give several examples of how prevailing public opinion has influenced governmental action.

5. Discuss this conclusion: "There has been an unnecessary growth in government power."

6. How do tax proposals affect business decisions?

7. Discuss this statement: "Tariffs involve as much government intervention as does labor legislation."

8. Indicate the highlights of antitrust legislation in the United States.

9. In your opinion, what is the distinction between reasonable and unreasonable restraints of trade?

10. What is the significance of the Standard Oil Case?

11. Why was the United States Steel Case important?

12. Describe the status of labor relations prior to the 1930's.

13. What did the Norris-LaGuardia Act accomplish?

14. What were the highlights of the Wagner Act?

15. What, in your opinion, would constitute coercion under our present labor laws?

16. What did the Employment Act of 1946 try to accomplish?

17. What is the nature of the constitutional role of government in the United States?

18. Comment on this statement: "The free enterprise system and government regulation are incompatible."

19. What was Adam Smith's attitude toward government?

20. How does the Federal government administer its regulations over business?

Circle the T or F (True or False) before each statement:

T   F   1. A merger may be considered illegal under the antitrust laws because of what a company might do rather than because of what it has done.

T   F   2. Administrative law may hamper a business more than the actual statutes on the books.

T   F   3. Legislation designed for good ends cannot injure business.

T   F   4. Employers are now barred from expressing any opinion about unions that are trying to organize their plants.

T   F   5. A company is only subject to antitrust action when it has more than 50 per cent of the market.

T   F   6. If a company pays its employees well above the minimum wage, a rise in the minimum wage will not affect it at all.

T   F   7. Dividends are taxed twice—once as profits to the company and then as income to the stockholders.

T   F   8. The government has little influence on the country's money markets.

T   F   9. Legislators pay little attention to letters from their constituents.

T   F   10. The tax situation within a state or a community may influence a company's decision to locate there.

ANSWERS

10. T	8. F	6. F	4. F	2. T
9. F	7. T	5. F	3. F	1. T

PART THREE

COMPARATIVE
ECONOMIC SYSTEMS

21

COMMUNISM: WHAT IT MEANS AND HOW IT WORKS

"A Communist[1] has no right to be a mere onlooker," said Nikita Khrushchev on February 14, 1956.

In our society we have the freedom to be active or passive, to be a doer or a spectator. We can choose to watch the world go by. That is our privilege; but, realistically, we can hardly afford to stand by. We must accept the responsibility and the opportunity for service to our community and country.

Communism is diametrically opposed to a system like ours, yet few Americans understand its philosophy, objectives, and methods. Throughout industrial history some groups have criticized free enterprise economies and have proposed communistic or socialistic systems. Some of these critics were motivated by ideals of reform, and they were content to establish their own communities. These earlier attempts at communism, featuring primarily a series of "model" and isolated communities, have been described as Nineteenth Century Utopian Socialism, because of the Utopian ideals motivating them.

Communists are quick to recite the economic and scientific advances of their society and the problems of ours. For example, it is commonplace for them to cite Soviet Russia's progress in space-age exploration. The important point to remember, however, is that a planned society allocates its resources in a dictatorial manner. Because of this fact the government can divert resources to a few national objectives and demonstrate outstanding achievements in these fields. What is often overlooked is that a controlled society is seldom capable of a balanced type of growth in all economic sectors—consumer as well as producer

---

[1] We have capitalized *Communist* and *Communism* whenever these terms are used in reference to Soviet Communism and its offshoots; they are not capitalized when used generically or in reference to Marxian communism.

goods. So a communist or socialist economy usually falls far behind when *all* goods and services are taken into account.

Today there is Communist activity in every part of the world—from the Near East to Southeast Asia, from Africa to South America. And as Communism has spread, its challenge to the Free World has become critical. Communist governments control over one and a quarter billion people, or over 35 per cent of the world's population. This compares with hardly any known Communists in 1903, 40,000 at the time of the Russian Revolution in 1917, and 400 million as late as 1950.

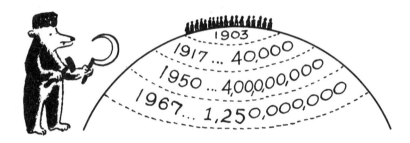

How do Communists gain control over so many people? What do they say? What do they do? To answer these questions this chapter describes Communist principles and practices.

WHAT COMMUNISM REALLY MEANS

Communism got its real start in 1848, when Karl Marx wrote the *Communist Manifesto*. The principles of Communism have not really changed since the *Manifesto* was published, although they have been interpreted and applied in various ways by Lenin, Stalin, Khrushchev, Kosygin, Mao Tse-tung, and others.

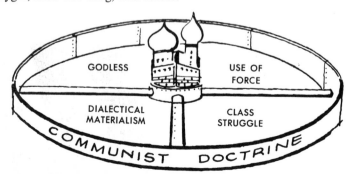

The Communists believe that human history is controlled by what they call "dialectical materialism." The dialectical theory was elaborated upon by Georg Hegel, a German philosopher, and was later adopted by Marx. Hegel believed that an "Absolute Spirit" was gradually realizing itself in human history. He contended that any existing condition in society (which he called "Thesis") automatically generated its opposite (called "Anti-Thesis"), and that the inevitable conflict between these two resulted in a "Synthesis," which represented a higher step in historical progress. In the long run, this progress by continuous conflict was to lead to the perfection of human society, at which time the dialectical process would cease to operate.

Marx believed that Hegel's dialectical approach was correct, but that he was wrong in believing in an "Absolute Spirit." Marx, therefore, put the dialectical method within a "materialistic" framework. He took the point of view that human history was really nothing more than a long-term economic struggle between opposing classes in society. These classes battle each other for purely economic reasons, and the most important of these are the means of production and the manner in which productive property is held.

In industrial countries, according to Marx, this inevitable class struggle takes place between propertyless workers, called "proletariat," and "profiteering" capitalists, called "bourgeoisie." According to Marx, the proletariat will reach their ultimate goal of peace and prosperity when the class struggle ends with the elimination of all capitalists. This will happen because, at the right time in history, the proletariat will take over all non-communist governments by subversion or revolution and will use their armies, police, and courts to exterminate the capitalist class.

Dialectical Materialism and the Class Struggle

Here, in greater detail, is Marx's version of the dialectical process.

Human history is nothing but a continuous struggle between opposing classes in society. In the beginning, there were conquerors and slaves, then feudal lords and serfs, and now capitalists and workers.

This historical class struggle always develops an *exploiting* and an *exploited* group. The exploitation of one class by another leads to open warfare and to the eventual destruction of that particular ruling class. Society then moves on to the next higher stage of historical progress, where a new class struggle takes place. At the present time, by Marxist standards, we are supposed to be at the point in history where the capitalists are the next class to be destroyed. Marx explains it this way. Capitalists are progressive in production methods, but backward in their social and economic thinking. Their technical changes result in sharp increases in the production of goods and services, but they underpay their workers to make a profit. Productive capacity then lies idle, and workers are laid off. As more and more workers become unemployed, the capitalists create the very disgruntled people who will destroy them. When that happens, *capitalism* gives way to *socialism,* the next higher step in the dialectical process—and then socialism gives way to *communism,* which Marx regarded as the final goal of humanity. When communism is achieved, the dialectical process comes to rest, because all productive property is owned by the state and is used for the benefit of the people rather than for an exploiting class.

Marx's theory rested on his conviction that the standard of living of industrial workers would get progressively worse as more factories were introduced. It apparently did not occur to him that the increased productivity made possible by more and better tools, in turn paid for by profits, would result in greater production with less physical labor, and that this increased production would be shared with workers and lead to higher living standards and better working conditions.

This is exactly what happened, because the standard of living of most industrial workers has risen more than 400 per cent since Marx wrote his *Manifesto.*

The Overthrow of Existing Governments

Marx regarded non-communist governments, anywhere in the world, as tools of the ruling class. He contended that the capitalists used the government's military forces, police, and courts to keep the proletariat in line.

For this reason, he believed that there would be a temporary form of socialism on the road to communism. This occurs when the proletariat seize an existing government and use its powers to get rid of the last survivors of a capitalist society. The communists then take over all education, all newspapers and magazines, all radio and television stations, and every form of art, literature, and science.

At this point, the society is socialistic because the government still exists as a means of persecution. So, by Marx's concept, Russia is socialistic today rather than communistic. Marx expected the government eventually to "wither away" after the exploiting class no longer existed.

The fact is, however, that the Soviet government shows no signs of withering away after some fifty years in power.

In any event Communists are taught to use any means—sabotage, assassination, or armed revolt—to overthrow existing non-communist governments. They use infiltration methods to get party members into key positions where they can obstruct the government's policies and spread anti-government propaganda. They are taught to conduct nation-wide strikes and to attack a government at a time of national crisis— such as during depressions, after wars, or when there is widespread dissatisfaction. They know that a well organized and militant minority with dedicated leadership can easily win over a confused and unorganized public.

Unfortunately, the record shows that the Communists have succeeded beyond their fondest dreams. They have taken over more than 25 countries in the last 27 years, and they now occupy about 30 per cent of the land area of the world. Communists are active in all countries, using every means to undermine existing governments.

Lack of Religion and Morality

Marx also believed that literature, art, and political and social ideals were nothing more than a "philosophical superstructure" that the ruling class used to justify its dominant position. He maintained that religion was "opium for the people"—an additional psychological tool used by the ruling class to keep the exploited people in line.

Also, Marx believed that a state of war already existed between the classes in society, and between communism and capitalism all over the world. He felt that real peace would come about only when communism was established all over the world. Revolution and violence were quite acceptable to Marx because anything that brought about communism was considered the highest form of cooperation with historical necessity.

People are shocked when Communists lie, murder, blackmail, start revolutions, or instigate wars. But these are perfectly consistent with their materialistic and atheistic philosophy. They believe a state of war already exists between the classes in society—and between communism and capitalism all over the world. They believe that their brand of peace will come about only when communism is established all over the world.

Revolution and violence are quite acceptable because anything that brings about communism is the highest form of cooperation with historical necessity.

Communism vs. Western Civilization

This summary of Communism shows how completely it is opposed to the moral, political, and economic principles of free enterprise and to the basic philosophy of the American Way of Life. The important points of difference include the following:

- We believe in the divine origin and inherent worth of each person, but Communism regards the individuals as a fragment on the tide of history—a fleck of dust without divine origin or destiny.
- We believe in religious freedom and in the brotherhood of man, but atheistic Communism destroys moral values and makes subversion and violence the main tools of their militaristic and materialistic society.
- We believe in private property and freedom of choice, but Communists believe in state ownership of productive property and government control of family life.
- We believe in democratic government with political power resting in the people, but the Communist Party runs the government without opposition by using secret police and terror tactics.
- We believe in human freedom and individual rights, in all of the legal protections of the Constitution, but these mean nothing to Communists except as legal loopholes for their illegal acts.

So much for what the Communists believe—and how their beliefs are opposed to ours. Now let's see what the Communists do once they get in power.

HOW COMMUNISM REALLY WORKS

Communists promise many things, including freedom, absolute equality, and a higher standard of living. But how faithful are they in carrying out their promises? The best way to answer that question is to see what Communists do once they take over a country.

Communist Society

Soviet Russia has a constitution which technically provides freedom of speech, press, and religion, but in practice it is nothing more than a piece of paper. Freedom of speech and of the press are controlled by the Communist Party. The press is used to attack anyone or anything the Party chooses, and is devoted largely to government propaganda.

In every school, from the lowest grades to the universities, students are indoctrinated in Communist philosophy. Everyone—including musicians, authors, and scientists—must keep within the Party Line, and there is little room for individual thought or action.

The Communists have tried to discourage church worship. But churches still operate on a limited basis because the Russian people have not completely accepted a way of life without God or religion.

What is more, the Communists maintain their position through constant fear and violence. To keep people true to the Party, a vast espionage network exists among Party members. People are encouraged to spy on one another. Children are taught to report anti-Party tendencies in their parents, and the secret police can enter homes and offices to seize individuals, records, or personal belongings without notice.

Communism's disregard for human values is apparent in Cuba, where Fidel Castro denied being a Communist, took over the government in a bloody revolution, held "kangaroo" trials that led to the execution of hundreds of Cubans, confiscated industrial plants and millions of acres of farm land with little or no compensation, and then finally declared himself to be a Communist in a nationwide telecast. He admitted lying all along the line to deceive the Cuban people into accepting his Communist revolution.

Communist Politics

Communist countries have lawmaking bodies and courts, but these are mere fronts for the Party, which is the real political force. In Soviet Russia there are only about 11 million Party members out of a total population of over 250 million people.

The Soviets boast of their unanimous elections, that are designed to prove that the Russian people are solidly behind their government. But this means nothing because there is only one party and a single slate of candidates.

Communist Economics

Communist economics has never produced a living standard comparable to ours or to that of Western Europe. The following special report on consumer goods was prepared by the Department of Labor's Bureau of Labor Statistics and covers the year 1959, the latest available comparable figures. It shows the lengths of time an American and a Russian had to work in order to earn each item in that year.

Hours Worked to Produce Consumer Goods

Item	In the U.S.A.	In the U.S.S.R.
Men's wool suit	23 Hours	275 Hours
Men's oxfords	7 Hours	61 Hours
Women's oxfords	5 Hours 10 min.	57 Hours 30 min.
Street dress	4 Hours 36 min.	73 Hours 30 min.
Salted butter (1 lb.)	21 Minutes	3 Hours 4 min.
Milk (1 qt.)	8 Minutes	31 Minutes
Potatoes (1 lb.)	2 Minutes	7 Minutes
Cigarettes (1 pkg.)	7 Minutes	27 Minutes
Tea (1 oz.)	6 Minutes	33 Minutes
Bread, rye (1 lb.)	6 Minutes	9 Minutes
Sugar (1 lb.)	3 Minutes	1 Hour 4 min.
Soap	3 Minutes	32 Minutes

In the U.S.S.R. food and clothing allowances are still inadequate, and there are few automobiles, refrigerators, washing machines, or television sets. These conveniences, along with the best housing, are reserved largely for Party members. Within the last few years public dissatisfaction with the small share of the Gross National Product allocated to personal consumption has stirred up sufficient unrest to cause top-level leaders to sit uneasily on their thrones of power. This has become evident in spite of ruthless and highly centralized control of individual expression.

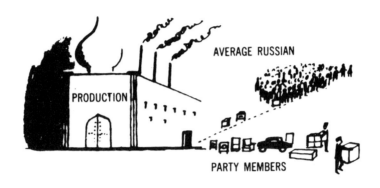

AVERAGE RUSSIAN

PRODUCTION

PARTY MEMBERS

There are no minimum wages in the U.S.S.R. A worker gets paid for what he produces, and his income is based on a production standard set by the state. When a worker consistently fails to meet the required standard, he is punished by imprisonment, because low productivity is considered a criminal offense.

Production standards are set each year from engineering studies made on specially trained "shock workers," called Stakhanovites. These carefully selected workers achieve high production records under artificially controlled conditions. Their records are then used to set higher production standards for the next year.

The government dictates pay and conditions of work, so there is no such thing as collective bargaining. The Russians do have labor contracts, but these simply outline what the state-controlled enterprise intends to accomplish, how many new machines must be paid for by increased productivity, and what the workers must do to meet their quotas.

The failure of state compulsion has become increasingly apparent in the last several years—and therefore we are seeing the introduction of incentives involving personal rewards of increased earnings to stimulate improved efficiency and increased productivity. Market pricing is also making itself felt to a far greater extent.

Russia has had good and bad results with state planning. It has made rapid progress in heavy industrial production but has done very poorly in consumer-goods production.

For example, in 1913, Russia ranked fifth as an industrial power, following the United States, England, Germany, and France. Today, Russia is second to the United States.

Between 1913–1966 the total Russian industrial output has increased more than 50 times:

- Output of steel has gone up 22 times.
- Output of pig iron has gone up 16 times.
- Output of coal has gone up 20 times.
- Output of cement has gone up 44 times.
- Output of oil has gone up 25 times.
- Output of electricity has gone up 272 times.
- Output of gas has gone up 7,250 times.

In 1913, as a military power, Russia was rated sixth—after Germany, France, England, the United States, and Japan. Today Russia is second only to the United States.

Perhaps Russia's most conspicuous failure has been in the field of agriculture. Today there is still a serious food shortage, even though the nation has had collective farms for over 35 years. Continuous shakeups have been made in the management of these farms, but with little success. Not too long ago, the Russian people were told that they had to eat more horse meat because there was a shortage of beef.

In 1913, Czarist Russia was an exporter of grain. Today Russia imports grain from the West. The per acre yield of all grains in Russia has risen by less than 50 per cent since 1913, and is only about a third of the yield in the United States. In the United States, with fewer people so employed, the output of sugar beets is about three times that of Russia, and of potatoes, it is about 2.5 as large.[2]

Contrast Russia's food shortage with the agricultural situation in the United States. With about 5 per cent of our work force on the farms, we have an abundance of farm products, and our problem for many years has been to get rid of the farm surplus.

We Americans are proud of our living standards, so we are inclined to compare our consumer-goods production with Russia's. But the real challenges of Russian Communism lie in the fields of scientific technology and in heavy industrial production, where the Russians have achieved surprising results—and for good reasons. A planned society like Russia's can best succeed when it plunges ahead toward a single, inflexible objective like producing materiel for war. It can allocate its best resources and finest manpower to natural resources development, heavy industrial pro-

[2] "What Russia Has Achieved—At What Price," *U.S. News & World Report,* Vol. LXII No. 11 (March 1967), p. 55.

duction, rocketry, and atomic energy, knowing full well that these areas are vital to its war-making potential.

Soviet Education

Russia's outstanding accomplishment has been in the field of education. Forty years ago most Russians were illiterate and had few opportunities for self-improvement. Today, over 60 million Russians take part in some type of education offered by 4,000 technical schools, about 950 institutions of higher learning, and some 55 universities.

The Russians regard mass education as the key to future progress and communist survival. Education is their way to indoctrinate the young and to infuse the old. More important, it provides the technicians, scientists, and engineers needed to move ahead of the United States and the free world. That is why Russia's schools operate on an extra long day, six days a week, the year around.

The Russians are fanatically upgrading the individual's ability and skills because they know there is nothing inevitable about progress. It must be planned for, worked for, and produced. The so-called "dialectical tide of history" just doesn't exist. Progress depends, as it always has, on a country's natural resources, the abilities and incentives of its people, and on the capital equipment needed for large-scale, efficient production.

Russia's educational system is also used to train foreign students from underdeveloped areas in Asia and Africa. Hundreds of these students attend Russian universities where they learn, among other things, Communist philosophy and tactics.

Russian Nationalism and Imperialism

In the U.S.S.R., physical punishment, banishment, and slave-labor camps are reserved for those who refuse to cooperate with the government. But the positive stimulus used with the people is national pride in Russia as the mother country. This is surprising because Marx considered nationalism a bad thing, for it was associated with capitalist societies. Communists were supposed to be worldwide in their thinking because theirs was the brotherhood of the working classes of all countries. But this, like many other ideas, was scrapped, and the Communists soon realized the value of nationalism as an incentive for their people. By glorifying Russia, and by constantly comparing her economic position with that of the United States, they give their people patriotic and positive goals for which to work. Their fundamental "whip" is psychological and is used in statements like, "We will surpass America by 1970."

Nationalism also comes in handy when the Communists take over an underdeveloped country. Their typical approach is to oppose an existing government as the puppet of a colonial power, beat the drums of nationalism within the country, with hopes of being able to infiltrate a coalition government and then gradually transform it into a Communist-type government favorable to Russia.

The underdeveloped continents of the world—Asia, Africa, and South America—are the prime targets for this kind of international Communism. The inhabitants live to a large extent in poverty in overpopulated countries where the ability to progress is held back by lack of capital, trained personnel, and competent leadership. People who live under such conditions are not inclined to question the logic of Communism. Its promise of a better future is music to their ears. Later—but too late, as in Cuba—they find out that they have been pawns in the power politics of Communism and that their "rainbow future" has been relegated to the junk heap of unfulfilled promises.

In any event, mass education and nationalism are the cornerstones of Russia's new economic and political order. They are the instruments for forging the Soviet man of the future. They are used to perpetuate the Communist society. They are the psychological forces with which the Communists intend to capture the minds of men.

CONCLUSION

Communist societies generally are the most aggressive and imperialistic powers in the history of mankind, yet they have succeeded in convincing many people in different countries that they are interested in helping the poor of the world. That's why Communism is a most serious challenge. Unless that challenge is met, we may well see the ebb tide of freedom in our generation.

The greatest danger to the free world is Communism's dialectical materialism, which claims to be inevitable economic progress in the making. The danger arises from the fact that a Communist is expected to do anything to make this dialectical progress a reality. Lacking a moral "balance wheel," no holds are barred and the only standard is success in getting Communism established—anywhere and everywhere. The key ingredients in their approach are propaganda and power used without moral or legal restraint. The main fuels that feed their progress are the hunger and hatred prevalent in the underdeveloped areas of the world.

We must never underestimate the serious challenge of Communism to human freedom all over the world. For there's nothing inevitable about freedom any more than there is about Communism. The world has known about twenty-one civilizations, and most of them have passed away because their people lost faith in the underlying principles of their society, or strayed from principles in the pursuit of personal pleasures, or simply did not have the courage to use national power to protect their way of life from internal subversion or external aggression.

If we're going to survive as a free nation, we must renew our dedication to the American way of life, not because it is a life of ease, but because it is a life of principles upon which free men can build a prosperous future based on a high regard for individual freedom and choice.

Discussion Questions

1. Why is Soviet Russia able to make such spectacular advances in space age exploration and heavy industry?

2. In your opinion, how extensive is Communist influence today?

3. Explain "dialectical materialism."

4. How did Marx modify Hegel's belief in an "absolute spirit"?

5. Describe the nature of the class conflict, as Marx saw it.

6. What did Marx mean by a "philosophical superstructure"?

7. Discuss this statement: "Communism is committed to peaceful co-existence."

8. Summarize the differences between central planning and decentralized decision making in a free enterprise system.

9. How are production goals achieved in Soviet Russia?

10. What has happened to education in Russia during the past fifty years?

11. How did Marx view nationalism?

12. Why didn't Marx expect communism to start in Russia?

13. Describe how economic activity is organized under communism.

14. How does present-day Russia fit into the picture of Marxian communism?

15. Why was Marxian communism described as scientific?
16. What do we mean by the "economic interpretation of history"?
17. What influence has the concept of the class struggle had on political thinking in recent years?
18. Describe briefly the various five-year plans in Russia.
19. What happens to labor unions under Communism?
20. Compare and contrast the philosophies of communism and socialism.

Circle the T or F (True or False) before each statement:

T F 1. Production can be planned without planning consumption.
T F 2. The Soviet Union has made its greatest strides in expanding heavy industry.
T F 3. Russia has sacrificed its current standard of living to increase productive capacity.
T F 4. Russia today is socialistic.
T F 5. Central planning is possible without force.
T F 6. Agriculture has been the most notable achievement of the Soviet Union.
T F 7. The Soviet economic system provides for substantial wage differentials.
T F 8. There are labor agreements between workers and state managers of industry in the Soviet Union.
T F 9. Illiteracy has been virtually eliminated in the Soviet Union.
T F 10. Communism is democratic because everyone has the right to vote.

ANSWERS

10. F	8. T	6. F	4. T	2. T
9. T	7. T	5. F	3. T	1. F

22

OUR AMERICAN ENTERPRISE SYSTEM: ITS HERITAGE AND FUTURE

Our economic system didn't produce its unparalleled results without continuous adaptations, yet its basic principles remain substantially the same despite political challenges and economic changes. This system is peculiarly American, even though it has borrowed from other societies and civilizations. We should remember, too, that our American way of life is more than an economic system; it includes a distinctive political philosophy and basic codes of moral behavior. These inseparable characteristics distinguish our way of life from societies that stress purely economic relationships and pay little attention to the dignity of man. So, when discussing our American heritage, we must consider political and spiritual values as well as the material considerations of earning a living.

OUR HERITAGE OF FREEDOM

At one time or another all of us have pledged "allegiance to the flag of the United States of America and to the Republic for which it stands." When we make that pledge, how many of us give serious consideration to what it means to be an American? For example, is an American determined by geography, nationality, race, or creed? Obviously our answer must be "No" because America has been a haven to all people regardless of their country of origin.

We might say, with some justification, that technical or scientific "know-how" is a peculiar American trait, but when you trace the origin of many chemical, physical, electronic, and atomic discoveries, when you see what the Germans, Japanese, and Russians are capable of doing, you hesitate to say that technical competence is a distinctly American characteristic.

When you analyze it, Americans are not distinguished by these things, important though they are, but rather by three sets of values concerning man and the society in which he lives:

1. We stress certain *moral* values that are stated in the Declaration of Independence and embodied in the Constitution. These values are based on a belief in the inherent rights of man, and from this belief flows the conviction that Man is more important than the State.

2. We believe in the *political* values summed up in the phrase "constitutional government." That is why we guarantee unalienable rights to the individual and place political power in the hands of the people and their elected representatives.

3. There are certain *economic* values behind our free enterprise system. This system requires that we believe in the fairness of competitive markets; that individuals and private companies have the right to manage their affairs; that we safeguard personal and corporate incentives; and that we preserve the self-reliance of our people.

Put these moral, political, and economic values together and you can quickly identify the characteristics of our American system. By living up to these values, our nation has weathered wars, droughts, fires, and depression—and has come back with increased vigor and determination. Put these values together and you have the heritage of freedom which has led us on to unparalleled progress as a nation. But impair these values and you literally destroy that which is characteristically American. With this in mind, let us consider these basic values in greater detail.

Our Moral Values

Some people see our way of life in a purely materialistic way. To them, our economy is a giant assembly line which turns out a large number of automobiles, washing machines, industrial equipment, and mechanical gadgets. As they see it, America is merely a set of statistics which prove that we produce about a third of the world's material wealth with less than 7 per cent of its population and resources.

Naturally, we are proud of our material progress because it has improved health, reduced physical toil, and has given us a standard of living higher than any people in the history of the world. But if this were all America stood for, if we didn't see behind our horn of plenty a spiritual order from which we derive our individual freedoms, there would be few differences between our way of life and materialistic communism or any other state-controlled society.

Perhaps the best statement of our nation's moral values is contained in the *Declaration of Independence:*

> We hold these truths to be self-evident, that all men are created equal; that they are endowed by their Creator with certain unalienable Rights, that among these are Life, Liberty and the pursuit of Happiness. That to secure these rights, Governments are instituted among Men, deriving their just powers from the consent of the governed. . . .

This short paragraph reveals the deeply religious base upon which our free society rests, the idea of a Creator above men and political institutions. And it is this belief which accounts for much of the respect that we have for the individual and his freedom.

For hundreds of years mankind has been trying to determine the proper relationship of the individual to the state. As a matter of fact, we could call this one of the fundamental problems of all times. In some countries the state has won out over the individual, and dictatorships have been the result; in other countries the individual has triumphed, and these have become republics or democracies of one kind or another. In our society the *individual counts*. He is the end purpose of the state, its main reason for existing. And for that reason we believe in limited, constitutional government and in maximum personal freedom.

Compare our deeply religious orientation and our respect for the individual with atheistic Communism or other forms of dictatorship, which deny religion, human rights, and morality, and believe that the individual exists only as a means to satisfy the needs of the state.

You then come up with a basic explanation of why America has been able to rise above economic, political, and environmental challenges to new heights of progress.

You then can understand why mob violence and the gun—and not the pen, plowshare, or individual initiative—have been the primary tools of many dictators, past and present. Stalin, the Soviet Communist leader, put it this way:

> What is the Soviet Union . . . but a base for the world revolution?
> . . . The scientific concept, dictatorship, means nothing more or less
> than power which rests on violence which is not limited by any laws.

Mao Tse-tung, the Chinese Communist leader, was even more emphatic:

> Every Communist must grasp the truth that political power grows out
> of the barrel of a gun . . . in fact, we can say that the whole world
> can be remolded only with a gun.

Our Political Values

Unfortunately, many people do not see a vital connection between
our moral values and our political and economic systems. They make
the mistake of thinking that our government can do anything it wants
without affecting our personal freedoms. The main reason for this widespread misconception is the belief that we have inherited political institutions which do not need our support or attention. We assume that
our political freedoms are completely protected by the Constitution, so
we tend to regard our Constitution like a Maginot Line behind which
we can retreat in political isolation.

But government does not take place in a vacuum. Men govern.
They pass and interpret laws, execute the government's policies, and
breathe reality into the structure of government. If we want to keep our
society virile and free, we must believe in and help preserve the basic
principles of government which guided the Founding Fathers:

- Respect for the individual
- Limited government based on law
- Periodic consent through free elections
- Peaceful change by intelligent legislation
- Federalism in government
- Separation of governmental powers

The Founding Fathers had a deep respect for the individual because they
had lived under arrogant royal governors, and were convinced that
government should be by law rather than by the whim of men. That is
why they framed the Constitution in the first place, striving to safeguard individual freedoms by a written instrument which set broad
boundaries on what the government could do.

The Constitution provides for the periodic consent of the people by
means of popular elections for most public offices. In this way there

can be frequent and peaceful change if the people desire it. But whether these changes are intelligent and constructive depends upon the knowledge and interest of the people themselves. The Constitution cannot guarantee good government. It was designed to protect us from arbitrary abuses of power.

The Founding Fathers went one step further and set up a federal system, in which political power is divided between a centralized national government and decentralized state and local governments. The sovereignty of the people is implied in this system, because all political power is assumed to reside in the people, who delegate portions of it to the Federal government.

Their deep suspicion of centralized power led the Founding Fathers to adopt the idea of "separation of powers." They divided up the *legislative, executive,* and *judicial* functions among a Congress, President, and Supreme Court, so that each branch of government would be in a better position to check and balance the others.

This brief review of our political ideals and governmental system emphasizes that our free society believes in the individual and his basic freedom. The American system shows a decided preference for limited government carried on by constitutional means. It is a society in which the individual can defend himself in court against abuses of power on the part of the state.

Our Economic Values

The American economic system is called "free enterprise" because it, too, serves the individual by leaving him free to pursue the means of earning a livelihood as he sees it, within certain overall restrictions applied by law and equally applicable to all.

There are six basic principles behind our economic system:

- Freedom of choice
- Private property
- Personal and corporate incentives
- Market competition
- Equal opportunities, but unequal rewards
- Productivity as the key to better living

Free enterprise permits us the freedom to work at a job of our own choosing, the right to go into business and earn a profit by furnishing goods or services which people are willing to buy, and the right to keep what we earn in the form of private property. Moreover, as an economy, the system does not force people to do any of these things. Rather, it encourages them with income and profit incentives.

Free enterprise believes in equal opportunities, but it takes into account that differences in individual abilities and ambition will permit some people to move ahead faster than others. As an economic system, it provides for the disabled, the unemployed, the sick and the elderly—but it expects the able-bodied to make their own way, knowing full well that this usually depends on personal talent, initiative, and hard work. A brief review of how our economy operates brings out the striking fact that free enterprise does not require a government agency to decide *what* or *how much* to produce of the goods and services we need or want. We as individuals make these decisions on the basis of how we spend our money in the market place. In a very real sense, the dollars we spend represent our economic votes. If we spend our money for automobiles, our economy produces autos. If we want appliances, it turns out appliances. By our dollar votes, cast daily in competitive markets all over the country, *we the people* decide what and how much our economic system will produce.

Just think how remarkably well it works. You can walk into a store, ask for a product, and get the brand you want in the size you desire without delay, and walk out with the item under your arm. This procedure is so efficient and so automatic that we take it for granted. Yet it represents a form of planning, keyed to consumer demands, but unlike government-made plans.

Finally, our free enterprise system's incentives are based upon the fact that our high standard of living is the result of our large national production of goods and services. For, in the last analysis, we can have more as a nation only if we produce more. Greater productivity, how-

ever, depends largely on machinery, plant, and equipment. To provide the tools for future progress, our economy encourages individuals and business firms to invest their savings by offering them the possibility of a return on their investment. This takes the form of interest on borrowed money or dividends paid out to stockholders.

Fundamentally, then, our free enterprise economy is an incentive system. Without the possibility of a profit, or fear of a loss, there would be no great push toward expansion or efficiency. There would be few tools, fewer jobs, and less goods and services for all of us to share. We should remember, too, that the profit motive applies to more than business firms. It is a natural desire in all of us. We want to improve and get ahead. We want our children to be better off than we have been. If we are reasonably ambitious, we want to profit over the years. The urge to profit is as old as man himself. That is why the communist Karl Marx spent most of his time attacking profits. He had to destroy a free society's fundamental economic incentive if communism were to succeed. His whole philosophy really represents an effort to prove that profits are extracted at the expense of the working man. Our progress as a nation proves he was wrong. The high and rising living standards we enjoy have been broadly shared through higher wages and increased benefits for workers, quality products at lower prices for consumers, and a rapidly growing ownership in American industry by approximately 20 million stockholders of publicly held corporations.

The following figures show how badly mistaken Marx was about our free enterprise system:

- From 1900 to 1967, the population of the United States rose from 76 million to 199 million people, an increase of almost 162 per cent. In the same period, however, our country's real total output of goods and services went up roughly 820 per cent.

- American workers shared in this outpouring of goods and services through higher real wages, better working conditions, improved hospitalization and pension plans, shorter hours of work, and longer vacations.

- The number of jobs increased from 27 million in 1900 to more than 75 million for 1966.

These figures emphasize that Americans are far better off than our critics ever dreamed we would be. We have more jobs, more income, more security, more leisure, and more opportunities—in short, a higher standard of living than ever before. We are fortunate to live in a country where a competitive enterprise system has, for the most part, been free to operate. Consider a few of our advantages:

- A large part of the world goes hungry every day. We do not.

- More than half of the world lives in constant fear of their governments. We do not.

- No one decides our "rightful place" in the scheme of things. We fashion our own destiny by our ambition and personal abilities.

THE FUTURE OF FREEDOM

Despite its almost miraculous achievements, the future of our free society is uncertain, because of powerful forces at work both at home and abroad.

Our Problems at Home

There are two serious domestic problems which will affect our free-doms and our ability to provide a rising standard of living for all of our people:

- Trend toward government control
- Population growth

Trend Toward Government Control . . . Today our free and com-petitive market system is endangered by increasing government inter-vention in farming, money and banking, labor negotiations, electric power, oil and gas production, transportation, pricing, communication, and in other areas too numerous to mention. The fundamental nature of this government intervention, and its effects on individual citizens, can be indicated by three trends. *First,* there is a decided drift toward the *welfare state.* In 1966 the Federal government spent well over $25

billion for items like housing, health and welfare, veterans' benefits, and general subsidies of all kinds. This amount represents twice the en-tire cost of operating the Federal government for the year 1940.

Second, there's a steady growth toward the *administrative state,* with its threat to popular control and individual freedom. About sixty different departments or independent agencies surround the President's Office, any one of which exercises vast powers over citizens, business firms, unions, and other organizations. This same pattern of administrative growth and power is evident in regulatory agencies like the Federal Trade Commis-sion, the Federal Power Commission, and the National Labor Relations Board.

Third, there is a trend toward a form of *garrison state* because of our defense requirements to meet the Cold War with the U.S.S.R. and Red China. In the past, wars had a beginning and an end, and when they were over, there was some semblance of normalcy. But today, there is no war as such, there is no peace, and there is no normalcy. When quasi-emergency conditions exist for long periods of time, the people come to regard government controls as the normal thing, and for this reason, they're apt to give up their freedom in bits and pieces.

Put these three trends together—the welfare state, the administrative state, and the garrison state—and you have a decided drift toward government control at the expense of the individual and our basic values.

Population Growth . . . Preserving individual freedom will be even more difficult because of the rapid increase in our population. The United States has a population of about 199 million people. By 1980 our population may increase to 250 million or more, which represents a rise of about 25 per cent in less than 15 years. This is true even though birth rates are now declining. Many people regard this as a guarantee of prosperity. They foresee more cars, larger homes, and longer vaca-

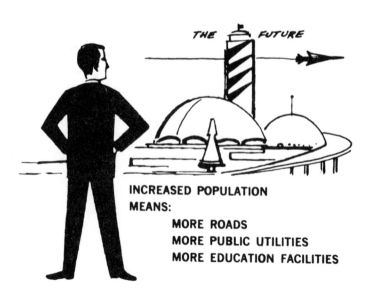

INCREASED POPULATION MEANS:

MORE ROADS
MORE PUBLIC UTILITIES
MORE EDUCATION FACILITIES

tions. But they overlook the many problems which lie ahead. Additional families mean more roads, public utilities, and community protection. The sharp increase in the numbers of school children and retired people will require more schools, recreational facilities, specialized hospitals, and economical housing. There will be a constant pressure to find employment for the increased labor force. The age distribution of our population may develop a greater percentage of nonproducers in the economy, who will constitute a drain on the output of the productive labor force.

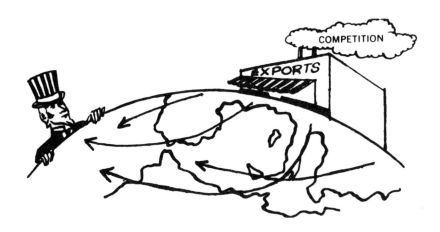

Our Problems Abroad

We are going to face vigorous competition in the world's markets, because of lower wage costs abroad, more modern and versatile production facilities, and the increased impact of common market areas. Moreover, for political reasons, Communist countries like Russia can hold down their production of consumer goods to build up their industrial capacity and long-term ability to compete. Perhaps, too, they will continue to pursue national policies intended to disrupt the world's markets and the operations of privately owned companies of the free world. Besides these economic problems we may face recurrent international crises fomented by Communists and fanned by local nationalist leaders.

A turbulent world, marked by violence and revolution, will force us to increase our strength if we intend to remain free. But this will require more resources than in the past.

THE KEY PROBLEM
OF ECONOMIC GROWTH

The combination of all of these domestic and foreign problems will encourage the local, state, and Federal governments to spend much more during the next 10 years, perhaps twice as much as we now spend for government services. This rapid rise in government spending has important implications for inflation and for our ability to maintain a sound dollar and adequate gold reserves.

To carry this increased load of government spending we must become more efficient as a nation and achieve a rate of economic growth sufficient to meet our added responsibilities.

To produce these goods and services, American business firms will have to invest billions in new capital equipment. This will be possible only if we provide a business climate favorable to growth in the American tradition. And this in turn requires profit incentives for companies and individuals working within the framework of our free enterprise system.

The best way to stop dictatorship and aggression is to strengthen the United States and the free countries of the world. This means strengthening our national defense; reducing unnecessary expenditures in non-defense areas; strengthening our economy through better incentives for economic growth; and preserving the individual freedoms inherent in our political system.

THE CROSSROADS OF FREEDOM

We are now in a period of history when all of our principles of Americanism are being seriously challenged. Our main goal, therefore, must be the preservation of freedom at home and abroad. The communists have been somewhat successful because of their singleness of purpose and willingness to use force. Their advance has been helped by our own apathy and lack of determination in standing up for the principles we believe in. Americans, as individuals, can make a vital contribution to the solution of our problems by:

- Understanding the nature of the challenges as well as the basic values of our free society.

- Improving and strengthening the United States in all of its aspects.

Unfortunately, people cannot preserve what they do not understand. Moral values, democratic government, and free enterprise are essential to our way of life, yet reliable surveys by national organizations reveal that few Americans understand what our society stands for or how it operates. Recently, a national task force on economic education studied our high schools for a year and came to this conclusion:

> 50,000 social studies teachers don't know anything about economics and . . . 95 per cent of our high school students never even get acquainted with such important areas as competitive prices, inflation, or taxes.

We cannot defend our free society unless we have a good grasp of its underlying values.

If we know what is basically American, and if we intend to remain free, we must understand the *moral, political,* and *economic* values behind this great nation of ours.

Discussion Questions

1. What is meant by our "American heritage"?
2. How are moral, political, and economic values interrelated?
3. How would you describe the roles of the individual and of the state in our American system of values?
4. Discuss this statement: "The economic system is a self-contained entity, independent of political values."
5. What is meant by federalism in government?
6. How does the separation of powers tend to assure the inherent freedoms of our society?
7. Describe the basic values of the American economic system.
8. Describe the key economic problems we face today.
9. Mention several ways in which population growth will affect our future goals as a nation.
10. Discuss this statement: "A competitive market system is the most free, efficient, and ethical system available today."
11. Discuss this statement: "Governmental power and control are killing the free enterprise system."
12. Discuss this conclusion: "Karl Marx was wrong in his basic predictions."

13. Discuss this conclusion: "The United States is self-sufficient and therefore need not concern itself with international economic problems."

14. Why is it necessary to increase the real Gross National Product, if the role of government increases?

15. Discuss this statement: "We are at the crossroads of freedom."

16. Discuss this statement: "If the United States is to move forward, its economy must be dynamic and ever-changing."

17. In your opinion, do the technically advanced or the backward countries make a more productive use of capital? Justify your answer.

18. Why is the study of national goals so important to the economist? To the political scientist?

19. Explain how competition has become a key factor in our economic development.

20. Why are "motivation" and "opportunity" important words in describing a private enterprise system?

Circle the T or F (True or False) before each statement:

T F 1. A progressively larger national income in constant dollars is a desirable national goal.

T F 2. There is no real difference between progress and change.

T F 3. A central issue with respect to our economic organization is decentralization of decision making authority.

T F 4. When a city provides its residents with band concerts, food for the needy, and sewage disposal—these should be properly classified as free economic goods and services.

T F 5. It is possible to have higher living standards and a decline in personal freedom.

T F 6. A big problem in history has been determining the proper relationship between the individual and the state.

T F 7. The American Constitution has been "read broadly" by the Supreme Court in recent years.

T F 8. The Constitution states definitively that the Supreme Court has the power of judicial review.

T   F   9. The economic system is independent of basic values, and therefore can be regulated without effect on personal freedoms.

T   F   10. The incentive system of reward is unnecessary when people are properly educated to perform a useful function.

ANSWERS

2. F	4. F	6. T	8. F	10. F
1. T	3. T	5. T	7. T	9. F

INDEX

INDEX

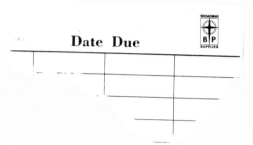

Date Due

BROADMAN
B P
SUPPLIES